Social Decision Making/Social Problem Solving

A Curriculum for Academic, Social, and Emotional Learning

Maurice J. Elias

Linda Bruene Butler

with

Erin M. Bruno

Maureen Reilly Papke

Teresa Farley Shapiro

GRADES 2-3

Research Press • 2612 North Mattis Avenue, Champaign, Illinois 61822

(800) 519-2707 • www.researchpress.com

Copies of this book may be ordered from Research Press at the address given on the title page.

Composition by Publication Services
Cover design by Linda Brown, Positive I.D. Graphic Design, Inc.
Printed by McNaughton & Gunn, Inc.

ISBN 0-87822-512-9
Library of Congress Control Number 2004097764

Contents

Tables

Foreword

Writing this foreword is an honor. I have known Maurice Elias since 1979, when we were both young psychologists who had just moved from Connecticut to New Jersey. Maurice was just joining the faculty at Rutgers University, and I had just started as an educator-clinician at the mental health center of the University of Medicine and Dentistry of New Jersey (UMDNJ). We were two young men from two different institutions with two different missions, but our interests and skills were complementary. Into the mix came Tom Schuyler, a seasoned principal with the Middlesex, New Jersey, Public Schools, another institution with another mission. The synergy worked. The three of us conceived and developed the wonderful project upon which the curriculum in this two-book sequence is based.

I have worked with Linda Bruene Butler since 1980. She relocated from Illinois and soon joined me at the mental health center at UMDNJ to devise approaches to help professionals learn to teach social decision making to children. For many years, we collaborated with a wonderful group of colleagues to provide professional development opportunities for educators across our state and across the country.

In August 2000, I accepted an exciting faculty position at the Robert Wood Johnson Medical School, where I teach behavioral science to family physicians. One of the exciting aspects of my present work is passing on the skills of social decision making to physicians in training. Maurice and Linda, at Rutgers and UMDNJ respectively, have continued to devote their careers to helping children, their parents, and their teachers develop the techniques to create psychologically healthy lives. It is rare in my experience that two professionals can not only stay the course of a particular content area over the long term but are still energetically inventive in moving the field further. These two books are testimony to Maurice's and Linda's long-term commitment to helping children.

One of the reasons that we need a program like the one detailed in this social decision making and social problem solving program is that parents and guardians have less help than they did before from the village of neighbors and local relatives to pass on the wisdom and culture. As a child in the 1950s and 1960s, I spent most of my time playing outside with other kids. As I remember it, it seemed that there were always some adults around, keeping an eye on things: "Does your mother know what you're doing?" We'd say yes. At times, a neighbor might even say, "Oh? Let's see." With that, we might be escorted off to a parent to check out the truth of what we had said. Remarkably, we would go with this neighbor, out of respect, even though it might have meant trouble for us. And our parents seemed to honor what these sentries of the neighborhood would report to them. It was a cultural arrangement that also made youngsters feel safe and secure. We knew that if there was some trouble we couldn't handle, we would be able to flag down one of these adults to help out.

But things have changed in our and in many other neighborhoods. In the cities and small towns of America today, adults who are fortunate to have jobs are anxious about keeping them. They are exhausted from working harder and for longer hours in order to support their families. Children are not only more isolated from adults but from one another. Kids today can entertain themselves in solitary ways with video, computer, or recorded music, and they have fewer opportunities to practice social skills and develop their emotional intelligence.

Something else changed along the way, too: You are only allowed to parent your own children. Although there may be an increasing number of organized recreational activities for children, structured group activities are very different from the free play with caring adult supervision that previous generations experienced. Today's parents have a much smaller village to rely upon to help raise thoughtful and responsible children. A neighbor who witnesses a child being bullied or a group of kids getting into trouble and wants to intervene would probably hesitate because this person wouldn't feel backed up or trusted by the parents of these children. Into this void steps the Social Decision Making/Social Problem Solving (SDM/SPS) program. Because while the village of some neighborhoods has gotten smaller, the village of the school has opened up.

Teachers have always been sanctioned to pass on the culture of relating in a civilized and caring way, but there are now recognized policies for instruction that go beyond the "hidden curriculum" of informal discussions. There are now formal programs in alcohol and drug abuse prevention, character education, and other topics. The SDM/SPS curriculum allows a school not only to address many problems, but also to influence positive development efforts in a comprehensive way. Children of the present generation have an advantage. There is now a science that did not exist years ago that helps adults know the skills and attitudes important for children to become moral decision makers. It is on this science that the SDM/SPS curriculum is based. There is no need to rely only on our intuition about what will help children. We now know what works.

This particular curriculum distinguishes itself from other programs with similar goals. Almost three decades in development, it offers instruction in the most comprehensive range of skills for teachers, students, and parents. In this curriculum, teachers will find ways to help children develop self-control skills—for example, to self-soothe when faced with stressful situations in the classroom. Teachers will also find ways here of teaching skills such as friendship development. In this program, the eight steps of critical thinking are taught explicitly, without mystery. These steps are woven into a wide variety of both social conflict and academic areas. The program also includes parenting materials that children can take home so their families can follow up with them and promote additional skill development.

Beyond the actual suggested instructional activities, this curriculum also distinguishes itself by attending to the art of teaching as well. Teachers who are new to the program can benefit from the experiences of the many master teachers who have gone before them. Readers will see many ways to teach social decision making that make it exciting and fun for children. The program's consistent, well-organized pedagogy provides an easy and soon-familiar flow and rhythm that repeats itself in engaging ways. The instructional tone of this work is respectful of teachers' professionalism—for example, instructional "topics" rather prescribed "lessons" are provided. Teachers are therefore encouraged to adapt and tailor the instruction to suit their own style and their students' educational needs and learning pace. This process is parallel to the program's goal to encourage independent and competent thinking on the part of children.

So, I invite you to settle back and confidently enjoy this collection of social decision making and social problem solving resources for children. This is a treasury of material developed through careful research, underscored by a pedagogy that invites enthusiasm from all, and refined on the basis of over 25 years in the classroom.

JOHN F. CLABBY, PH.D.

UMDNJ–ROBERT WOOD JOHNSON
MEDICAL SCHOOL

Acknowledgments

As our work enters its third decade, we look back with amazement and gratitude at the hundreds of colleagues who have been instrumental in the development of our work. We cannot possibly mention them all, but we hold them all in our hearts with tremendous gratitude and admiration. Those whose role in getting the SDM/SPS work started deserve special mention. These are Myrna Shure, George Spivack, and Steve Larcen, who generously shared their initial work with Interpersonal Cognitive Problem Solving, and Tom Schuyler, John Clabby, and Charlotte Hett, whose collaboration, vision, commitment, and enthusiasm in the first decade of the work helped it flourish despite many obstacles.

In subsequent years, we have been blessed with being able to work with many talented colleagues who have taught us so much and lent their expertise to our work. Again, there are too many to name, but we want to note several whose ongoing work with us has gone above and beyond any reasonable expectation and whose ideas have come to mesh with our own in ways very hard to disentangle. These include Jacqueline Norris, Phil Brown, Vicki Poedubicky, Judy Lerner, Lois Brown, Frank Fehn, Karen Welland, Bruce Ettinger, Larry Leverett, Joseph Sperlazza, and Robin Stern. Linda would like to give special acknowledgment to Bruce Stout of University of Medicine and Dentistry of New Jersey–University Behavioral Health Care for his continuing mentorship and tangible and logistical support, and Maurice would like to extend the same to Lew Gantwerk of the Graduate School of Applied and Professional Psychology–Center for Applied Psychology.

We also mention with deep appreciation and awe Erin Bruno, Maureen Papke, and Teresa Shapiro, who tangibly assisted us in compiling this volume and who carry the legacy of SDM/SPS work so brilliantly every day. They, along with other long-time SDM/SPS staff members Jeff Kress, Carl Preto, Lisa Blum, Margo Hunter, Mary Ellen Taylor, Ronda Jones, and Deborah Mosley, as well as Steven Tobias and Brian Friedlander, have developed the ideas that appear in our curriculum in the spirit of continuous improvement.

Finally, we thank the remarkable team at Research Press, who believe in our work so deeply and care so much about how it is presented to the world. Ann Wendel, Russ Pence, Karen Steiner, Dennis Wizeicki, Hilary Powers (our capable freelance copyeditor), and an incredibly talented production staff have made it possible to put our best work forward and provide materials to our colleagues in schools about which we are very, very proud. The effort represented in this curriculum will have the ultimate effect of helping children, and that is the point of all of our work.

A personal note from Maurice: I am filled with gratitude for so many people, immediate and extended family, friends, close colleagues, and amazing students, past and present, who have been so supportive of my work. Your contributions, tangible and intangible, have made the best of this work better and have helped keep me refreshed, enthused, and ready to persist and create in the service of improving kids' lives. A special thank you to cherished friend, source of mirth and chocolate, and collaborator Ed Dunkelblau; the incredible team at the Collaborative for Academic, Social, and Emotional Learning; my parents, Agnes and Sol; my in-laws, Myra and Lou Rosen; and last, and most of all, my wife, Ellen, and daughters Sara Elizabeth and Samara Alexandra—all three of whom are my best sources of feedback, support, and kvelling.

A personal note from Linda: I would like to thank Dr. John Gottman for his mentoring and making me so aware at an early and foundational stage of my career of the critical importance of a child's social and emotional competency. I also want to thank my amazing circle of family and friends for all of their love and support and for so richly filling the much too little time I have to play. My inner-circle family support group includes my mothers, Joan and Edna; my Aunt Marcy; Kay; Joannetta and Mern; my twin sister, Laura, and sisters Diane, Carrie, Linda Bruene II, Jane, Pat, Jeannie, Jennifer, and Amy; my brothers, John and Bob, and my uncles, Mike and Bud. I could not work or survive without my amazing circle of friends, which includes Nancy, Andrew, Annette, Val, Lois, Lizzie, Howard, Freddie, Donna, Sandra, Riki, Vicky, and Teff. Last of all, thanks to my loving husband, Chris, who continues to capture my respect for his emotional intelligence, and to my most adoring buddy/golden retriever, Josh.

Introduction

Guide to Instructional Design and Implementation Procedures

> For students to enter the community of responsible adults prepared for a diversity of social roles, they must possess critical-thinking and problem-solving skills, as well as interpersonal sensitivity. Their future success in citizenship, parenthood, family life, and the workplace will require them to find appropriate answers to numerous difficult questions, and it is up to the schools to help provide a foundation from which to answer them.
>
> —M. J. Elias & S. E. Tobias, *Social Problem Solving Interventions in the Schools* (New York: Guilford Press, 1996, p. iii)

The Social Decision Making/Social Problem Solving (SDM/SPS) curriculum is an evidence-based approach to building skills that students need for success in school and in life: the skills required for effective work in groups, persistent work on projects, constructive handling of frustration and challenge, and nonviolent conflict resolution. Students learn both how and why to care about classmates and teammates; to feel and show empathy; and to practice perspective taking, emotional regulation and self-control, and participation in democratic institutions, workplaces, and family life. In other words, SDM/SPS teaches essential life skills, skills that were once the province of family life but are, for many children, no longer routinely covered in the course of normal growing up. Much as we can lament that this is the case, we also must do something about it. When we do not, our classrooms are chaotic, our schools suffer, and many of our children emerge from education as social casualties, either unwilling or unable to take productive roles in society and lacking the moral character to put their talents to use for good in the world.

STUDENTS NEED SKILLS, NOT SLOGANS

Students need skills, not slogans, and so SDM/SPS is geared to build skills. Ideally, students will have several years of exposure to the curriculum in elementary and middle school, but even one solid year can have benefits. This Introduction is designed to give you a brief overview of the curriculum, the structure of its activities, and a selection of ways you can use the teaching skills you already have to carry out what is required.

The SDM/SPS curriculum is best thought of as a launching pad. Students cannot learn skills merely from engaging in activities on a topic. The curriculum provides a structure for introducing the skills, ensuring their relevance to students and a connection to their everyday lives, and providing numerous opportunities for practice and feedback. It is through this practice and feedback process that skills come to be internalized—but it takes months, not days. The pedagogy of the SDM/SPS curriculum extends beyond the actual delivery of formal activities in the classroom. Teaching of SDM/SPS skills becomes infused into virtually all aspects of the school day, because there really is no part of the day when having solid life skills and exhibiting good character are irrelevant.

The SDM/SPS curriculum is included in the list of Model and Promising Programs from the U.S. Department of Education's Expert Panel on Safe, Drug Free Schools, and has been designated as a Select Social-Emotional Learning (SELect) program by the Collaborative for Academic, Social, and Emotional Learning. (See the "Safe and Sound" guide to selection and implementation of SEL programs, updated periodically, at the Collaborative's Web site, www.CASEL.org.)

The instructional design is as important as the skills targeted in each topic area. Systematic skill-building procedures are used for all curriculum units.

SYSTEMATIC SKILL-BUILDING TOOLS
FOR SOCIAL DECISION MAKING/SOCIAL PROBLEM SOLVING

The program focuses on teaching self-control and social awareness skills as important tools for decision making.

Format for Each Topic

Activities are organized into Topics rather than lessons. This identifier is preferred because of the emphasis on skill building. Teachers must have the flexibility to stay on a topic for the length of time necessary for a sufficient proportion of the class to grasp the concepts and be ready to move on.

Topics begin with a statement of objectives, followed by materials and preparation needed to carry out the main activities. A number of activities involve materials that are handed out to students, which are collectively referred to as worksheets. Except for a few items readily available at school or in the community, these are included at the end of the first Topic to call for their use, with cross-references from later Topics if they are used more than once. Among the materials are various kinds of assessments and charts to be completed by students and teachers, Problem Diaries, and take-home materials for parents.

The next part of the Topic format is a set of instructional activities that incorporates the following components:

- Introducing the skills and concepts and providing motivation for learning; skills are presented in concrete behavioral components.

- Modeling behavioral components and clarifying the concept by descriptions and behavioral examples of using and not using the skill.

- Providing opportunities for practice of the skill in kid-tested, enjoyable activities, to allow for corrective feedback and reinforcement until skill mastery is approached.

- Labeling the skill with a prompt or cue to establish a shared language that can be used to call for exercise of the skill in future situations, to promote transfer and generalization.

- Assignments for skill practice outside the structured lessons.

- Follow-through activities and planned opportunities for using skill prompts in academic content areas, classroom management, and everyday interpersonal situations at school and in the home and community.

- Occasional take-home activities or information sheets for parents.

The Reflective Summary

Each set of instructional activities includes a Reflective Summary. The purpose of this summary is to give students a chance to think about what they have learned from the Topic, as well as to allow teachers to see what students are taking away with them. Sometimes, the Reflective Summary can show when students have misunderstandings or uncertainty about what they have learned, suggesting the need for additional instructional activities before moving on in the Topic sequence. Here is the procedure:

Ask students to reflect on the question "What did you learn from today's lesson?" You can do this with the whole group, in a Sharing Circle format (described later in this Introduction and in more detail in the first Topic for each grade level), by having students fill out index cards, or by having them respond in other formats if you prefer. We recommend that you have some variety in formats. For example, sometimes you might ask, "What are two or three things you will most remember from today's lesson?" After getting a sense of what the students have learned, reinforce key themes that they mentioned and add perhaps one or two that you would like them to keep in mind. Also discuss any follow-up assignments or take-homes.

Tips for Teachers

After the instructional activities you will find a Tips for Teachers section, with specific, practical suggestions for carrying out the activities most effectively, based on feedback from teachers who have used SDM/SPS in various settings. This section is followed by specific worksheets called for in the Topic for the first time.

SYSTEMATIC SKILL BUILDING FOR SOCIAL-EMOTIONAL DEVELOPMENT

The set of skills that students learn does not change from Grades 2 through 8. They are listed in Table 1. Think of these skills as a sort of alphabet. The basic set of letters does not change, but new combinations of the same basic letters become both possible and necessary as children develop and face new and more complex situations. Ultimately, the goal is for students to use their new social and emotional skills independently in the context of the new, increasingly complex, and ever-changing problems and decisions they will encounter. The activities in this curriculum start from the social and emotional skills your students have learned up to this point and build upon them to help your students learn to make socially competent and successful social decisions.

Primary Skill Area for Grades 2 and 3: Readiness

Readiness refers to a climate that must be established and a set of skills that must be learned as prerequisites to thoughtful decision making. To create the climate, students need to think of themselves as being part of a problem-solving team, and the first units of the curricula in Grades 2, 3, 4, and 5 all begin with that focus. To accomplish this, we recommend using a group gathering called a Sharing Circle to begin class discussions and skill-building activities. In the Sharing Circle, students are asked to share their name and answer a question or two, beginning with simple things such as naming a favorite restaurant and moving on, after a certain level of trust is established, to describing feelings about a school or classroom issue. This deceptively simple process allows students to share with one another, to learn to listen to and care about their classmates, to get some "air time," and to foster positive transitions from the pressures of home and the pace and action of lunch and recess during the school day. It is a format for

Table 1   Skills Taught in the SDM/SPS Curriculum: Grades 2–8

SOCIAL COMPETENCE SKILLS

Self-Control

Effective listening
Memory strategies
Following directions
Identifying personal stress triggers
Self-monitoring (stress management)
Self-calming
Assertive communication
Giving constructive criticism
Resisting provocations
Role-play for behavioral rehearsal
Self-evaluation

Social Awareness

Working as part of a team
Expressing oneself in a group
Perspective taking
Choosing and caring for friends
Giving and receiving praise
Asking for and giving help
Conversation skills
Joining a group

DECISION-MAKING AND PROBLEM-SOLVING SKILLS

Feelings awareness (self and others)
Articulating feelings
Problem definition
Realistic goal setting
Flexible and creative thinking/generating alternatives
Consequential thinking:
    short- and long-term
    positive and negative
    for self and others
Decision making
    in service of a goal
    positive choices
Planning
Anticipating obstacles
Behavioral rehearsal
Overcoming setbacks
Utilizing previous experience for future decision making

reflection on the weekend past, the day or week ahead, and the weekend to come.

We also find it essential to have a visible, clear rule structure in the classroom. One format for this is the Classroom Constitution. The constitution allows parallels to academics by introducing the idea that, just as is true for the nation, a classroom functions with a set of rights and a set of rules. Students are involved in making these rules, and the list of rules is posted visibly in the classroom. Typically, when visitors walk in and view the constitution, they sense the pride embodied in the values and priorities of the classroom. The constitution should be phrased in positive terms, although some educators maintain that a couple of clear "Thou shalt not's" are also worthwhile. When problems such as classroom disruption, lack of effort, or poor group work are observed, the constitution is invoked and an improvement plan is created.

Parents are highly supportive of Classroom Constitutions and other visible, explicit rule structures, as these enable clear home-school communication about expected behaviors in school. This is an important point, in that teachers do not want to get into conflicts with students about different values and messages they may be getting from home. The Classroom Constitution or other rules for school are exactly that—expectations for how students will act in school and in school-related situations (for example, on the bus, on school grounds, on the way to and from school, on school trips).

Against the backdrop of a climate that fosters social and emotional learning, specific readiness skills can be built—all of them prerequisites for thoughtful social decision making and problem solving in all aspects of life. In addition to the skills needed to become a problem-solving team, readiness also includes skills in feelings—that is, understanding one's own feelings and those of others, as well as learning how to manage strong emotions in everyday situations. This awareness requires students to focus on the areas of self-control and social awareness. *Self-control* refers to the personal skills necessary for self-regulation and monitoring of emotions and interactive behavior; *social awareness* focuses on the skills and knowledge linked with successful participation in a group. Readiness is the focus of Grade 2 and much of Grade 3 content, especially in the units focusing on becoming a problem-solving team and dealing with feelings.

The Instructional Phase: Instruction in a Social Decision Making Process

The cornerstone of SDM/SPS, like any life skills, character education, or social-emotional program, is to provide students with a problem-solving and decision-making strategy they can internalize to use in a variety of everyday and challenging situations they encounter. This is accomplished through a combination of (a) introducing an overall strategy for guided self-talk, summarized with the mnemonic "FIG

TESPN," (b) exploring each element of FIG TESPN as a separate skill, and (c) practicing the FIG TESPN strategy in the context of a variety of hypothetical, age-appropriate, and open-ended choice and conflict situations. As each skill is emphasized and practiced, its link to the chain of skills that forms the overall strategy is strengthened.

The "FIG TESPN" acronym reflects the following skills:

F —Find the feelings

I —Identify the problem

G —Guide yourself with a goal

T —Think of many possible solutions

E —Envision consequences

S —Select the best solution

P —Plan and be prepared for pitfalls

N —Notice what happened (Now what?)

The skill areas can be summarized by stating that when children and adults are using their social problem solving skills, they are engaged in the following activities:

1. Noticing and labeling signs of feelings in themselves and others.

2. Identifying issues or problems and putting them into words.

3. Determining and selecting personal goals.

4. Generating alternative solutions—brainstorming.

5. Envisioning—getting a mental picture of—possible consequences (in the short and long term, to themselves and others).

6. Selecting the solution that best meets their goal.

7. Planning and rehearsing the details of carrying out the solution, making a final check for obstacles, and anticipating what to do if they occur.

8. Noticing what happened and using the information for future decision making and problem solving.

In Grades 2 and 3, the emphasis is much more on readiness than on teaching FIG TESPN. Students work briefly with the "FIG" part of the system in Grade 2 (Topic 26) and are formally introduced to the whole FIG TESPN in Grade 3, in the SDM/SPS unit beginning with Topic 22. However, precursors to the FIG TESPN strategy are embedded in the context of many activities. This is especially true in areas that have academic application, which is a part of activities in most Topics and related Supplemental Activities (Topics 27–29). The latter can be introduced any time after the first six or eight weeks of the school year and used repeatedly with changing content. Tables 2 and 3 contain a specific topic-by-topic outline of how SDM/SPS is integrated with and includes a range of academic, standards-linked content areas.

Table 2 Social Decision Making/Social Problem Solving (SDM/SPS): Academic and Home Application Activities (Grade 2)

TOPICS	Language Arts	Social Studies	Health	Behavior Management	Interpersonal and Personal Real-Life Situations	Home	Other
1. Introduction to Social Decision Making/Social Problem Solving	X	X		X		X	Sharing Circle; group rules; Speaker Power
2. Listening Position	X	X	X	X	X	X	Assemblies; line position
3. Effective Listening	X	X	X	X	X	X	
4. Listening Power	X	X	X	X	X	X	
5. Strategies for Remembering				X	X		Tests; math facts; spelling words; homework
6. Following Directions				X	X		
7. Be Your BEST. S = Speech (Say Something Nice)				X	X		

#	Lesson						
8.	Be Your BEST: *T* = Tone of Voice			X	X		
9.	Be Your BEST: Putting *S* and *T* Together			X	X		
10.	How to Give Praise			X	X		
11.	How to Receive Praise			X	X		
12.	Asking for Help and Giving Help to Others	X		X	X		Art
13.	Selecting and Caring for Friends			X	X		Teammate behaviors
14.	Packing Your SDM/SPS Toolbox			X	X		
15.	Pull Your Class Together			X	X		
16.	Identifying Personal Feelings	X	X	X		X	
17.	Identifying Feelings in Others	X	X	X	X		

Table 2 (continued)

	TOPICS	Language Arts	Social Studies	Health	Behavior Management	Interpersonal and Personal Real-Life Situations	Home	Other
18.	Identifying Personal Feelings and the Feelings of Others	X	X	X	X	X		
19.	Identifying Feelings in Stories	X	X		X	X		
20.	Things That Bug You and How Your Body Responds			X	X	X		
21.	A Strategy for Keeping Calm			X	X	X		
22.	Be Your BEST and Keep Calm				X	X		
23.	Introducing Problem Diaries in Our Lives				X	X		
24.	Problem Diaries and Literature	X						

10

#	Lesson					Technology
25.	Using Problem Solving to Reduce Tattling		X	X		
26.	Review SDM/SPS Tools and Celebrate Success		X	X	X	
27.	Using Problem Diaries to Solve Playground Problems					
28.	Learning How to Use the Problem-Solving Corner					
29.	Using Technology to Practice Identifying Feelings and Develop a Vocabulary for Feelings					

**Table 3 Social Decision Making/Social Problem Solving (SDM/SPS):
Academic and Home Application Activities (Grade 3)**

	TOPICS	Language Arts	Social Studies	Health	Behavior Management	Interpersonal and Personal Real-Life Situations	Community and Service Learning	Home	Other
1.	Introduction to Social Decision Making/Social Problem Solving	X	X	X	X	X		X	Physical education
2.	Learning to Listen Carefully and Accurately				X	X		X	Transitions
3.	Exercises to Pull Your Team Together				X	X			
4.	Listening Power				X	X		X	
5.	Strategies for Remembering				X	X		X	Tests; math facts; spelling words; homework
6.	Following Directions				X	X		X	Spelling; math facts
7.	Learning to Role-Play	X	X		X			X	

No.	Topic							Notes
8.	Be Your BEST				X	X	X	
9.	Using Your BEST to Stop Bullying and Teasing	X			X	X		
10.	Using Your BEST to Give and Receive Praise	X			X	X	X	Media; peer tutoring
11.	Using Your BEST to Give and Receive Help					X		
12.	What Makes a Friend a Friend?				X	X	X	
13.	Packing Your SDM/SPS Toolbox	X	X		X	X	X	
14.	Identifying Feelings	X	X	X	X	X	X	Art
15.	Looking for Signs of Different Feelings	X	X	X	X	X		
16.	Identifying Feelings in Stories	X			X	X		
17.	What Are Your Feelings Fingerprints?	X	X	X	X	X	X	Games

Table 3 (continued)

	TOPICS	Language Arts	Social Studies	Health	Behavior Management	Interpersonal and Personal Real-Life Situations	Community and Service Learning	Home	Other
18.	A Strategy for Keeping Calm			X	X	X	X		Transitions; tests; physical education; playground
19.	Introduction to Problem Diaries	X			X	X			Prereferral intervention
20.	Using Problem Diaries in Our Lives (Part 1)								
21.	Using Problem Diaries in Our Lives (Part 2)								
22.	Introduction to FIG TESPN	X	X		X	X		X	
23.	Using FIG to Give Constructive Criticism	X	X		X	X		X	
24.	Using FIG to Understand Different Points of View	X	X	X	X	X			Conflict resolution

#	Topic								Notes
25.	Practice Using FIG to Tackle School and Life Problems			X	X				
26.	Review SDM/SPS Tools and Celebrate Success				X	X		X	Assessment and goal setting
27.	Using FIG in Language Arts	X			X	X		X	
28.	Using FIG in Social Studies		X		X			X	Science
29.	Joining a New Group	X			X	X			

The SDM/SPS–Academics Connection

Integrating SDM/SPS into the academic work of students builds their social-emotional learning (SEL) skills and enriches their academics by linking cognitive, social, and emotional processes. Readiness skills are essential for students to accomplish the following academic and learning tasks, among many others too numerous to list here:

- Understand assignments and test instructions accurately.
- Examine passages of text patiently and extract necessary information across a wide range of academic subject areas.
- Delay gratification long enough to think about difficult choices on exams or to prepare well for those exams.
- Participate in cooperative learning groups.
- Complete homework and short- and long-term projects in an organized way.

Beyond the readiness skills, the critical thinking skills denoted by FIG TESPN are the cornerstone of academic understanding and sustained achievement. This is true both in terms of mastering the intricacies of any subject area and in terms of addressing the numerous everyday decisions that are part of life in school and among peers and family. Consider how well a student would function with deficiencies in any one, two, or three FIG TESPN skills. Imagine if the deficiencies occurred in only two or three school or home situations. Is there any doubt that the student would be at risk for academic difficulty, for substance abuse, and for not functioning as a healthy, productive adult citizen? Hence, applications to academic contexts are a regular feature of SDM/SPS, building a broad array of literacy skills in students. As noted earlier, Tables 2 and 3 outline how each of the Topics in the Grade 2 and 3 curricula link with a range of academic areas.

THE SDM/SPS INSTRUCTIONAL AND PEDAGOGICAL APPROACH

In addition to direct instruction and application of a decision-making process, students also benefit from having external coaching and facilitation of their learning. This process is carried out through a form of pedagogy refined over many years to help teachers systematically guide and coach students to use their SDM/SPS skills in a variety of situations. For this reason, the pedagogy of SDM/SPS is of equal importance to the activities and essential if SDM/SPS is to be implemented effectively and internalized by students.

Gathering: The Sharing Circle

Whether one calls it a Sharing Circle, Morning Meeting, Sharing Time, Advisory Group, Circle Time, or any of a number of related titles, the reality is that students welcome the chance to come together informally to address issues of emotional concern. Students benefit from a buffer between socially challenging parts of their day—preparation for and trip to school, lunch and recess, and dismissal—and applying themselves to serious academic work. For this reason, schools find it useful to have gatherings to start the school day, after lunch and recess, and at the end of the day. Such activities recognize and help to implement three essential SEL principles (from the "Lessons for Life" Video-Inservice Kit for staff members new to SEL, National Center for Innovation and Education, www.communitiesofhope.org):

- *Caring relationships form the foundation of all lasting learning:* Gatherings bring everyone together and make a statement that while agendas are important, relationships come first. They also set a climate in which learning is most likely to be internalized and lasting.

- *Emotions affect how and what we learn:* Academic work cannot proceed when students' emotions are churned up, when they are anxious, fearful, or angry. The group focus during start-of-day gatherings is on providing an opportunity for some expression of concern, or at least using a ritual beginning to give students a chance to get their own emotions regulated a bit. By so doing, they are better prepared for the academic tasks ahead of them. At the end of the day, addressing students' emotions makes it more likely that the day's learning will stick, and good intentions with regard to homework and projects and such will get followed through on.

- *Goal setting and problem solving provide direction and energy to learning:* Gatherings provide a chance to reaffirm common goals, set personal goals, work on issues of general concern, or make the transition into the SDM/SPS activity about to be undertaken. Gatherings also reinforce goals by providing opportunities for testimonials about progress on projects and attempts to use new skills, and for students to get feedback on aspects of SDM/SPS that are proving difficult.

It is this flexible use of gatherings that led the activities in the SDM/SPS curricula to be called Topics rather than lessons. Sometimes the immediate needs of the group, including the need to review what went on in the prior meeting, will make it impossible to complete the day's planned activities. However, because the emphasis on SDM/SPS is in long-term, generalizable skill development, when a choice exists between deep learning and coverage of more topics, the former is preferred.

Caveats: Taking Care with Student Disclosure and Student Hurt

In Sharing Circles or other gatherings, as well as in problem-solving discussions, some students are likely to want to share family or other personal home circumstances with peers. It is important to set up ground rules, from the very beginning, that family matters should not be topics of general discussion. Further, many groups establish a rule that they will not talk about people who are not in the room at the time. That being said, you will also want to be sure to convey to students that they can and should individually approach you, a counselor, school psychologist or social worker, or other school professional whenever they are facing difficult personal or interpersonal problems or circumstances.

These considerations are especially powerful when students are coming to class with a great deal of emotional hurt. Often, they are in need of opportunities to express their strong feelings. And they may try to do so despite warnings that such personal disclosures are not appropriate for the group. Try to be aware of what is happening in the lives of students and offer those who are dealing with difficulties chances to meet with you or another member of the school staff on an individual basis. Your alertness to both quiet and overt signs of distress can make a large difference in the lives of students. The work of the PassageWays Institute is a valuable resource to teachers in addressing these concerns (www.passageways.org).

The Facilitative Approach of Open-Ended Questioning

From the SDM/SPS point of view, the main role of the teacher is neither to solve students' problems nor to make decisions for students. Instead, teachers are facilitators of students' own decision-making and problem-solving skills. (This approach is analogous to the old adage about the relative merits of teaching people to fish and of catching fish for them.) The facilitative approach involves asking questions, rather than telling. However, questions are not all the same. Consider four types of questions:

- *Closed:* "Did you hit him?"
- *Interrogative:* "Why did you hit him?"
- *Multiple choice:* "Did you hit him because he was teasing you or because of something else?"
- *Open-ended:* "What happened?"

Closed questions require a yes or no or other one-word response from students and do not elicit much reflection. "Are you angry?" will elicit much less information than a question phrased in an open-ended manner, say, "What feelings are you having?" Students often do not react well to "why" questions because their insecurity can lead them to feel defensive and blamed. Most students are usually not aware of, or able to articulate, the deep reasons behind their actions; this is especially true of students with behavioral and emotional difficulties.

An honest response to "Why did you hit him?" is something very few students will offer: "Because I lack self-control and have an inconsistent social learning history with regard to getting negative consequences as a result of my violent actions" or "I think it comes from a chaotic home, some poor parental modeling, and an overexposure to movies, TV, and videogames that glorify aggression, with inadequate adult supervision." By contrast, open-ended questions such as "What happened?" are apt to maximize a student's own thinking about the problem. Further, getting students more invested in the problem-solving process leads them to feel more ownership of and responsibility for the solution.

Giving students several choices from which to select certainly still has its uses—for example, with students who need to be brought along as problem solvers, are immature or have cognitive limitations, or are initially resistive or draw blanks to open-ended questions. And at times, teachers will have to tell students the answer in an authoritative way. What SDM/SPS pedagogy recommends is that teachers first try to *ask* open-ended questions, then *suggest* options from which students can choose, and then *tell* students, if necessary. Cognitive choice is good exercise for students' intellects, as well as for their social-emotional skills. SDM/SPS activities accomplish this by structuring the initial questions teachers ask, both verbally and in written formats, to be open-ended.

The Two Question Rule: A Specialized Questioning Approach

The Two Question Rule is a powerful, simple way to stimulate students' thinking. In leading a group discussion, the rule is to *follow up a question with another question.* It reminds the teacher to stay in a questioning mode and it serves notice to students that the teacher is genuinely interested in hearing details. For example, "How are you feeling?" can be followed up by "What other feelings are you aware of?" "What are you going to say when you go up to the lunch aide?" can be followed up by "How exactly are you going to say it?" In an academic context, "Why do you think the character in the book acted in that way?" can be followed up by "What do you think the character will do next?" Or "What are the ways that the body regulates temperature?" can be followed up by "How do you know that is true?" That last follow-up probe—"How do you know that is true?"—is an especially useful tool for grounding and clarifying students' thinking. Overall, the more students elaborate on their ideas about a problem or issue under consideration, the better understanding teachers have of what students mean and what they are taking from the discussion. The Two Question Rule is valuable for clarifying students' thoughts, feelings, goals, and plans.

Role-Playing, Rehearsal, and Practice

Role-playing provides an opportunity for students to rehearse and practice the responses they would make in actual interpersonal situations. Many students find this activity an enjoyable and valuable supplement to classroom discussions. For teachers, it is an opportunity to give students supervised practice and feedback in reacting to a simulation of everyday events. Four basic steps are involved in a role-play, and these can be explained to students:

- Prepare the script.
- Run through the action.
- Action on the set.
- Review the performance.

Prepare the Script

Select a relevant interpersonal situation and establish the problem and conflict. Choose participants who are willing to accept roles and are likely to handle the roles successfully. Do not place students in roles that reflect their typical situation or approach. Carefully explain the overall situation and the expected actions of each character. Characters should have distinct feelings, motives, and goals in the situation. Where applicable, students should know what alternatives to state and what consequences to expect. There is a clear analogy here with the script of a play.

Run Through the Action

This rehearsal has two aspects. First, have the class discuss the situation and encourage audience participation and constructive suggestions during the run-through process. Be prepared to model, or to have students model, specific examples of any desired behavior that will be the focus of the role-play. Then have the actors discuss among themselves what they will say and do and how they will do it. Have them practice expressions of feelings, verbalize alternatives, or run through any other parts of the overall situation that you feel require emphasis.

Action on the Set

Have the students enact the situation. Teachers are director-coaches and should feel free to help the actors portray their roles as the action is occurring. By actively coaching, you are providing students with feedback and support. This makes role-playing less threatening and confusing for them and also helps move the action along. Discontinue role-playing if a student shows any sign of emotional upset or if the actors (or children in the audience) begin acting in a silly or off-task manner.

Review the Performance

After the performance, have the audience share their views of the thoughts, feelings, and actions expressed by the characters. Students can also be asked how it felt to be involved in, or to watch, the role-play. A valuable way to provide closure is for the teacher to discuss how the role-play could be done differently in the future, emphasizing how the various skills the students are learning fit together.

To help students get started, you can share the four-step outline with them and then proceed by introducing a situation to role-play. Choose a situation such as one of these:

- You have a new student in your class and you want to make that student feel welcome.
- You are having trouble doing a math problem and you want to ask the teacher for help.
- You are a new student in the class and want to make friends.

Choose volunteers and brief the role-players on their parts. Have them plan what they will say and possibly let them rehearse by themselves. Many topics will feature role-play as part of skill building and practice for generalization.

Questions About Role-Playing

Teachers new to role-playing often have questions about how it will fit into classroom activity. For example:

- When would I use role-playing?
- What exactly does the audience do during the role-play?
- What if students are reluctant to become involved or are not ready?

When would I use role-playing?

Role-playing is useful to:

- Highlight personal feelings and those of others when involved in a problematic situation.
- Act out a possible solution to a problem and make it more real.
- Compare two or more solutions.
- Teach planning skills.
- Teach reactions to obstacles.
- Help children integrate their various social decision making and social problem solving skills.

What exactly does the audience do during the role-play?

Members of the audience should be assigned specific points to observe. This focus will keep them actively involved in the process so they don't just watch it like something on TV. Here are some of the major categories:

- Verbal or nonverbal behaviors such as BEST: body posture, eye contact, content of speech, and tone of voice. (See Tables 2 and 3 for topics in which BEST is presented.)
- Specific social decision making and social problem solving steps. (Specify which ones to watch for.)

- All social problem solving steps.
- One actor. (Specify which one.)
- All actors.

Of greatest importance is that students learn to give positive feedback before making any critical comments or suggestions. Teachers should be sure that reviews of performances begin on a positive note. Over time, this encourages the class to work as a problem-solving team and to participate in the role-plays.

What if students are reluctant to become involved or are not ready?

By following the procedures outlined earlier, especially running through the action and coaching while the action is occurring, teachers ensure that most students will wish to be involved. It is also important to establish a positive working atmosphere in which students know that teasing or ridicule is not tolerated. Beyond this, teachers should attempt to gradually phase students into more and more direct involvement. Role-playing with puppets is often a good beginning point for a reluctant class. Students also enjoy making the puppets. Observation of a videotaped interaction also helps sharpen students' skills at observing and giving feedback. A student can also be assigned a specific observational task, such as watching for signs of feelings or for verbal behaviors. The student can be asked to report these observations during the review. Finally, reluctant students can play the parts of extras—people in nonspeaking parts, such as bystanders or passers-by. One of the most successful ways to gently encourage participation is to say to a student, "Do it as if you were . . . [a sports figure, actor or actress, cowboy, musician, school principal, or some other role the student will be able to identify with]." Teachers can judge from students' reactions to these gradual steps when they might be ready to move into greater involvement.

USING THE FOUR "R'S" TO AID RETENTION

Forgetting and confusion will inevitably interfere with learning, much as occurs in the context of other school instruction. Therefore, activities are designed to reflect four "R's" that can increase retention: review, repetition, reminders, and reinforcement.

Review

Each meeting should include a review of both group discussion rules and what occurred in the preceding meeting. This helps bring people who missed that session up-to-date and also lets the teacher accurately gauge the group's starting point.

Repetition

Especially with youngsters in lower elementary grades, our recommended procedure is to maximize tolerable repetition. Many students' attention, memory, or depth of understanding is not sufficient to permit one-trial learning. They benefit from repetition through different modalities (speaking, reading words, viewing pictures, pantomiming, singing, and whispering) and from different sources (teacher, group of peers, dyad).

For the most part, teachers do not repeat *all* the lessons from one year to the next. Rather, a developmentally sequenced flow is designed for each grade. However, a key aspect of instruction, we have found, is children's own maturing ways of responding to situations. Therefore, there will be times when similar content is presented from one year to the next, with the goal of helping children deepen and elaborate their repertoire of feelings, thoughts, and actions around that content. It is also the case that students tend to appreciate structure. Therefore, instruction in most topics begins with a Sharing Circle and a review of the previous session. These features are not described in detail in the instructional activities sections because the review segment will be tailored to each unique classroom context.

Reminders

In our view, the elementary school years are best viewed as a skill acquisition period. It is not consistent with developmental or educational expectations to look for significant internalization and generalization of skill concepts based solely on their presentation in the classroom lessons. The more children are reminded by group leaders, classroom teachers, aides, peers, bus drivers, building administrators, counselors, and others to use their new skills, the more likely they are to find them salient and worth remembering and developing further. The most effective reminders are tangible ones, such as posters depicting the skill components (such as keeping calm, having a successful conversation, or going through the steps of making a sound decision). As an example, teachers using our program have made signs showing ways to get help, both in words and in pictures, and have referred students to these signs when they seem in need of help. Posting stories, worksheets, or other products generated from SDM/SPS activities also serves as a tangible reminder of the skills. In addition to the classroom, other good locations include guidance offices, group rooms, the main office, and hallway bulletin boards.

Use of Prompts and Cues

Prompts and cues are defined as special types of reminders composed of verbal requests or directives to use a certain set of skills. The set of skills generally has components that have been taught in formal group meetings, and the total sequence of these components is given a label. (For example, the components of the skill of self-calming are given the label "Keep Calm.") Nearly all the readiness topics contain labels that can be used as prompts or cues. Here are some examples, along with indications of when to use them:

- *Speaker Power:* A sign not to talk out of turn.
- *Listening Position:* A cue to sit up and orient attention appropriately.
- *Keep Calm:* A prompt to use deep breathing and "self-talk" to calm down.
- *Be Your BEST:* A prompt to behave in a polite, socially acceptable way, attending to body position, eye contact, speech, and tone of voice.
- *Problem Diary:* A way of monitoring personal problems and a tool for thinking about them (by writing a diary) and, at times, for planning ways to handle them.
- *Role-Playing:* A set of behaviors to enact a problem-solving situation and to take others' points of view.
- *Friendship Behavior:* A prompt to think about how one relates to others and how to maintain a positive relationship or change an unsatisfying one.
- *Giving and Getting Help:* A prompt to share one's problems and to be willing to help others solve theirs as well.

Examples of situations in which to use prompts include these:

- Two children are arguing over a pencil; you see the situation escalating.

  Prompt: "I would like to see you both use Keep Calm. . . . Now, let's see what happens if you two try to Be Your BEST."

- One child is squirming around while you are reading something to the class.

  Prompt: "I will continue when everyone is in Listening Position."

- A child runs to you, upset about a problem; you are not able to deal with this outburst right now.

  Prompt: "I can see you were really hassled. Please go fill out a Problem Diary and then come back and see me, and we can talk about it."

- One child is being led astray by another, and you are concerned about it.

  Prompt: "Is Billy your friend? What does it mean to be Billy's friend? What friendship behaviors does he use that you like? What does he do that are not good Friendship Behaviors? How do you feel when he does these things?"

Testimonials

To capitalize on the known potency of peer modeling as an influence on learning, it is advisable to regularly incorporate testimonials into readiness lessons. Testimonials are opportunities for students to tell about situations in which they used skills that they have been taught. A teacher might say, "Let's go around and have everyone share a time in the past week they used 'Keep Calm' or tell about something that happened to you or something you saw where 'Keep Calm' or 'Be Your BEST' might have been helpful."

The reports of the students sharpen their recognition of suitable times to use the skills, provide examples of how the skills can be used in practice, and, for the teacher or group leader, give an opportunity to provide feedback and encouragement that will help promote further skill use. Testimonials may be conducted as part of the Sharing Circle or as a second activity. Some teachers prefer to elicit testimonials on non-lesson days as a way of extending students' involvement with the material.

Reinforcement

The fourth "R" reflects learning theorists' belief that, in the absence of incentives and feedback, proper skill learning is unlikely to occur. Group leaders and others in the students' environment should be alert to their attempts to use their skills. At such times, the attempt should be reinforced with praise or whatever tangible rewards may be applicable in the setting. The opportunity should also be taken to provide specific feedback about which of the students' behaviors would be worth remembering and repeating on future occasions.

If the students can handle it, it would be beneficial to add constructive feedback about what might be useful to try next time to make achievement of goals more likely.

THE APPLICATION PHASE: INFUSION INTO ACADEMICS AND EVERYDAY INTERPERSONAL INTERACTIONS

A particular area in which the SDM/SPS approach is distinctive is the way in which the skills are integrated into everyday academic and interpersonal contexts in classrooms and schools. A teacher who wants to build students' SDM/SPS skills during language arts, health, social studies, civics, science, art, gym, or music will find well-articulated strategies and activities to help this take place in what we call the application phase.

The application phase of SDM/SPS instruction provides students with ongoing opportunities to apply and practice skills taught in the readiness and instructional domains in real-life situations and within the context of academic content areas. Practice is accomplished through a combination of structured practice activities and lessons and facilitative questioning on the part of adults.

Structured Practice Opportunities

Relevant curriculum materials can be found within many of the Topic areas (see Tables 2 and 3) and are emphasized in Supplemental Activities. They take the form of a wide variety of sample structures, frameworks, and materials for infusing a decision-making approach into instruction in almost any subject area, as well as a method for addressing real-life problems and decisions. These lessons and methods are easily adapted to address specific instructional objectives and are flexible enough to use with a variety of content themes, topics, stories, and situations.

For example, worksheets and procedures from Topics for a decision-making approach to social studies or for analyzing literature can be used, with minor variations, with a wide variety of specific topics addressed in social studies or history or for a variety of authors and works of literature.

The FIG TESPN framework can be used to help students think more deeply about and personalize issues in a way that strongly fosters retention and internalization of knowledge. Brain research has provided many insights about how to create more vivid and sustained learning situations, and these are built into the SDM/SPS approach. Consider a series of FIG TESPN–derived questions focused on the topic of immigration or explorers:

1. How did the people feel about leaving their countries? How might you have felt?

2. What countries were they leaving?

3. What problems were going on that made them want to leave?

4. What problems would leaving bring about?

5. What would have been their goals in leaving or staying?

6. What were their options, and how did they envision the results of each possibility? What do you think you would have done?

7. What plans did they have to make? What kinds of things got in their way at the last minute? How did they overcome these roadblocks? How else might they have tried to deal with their situation and solve their problems?

8. Once they arrived, how did they feel? What problems did they encounter at the beginning? What were their first goals?

To help students find fact-based answers to questions posed and check their own views, further reading and research can be assigned. And there are obvious parallels to be drawn in the context of understanding the current diversity of one's classroom, school, or community. Note that students from Grades 2 through 8 can answer the same basic set of questions, bringing to it knowledge, experiences, concerns, and ideas that reflect their developmental differences.

Consider an application-phase approach to holidays or ethnic and cultural commemorations, such as African American History or Latino Heritage months. After students learn some background, you can use FIG TESPN questioning to help students think—as a whole class, in cooperative learning groups, or individually—about how members of different groups feel about the holiday and how they might celebrate it. First, students begin with the group's celebrating the holiday. Then, to broaden their perspectives, they are asked to take the perspectives of other groups—for example, those who are not African Americans, African Americans who lived before the Civil War, people in the United States from different countries. Students can think about alternative ways to recognize events and the consequences of doing so, and then can plan their own way to recognize the event.

The application of frameworks taught in the curriculum can extend to unanticipated events in the life of the classroom, school, or nation. Although the evidence is only anecdotal, there is reason to believe that schools in which SDM/SPS and related SEL programs already existed were well able to address and respond to the events of September 11, 2001, at the World Trade Center in New York, the Pentagon in Washington, D.C., and a field in rural Pennsylvania. Teachers were prepared to address the social-emotional needs of students while the mental health and crisis teams were still being organized and mobilized. FIG TESPN and related problem-solving strategies were used as tools to help students sort through an incredibly complex and charged set of facts and feelings at appropriate developmental levels. Perhaps most important, the tools of SDM/SPS were found to be instruments not only of reflection but also of action. Students were helped to think through how they would cope with the situation immediately and then what they could do to help. And the problem-solving and decision-making approach continued to be used regularly in the days afterward to continually enhance children's understanding and channel their need for contribution.

Similar applications have been made in the context of bullying and school tragedies, as well as in planning positive schoolwide events.

Encouraging Students to Be Thoughtful Decision Makers and Problem Solvers

The SDM/SPS approach is built on promoting generalization and application, and for this, confidence building is essential. Foremost, teachers, counselors, other implementers, and parents are encouraged to communicate with students in a manner that stimulates students' own thinking. Through the use of open-ended questions and dialogue that facilitates students' higher order thinking skills ("What are all the ways that you can think of to handle that problem with

Lee?"), adults keep the channels of communication open. They let students know that they *can* solve their own problems and that their ideas are worthwhile. Moreover, students see adults around them listening to them and caring about and respecting what they say. In this situation, students feel a sense of empowerment. In addition, they are learning skills they can use every day. They are prompted, coached, and guided to practice the skills, and are given feedback aimed at helping them increase their effectiveness. Success is an important source of confidence, but so is praise for effort and progress that gives students the expectation that they are on a pathway to success. This is an important message for self-doubting students who may be prone to see even a 90 percent full glass as 10 percent empty.

Because SDM/SPS is grounded in the social world of students—even when applied to academic areas—students who otherwise seem disaffected, unengaged, or at high risk feel included. Many teachers find that social decision making activities lead to increases in students' involvement in cooperative learning activities. Thus it is more than the content of social decision making that is important in skill building. The instructional principles built into every activity that follows from the social decision making tradition are designed to enhance a range of social and life skills and build self-confidence by helping students recognize that they are valued members of something that is worthwhile. Whether it is being used in a classroom, group, club, advisory, counseling, or clinical context, or in after-school programs, the SDM/SPS approach helps students (and adults) become part of a cooperative problem-solving and decision-making team. It is the powerful combination of direct instruction and external support that has led to significant and lasting student skill gains using the SDM/SPS curriculum.

Modeling

Instruction is important, but seeing adults use problem-solving skills is much more effective than just telling students to problem solve on their own. As students hear adults try to use SDM/SPS skills, they realize that it is normal to have negative feelings, that adults do not always have the perfect solution right at their fingertips, and that adults turn to problem solving when they face difficult situations or choices. Teachers need to find ways of modeling aspects of the program. When introducing a skill, teachers can discuss times they used the particular skill in their own lives. When a conflict takes place, teachers can talk about how they are calming themselves down and using the skills in the curriculum to address the situation. And when staff members interact with one another in the presence of students, it is important to take a positive, respectful, problem-solving approach, even during disagreements.

GETTING STARTED: PREPARE YOUR STUDENTS, THEIR PARENTS AND GUARDIANS, AND YOUR COLLEAGUES

The first Topic in the curriculum at each grade level is an introduction to SDM/SPS and the way activities will be structured. It is essential to set a regular meeting time because students will come to look forward to this part of the school routine. In addition, as students develop more experience with the SDM/SPS pedagogy and as they build their skills, they will be able to save a discussion of problems, conflicts, or other interpersonal issues for the regular SDM/SPS meeting time.

SDM/SPS is built on having a set of classroom rules and procedures, ideally developed with students' input. If there is no order and organization in the classroom, it will be difficult to carry out SDM/SPS or any academic or social development activities. Hence, time is taken in the beginning to establish a climate of mutual respect and teamwork. These procedures are outlined in the first few Topics at each grade level. At the end of this Introduction is a sample letter that can be modified and sent to parents on school letterhead or via e-mail to introduce them to the SDM/SPS curriculum and explain any details you would like them to know as you begin.

Also essential is communication of SDM/SPS to parents and guardians. At the beginning of the year, send an e-mail note, letter, or other communication to parents and guardians, letting them know what you are about to begin and when and how it will take place.

At the end of this Introduction is a sample letter that can be modified and sent to parents on school letterhead or via e-mail to introduce them to the SDM/SPS curriculum and explain any details you would like them to know as you begin.

The curriculum incorporates other communications to the home. These take the following forms:

- Pages to send home that help parents and guardians reinforce skills taught in class
- Activities that students can do with their families
- Suggestions to parents and guardians of ways that they can build their children's SDM/SPS skills by making some small changes in their home routines

Also strongly recommended is a paperback book for parents and guardians that supports all of the skills instruction in this curriculum: *Emotionally Intelligent Parenting: How to Raise a Self-Disciplined, Responsible, Socially Skilled Child,* by Elias, Tobias, and Friedlander (2000).

Finally, be sure your colleagues know what you are doing. Let teachers of special subjects and student support services personnel know what you are covering and how they might be able to use the prompts and cues the students are learning. Find time to share about the activities during grade-level and general faculty meetings. Begin to create a conversation about character in your school so that it becomes as clear to others as it is to you that school is not just about preparing students for tests in school, but also about preparing them for the tests of life.

QUESTIONS AND ANSWERS: EVERYTHING YOU ALWAYS WANTED TO KNOW ABOUT SDM/SPS

Those working with SDM/SPS—including teachers, other educators, parents, school board members, and community partners—often have questions about the curriculum and the overall approach. The "big question" concerns how SDM/SPS relates to other forms of character education and to emotional intelligence. That question will be addressed first; a list of other frequently asked questions and their answers will follow.

Relationship to Other Forms of Character Education

SDM/SPS is considered to be a primary example of a social-emotional learning (SEL) curriculum, that is, a curriculum that builds students' social, emotional, cognitive, and academic capacities in an integrated manner. This curriculum, developed over three decades, is also linked to many other related curricula. For example, SDM/SPS is recognized by the Character Education Partnership as a model program. It is also considered a Promising Program for prevention of violence and substance abuse by the U.S. Department of Education's Expert Panel on Safe and Drug Free Schools, and a winner of the Lela Rowland Prevention Award by the National Mental Health Association as an outstanding program. As noted earlier, SDM/SPS is recognized for excellence by the National Association of School Psychologists and the Collaborative for Academic, Social, and Emotional Learning (www.CASEL.org). Even a cursory look at the FIG TESPN skills (described in the section titled "The Instructional Phase: Instruction in a Social Decision Making Process" earlier in this Introduction) makes clear that students cannot have skill deficits and expect to achieve meaningful academic and social success, sound character, and the ability to engage in nonviolent conflict resolution and to resist pressures to become involved in substance abuse.

SDM/SPS is most directly related to the Interpersonal Cognitive Problem Solving (ICPS—"I Can Problem Solve") approach developed by Spivack and Shure in the early 1970s and described as it relates to preschool through intermediate grades in three books by Shure (2000, 2001a, 2001b). SDM/SPS is completely compatible with and an excellent follow-up to the ICPS curricula. SDM/SPS principles can be found in other empirically based social-emotional learning curricula, such as Lions-Quest, Second Step, Open Circle, PATHS, and TRIBES.

Relationship to Emotional Intelligence

In 1995, Daniel Goleman published his book *Emotional Intelligence*. In it, he summarized years of work done in schools, hospitals, workplaces, and families showing that intellectual abilities alone were not sufficient to account for life success. The skills of emotional intelligence—referred to in most schools as social-emotional learning—are needed for our success as students and as workers, as citizens, and as parents. SDM/SPS is one of six programs that formed the conceptual and empirical basis behind Daniel Goleman's work.

What are the skills of emotional intelligence? Goleman defines five overlapping areas:

- *Self-awareness:* Recognition of one's emotions, possessing an adequate emotional vocabulary, understanding the reasons for feeling as one does in different situations

- *Self-regulation of emotion:* Capacity to verbalize and cope positively with anxiety, depression, and anger and to control impulses toward aggressive, self-destructive, antisocial behavior

- *Self-monitoring and performance:* Short-term and long-term goal setting, focus on tasks at hand; mobilization of positive motivation, hope, and optimism; and ability to work toward one's optimal performance states

- *Empathy and perspective taking:* Listening skills, sensitivity to others' feelings, and understanding of others' points of view, feelings, and perspectives

- *Social skills in handling relationships:* Assertiveness; the ability to express emotions effectively and to show sensitivity to social cues; skills and strategies for working in groups; leadership; social decision making strategies; and the ability to respond constructively to interpersonal obstacles

Emotional Intelligence/SEL and SDM/SPS are entirely compatible. The steps of FIG TESPN are part of social skills for handling relationships; the first step, of course, is part of self-awareness. The readiness skills are interspersed throughout all aspects of emotional intelligence. What was not present in Goleman's work, including the sections on education, was a detailed discussion of implementation. This curriculum operationalizes what is necessary to bring emotional intelligence to every elementary school and classroom.

Effectiveness of the SDM/SPS Curriculum

Evaluation data on SDM/SPS, gathered over the last three decades, strongly support the effectiveness of the curriculum with regard to teachers' ability to facilitate students' social decision making and social problem solving. The evaluations also show students' improved social decision and social problem solving skills; increased prosocial behavior in school and better ability to cope with stressors; and retention of positive effects, as indicated in a high school follow-up. A summary of the evaluation data is provided in Appendix A.

Educators are likely to have specific requirements for assessing the effectiveness of the SDM/SPS program as provided in their own educational environments. However, we include in Appendix B two instruments that we have found helpful in evaluating the Grades 2–3 curriculum at the individual program level. The first is a curriculum feedback form designed to obtain educators' opinions of specific SDM/SPS lesson material. The second, the Profile of Social Decision Making/Social Problem Solving Strengths, may serve as a pretest and posttest to provide information about students' skill learning as a result of program participation.

Other Frequently Asked Questions

Looking at the SDM/SPS program for the first time, many teachers share the following concerns:

- How does SDM/SPS integrate into classroom lesson plans and curricula?
- How does SDM/SPS use multiple methods of delivery to make its points?
- How does SDM/SPS promote engaging and experiential learning?
- How does SDM/SPS encourage higher-level thinking skills that spur moral development?
- How does SDM/SPS provide opportunities for moral action?
- How does SDM/SPS reach students in a developmentally appropriate manner?
- How does SDM/SPS apply to diverse student populations and cultural backgrounds?
- How does SDM/SPS appeal to diverse learning styles?
- How does SDM/SPS support cooperative learning?
- How does SDM/SPS address decision-making skills in the context of high-risk activities?
- How does SDM/SPS encourage positive core values?
- How does SDM/SPS enhance social skills?
- How does SDM/SPS promote a caring school climate?
- How does SDM/SPS complement extracurricular activities?
- How does SDM/SPS include parents and family members?
- How does SDM/SPS encourage school-business partnerships?
- How does SDM/SPS address the effects of mass media?
- How does SDM/SPS link with academic achievement?

How does SDM/SPS integrate into classroom lesson plans and curricula?

SDM/SPS can be readily infused into most existing academic content areas and is aligned with core curriculum standards in such areas as health, language arts, and social studies. Rather than changing lesson content, SDM/SPS uses a pedagogy in which teachers develop an approach that is active in facilitating students' use of sound problem-solving and decision-making strategies and social and emotional competencies.

SDM/SPS is designed to become a strategic part of the teaching process, influencing behavior, academic learning, and social and emotional life in the school setting. Behavioral and cognitive-emotional skills taught have a broad-based range of applications that can extend to community and home situations as well. The formal curriculum activities are most effectively conducted in a regular, consistent time period, usually at least once per week. Because SDM/SPS provides a foundation of prosocial, critical thinking and life skills learning for all students, it is often a useful structure for organizing existing character education, prevention, social skills, and related school programs.

How does SDM/SPS use multiple methods of delivery to make its points?

Teachers using SDM/SPS with their students make use of multiple methods to teach the skills, including direct instruction, worksheets, group discussions, role-playing and rehearsal, and videos and literature as stimuli for discussion.

Ideally, teacher training sessions will be available to prepare teachers to lead these classes, based primarily around small-group experiential activities. Video clips of master teachers in the classroom and live modeling of teacher skills can help to inform participants prior to role-play practice and performance feedback activities. Lecture components include program history and overview. Print and media are used to support the training, and field testing of new skills is processed in follow-up consultation. (See www.2umdnj.edu/SPSweb for additional information.)

How does SDM/SPS promote engaging and experiential learning?

Through application and generalization activities and supplemental topics, students apply SDM/SPS skills to curriculum content and real-life situations. They learn to see literature and historical events through the eyes of the protagonists and to understand the feelings involved. Many activities involve cooperative learning groups and movement on the part of students. Students are encouraged to use skills in brainstorming and planning to develop creative methods for presenting material (for example, learning about caring for the environment or reducing vandalism through a community-based project). Further, the final step of the FIG TESPN decision-making framework —Notice what happened (Now what?)—is a blueprint for learning the skill of self-reflection and exercising the ability to learn from personal experience.

How does SDM/SPS encourage higher level thinking skills that spur moral development?

A primary goal of this approach is to help students develop the ability to think clearly, even under stress. By providing a combination of direct instruction and multiple and varied opportunities to practice a strategy for thinking through a problem, decision, or life conflict, the program helps students internalize this ability. Although the skills are essential for processing understanding in academic areas, the focus of much of the instruction and practice is on everyday moral and interpersonal choices that students face. These skills are the cornerstone of self-reflection, which is a central aspect of emotional intelligence, moral development, and moral action.

How does SDM/SPS provide opportunities for moral action?

The SDM/SPS approach requires students to develop plans for action and evaluate the results of what they have done. This requirement results in a range of life applications in wide and diverse areas of moral action. For example, educators are trained to help students whose behaviors result in a disciplinary action or have hurt another person develop a personal plan for restitution.

Educators implementing the SDM/SPS approach have also developed a diverse variety of school and community service projects that promote moral action. These applications include the following:

- Classroom (students solving interpersonal conflicts within the classroom).

- School, community, or peer mediation applications to promote moral action on the playground and in the school bus, cafeteria, and other less structured school community situations.

- Community service projects. (Examples include a project that resulted in the recycling of plastics, inspired by student presentations to a town council, and a "Community Sharing Circle," involving students from public and private schools within a township that led the recreation department and the mayor's office to develop a three-year plan to reduce vandalism in the community.)

The SDM/SPS approach focuses on providing students with a foundation for moral action. They learn basic skills that are then applied to endless and ongoing opportunities to stop and reflect on choices made and the impact these choices have on oneself, on others, and on the community.

How does SDM/SPS reach students in a developmentally appropriate manner?

SDM/SPS uses a developmentally sensitive scope and sequence of skills to provide students with social-emotional competencies they can use at once. The program is built on foundations of research and practice from the fields of child development, child clinical psychology, the cognitive sciences, brain and emotion research, educational practice, and primary prevention. Professional psychologists developed the curriculum, which was then field-tested and revised by teachers working within the school systems over a period of three decades. SDM/SPS is used, and has been adapted for use, with all students (general and special education) in elementary and middle schools, regardless of ability level, ethnic group, and socioeconomic status.

How does SDM/SPS apply to diverse student populations and cultural backgrounds?

Many of the SDM/SPS skills are also key components of promoting a multicultural perspective in students. Instruction in SDM/SPS includes learning to care about and respect one's classmates (regardless of issues of difference), to listen and learn from one another, and to comfortably share diverse opinions and backgrounds. Activities are included to build group cohesion, acceptance of differences, and the ability to understand different points of view. In this way, respect for diversity moves beyond knowledge acquisition and into the realm of systematic skill building to develop students' ability to perform successfully according to established classroom norms and expectations.

How does SDM/SPS appeal to diverse learning styles?

An awareness of diverse learning styles was a part of the authors' original goals for program design and is built into the activities, pedagogy, and Tips for Teachers. Because of the nature of the content, almost all areas of instruction lend themselves to the use of varied modes of content delivery and application across the modalities of the multiple intelligences.

Curriculum-based activities include the use of a wide range of instructional methods to ensure that students who favor imaginative, analytic, commonsense, and dynamic learning styles are all addressed. Instruction includes these methods:

- Visual displays
- Mnemonic devices for remembering skills and concepts
- Hands-on activities
- Storytelling
- Role-play and real-life practice
- Live modeling
- Reflective discussions to highlight the purpose of a lesson after experiential activities
- Activities that allow students to teach others
- Multimodal formats for presentation of projects and other learning

Much of the curriculum consists of innovations developed by teachers to match students' different learning styles and needs.

How does SDM/SPS support cooperative learning?

The SDM/SPS model supports cooperative learning in two ways. First, the initial phase of the curriculum is focused on helping students treat their classmates as a problem-solving team. By learning and practicing these skills in a controlled situation, students become better prepared to be productive and to behave acceptably in a cooperative learning group. Second, both skill-building lessons and the ongoing infused application of these skills are conducted by using a wide range of cooperative learning methods, such as pair shares, small-group brainstorming, problem solving, and role-playing activities.

How does SDM/SPS address decision-making skills in the context of high-risk activities?

Traditional prevention programs tend to be organized around a single problem area, such as substance abuse, handgun violence, or risky teenage sex. SDM/SPS serves as a research-validated framework for prevention programs that are not limited to specific problems but rather are more unifying in their prevention messages. This unifying framework teaches students to become more socially aware and socially skilled decision makers in both routine and high-risk problem situations.

How does SDM/SPS encourage positive core values?

A number of positive core value areas are encouraged and supported by the SDM/SPS curriculum. The program focuses on building skills that will enable a person to be a caring, compassionate, responsible, and respectful friend and classmate, thus preparing students to become positive and productive citizens. Students are taught to be reflective, nonimpulsive, and responsible decision makers and problem solvers who consider the way in which their actions will affect both themselves and others. The basis of the curriculum at each grade level is teamwork, operationalized by activities that build the skills that underlie this value, such as self-control, listening, respectful communication, giving and receiving help and authentic praise, working cooperatively and fairly in small groups, and understanding and respecting others' different points of view.

How does SDM/SPS enhance social skills?

The purpose of the SDM/SPS program is to develop the social and decision-making skills children need to cope with stress, make sound choices, avoid self-destructive behaviors, and resolve conflicts peacefully. These are the goals of the program:

1. Develop children's self-control and social awareness skills (including monitoring and regulating stress and emotions, group cooperation, and the ability to develop positive peer relationships).

2. Improve students' decision-making, problem-solving, and conflict resolution and mediation skills.

3. Increase students' academic and interpersonal self-efficacy by providing them with a problem-solving framework and social-emotional competencies upon which they can rely in stressful situations.

4. Enhance positive social behaviors and healthy life choices.

How does SDM/SPS promote a caring school climate?

The SDM/SPS curriculum has many activities and strategies for building class cohesion and transforming classrooms into problem-solving teams. Moreover, when SDM/SPS becomes part of schoolwide procedures, changes occur in the way problems and discipline are handled in the school. The focus shifts to setting positive behavioral norms and to dealing with violations as problems to be solved. Students develop and make agreements to follow a new plan for action in the future.

How does SDM/SPS complement extracurricular activities?

Ideally, SDM/SPS becomes an integral part of the overall school climate and easily complements the school's extracurricular activities. Coaches of both school- and township-sponsored athletic programs have been trained to reinforce the SDM/SPS skills that the children are learning in their classroom-based program. For example, coaches can call upon the self-control skills, such as "Keep Calm," when athletes have difficulty controlling their emotions during a game. Constructive criticism and team building are also important sportsmanship skills. After-school and summer programs also can provide both direct instruction and reinforcing practice activities in social and decision making skills. Workshops have been developed to incorporate SDM/SPS as foundation skills for training of students involved in student government, peer leadership, peer mediation, and service learning.

How does SDM/SPS include parents and family members?

Parent and family involvement is a critical area for extending classroom-based instruction to the home and family. Two widely available paperback publications by Elias, Tobias, and Friedlander, *Emotionally Intelligent Parenting* (2000) and *Raising Emotionally Intelligent Teenagers* (2002), and a related Web site (www.eqparenting.com) have helped us to reach parents. The University of Medicine and Dentistry of New Jersey's Social Decision Making Program has developed the *Leader's Guide for Conducting Parent Meetings,* which provides a detailed plan to conduct a sequence of parent workshops on social decision making.

In addition, we have collaborated with district teams in the development of a wide variety of outreach activities and materials, based on the creative problem solving of educators and our staff. For example, a variety of local cable video programs have been produced as successful ways to reach many parents in a community. A parent survey to assess the best times for parents to tune in can help set a schedule in line with a variety of viewing times for busy parents. No baby-sitter or other logistical planning is needed for participation. Copies of the video are then distributed by the school for home viewing. In addition, we help districts adapt a brochure for parents describing the program, based on some standard prototypes we have designed in the past. Parents are also reached through materials incorporated into the curriculum that are designed to provide information that parents and guardians can post on their refrigerators for easy, regular viewing.

A wide variety of school-based events have also been effective in some communities, such as evening sessions including dinner and baby-sitters and bagel breakfasts in which parents are invited to join a morning class session where children help their teachers share what they are learning. Such events are designed and marketed in collaboration with our school colleagues, who are most knowledgeable regarding the local needs, access points, and obstacles in the community.

How does SDM/SPS encourage school-business partnerships?

Local businesses and corporations are very interested in working with schools to prepare students to enter the workforce. Recent studies have shown the importance of social and emotional competencies in the workplace. Learning these skills early in life has been shown to be beneficial in finding employment and in receiving promotions throughout a whole career. Local businesses have supported meetings at which students have displayed work done as part of the SDM/SPS curriculum, provided mentors for projects, visited classrooms, and provided resources in support of various projects and activities.

How does SDM/SPS address the effects of mass media?

SDM/SPS addresses the media in constructive ways. Students are taught critical viewing skills and to recognize situations in which they are being persuaded to buy a particular product or to agree with a certain point of view. In the Grade 5 materials, specific emphasis is placed on teaching students to recognize how advertisements play on their emotions and vulnerabilities. Mass media are also useful tools in teaching social and emotional learning. Various movies, television shows, and videos can present real-life and hypothetical situations that can be used to teach problem-solving and decision-making skills. Part of the SDM/SPS pedagogy is the TVDRP technique, a combination of television (or other audiovisual or digital media), discussion (that will facilitate thoughtful decision making), and guided rehearsal and practice (or other forms of experiential activity).

How does SDM/SPS link with academic achievement?

SDM/SPS and academics have strong empirical and conceptual links. Research studies carried out over the past three decades are summarized in Appendix A.

SUMMARY

SDM/SPS can help schools meet their mandates and perceived needs in a broad variety of areas. The skills it establishes are an essential part of developing a safe, caring school. The program helps educators build learning communities with character and lay a foundation for students' social-emotional development and for prevention of violence and substance abuse.

Sample Letter to Parents and Guardians to Introduce SDM/SPS

Dear Parents or Guardians:

I would like to take this opportunity to introduce you to a program that we are initiating in our school. The program is called Social Decision Making/Social Problem Solving (SDM/SPS). It teaches children valuable skills in the areas of self-control, problem solving, decision making, and getting along with others. We will be doing SDM/SPS lessons once a week, usually every _____ at _____ .

These skills require time and practice to develop. You will be receiving information and ideas for activities that will assist you in helping your child practice these skills. I would like to encourage you to reinforce these skills when your child is at home and during extracurricular activities. Your continued support and encouragement will enable your child to gain strength in this area and experience success now and in the future.

I am excited about implementing this program in our school. Please feel free to contact me or our building principal with any questions or ideas.

Sincerely,

_____   _____
(Teacher signature)   *(Date)*

RECOMMENDED TOPICS FOR GRADE 2

Becoming a Problem-Solving Team

Feelings

Supplemental

Grade 2 Worksheets

BECOMING A PROBLEM-SOLVING TEAM

Topics 1–12

1 Introduction to Social Decision Making/Social Problem Solving (SDM/SPS) Lessons

OBJECTIVES
- To introduce and orient students to SDM/SPS meetings
- To establish ground rules for SDM/SPS meetings
- To introduce and participate in a *Sharing Circle*
- To introduce and provide opportunities to practice Speaker Power, and to establish *Speaker Power* as shared language and a skill prompt
- To build a sense of group trust, belonging, and cohesiveness

MATERIALS
Chalkboard or easel pad

Speaker Power object

Poster board and markers

"Suggested Sharing Circle Questions" (Worksheet 2.1.1)

Copies of the "Introduction to Sharing Circles" Take-Home (Worksheet 2.1.2)

PREPARATION It is helpful to have chairs in a circle for a Sharing Circle, or if this is not possible some arrangement that will allow the children to see one another. This format will eventually be used as a vehicle for working through the problem-solving steps during formal lessons and class discussions of problem solving. Determine the location and arrangement of the Sharing Circle and decide how to have the children settle into it. Many teachers have found it successful to ask the students for ideas about efficient ways to move into a Sharing Circle.

NOTE After the group has compiled a list of rules, write them on a sheet of poster board and display them prominently. As rules are refined and new rules added, change the list accordingly. (Students can help by adding drawings or decorations to the poster.)

INSTRUCTIONAL ACTIVITIES

1. Describe the meetings.

Have children sit in a circle so they can see one another.

Begin by telling students that they will be having lessons that will help them learn skills for getting along with other people and making good decisions. Knowing how to make decisions that will help solve problems and being able to get along with other people are important in second grade and will also help them be successful and healthy as they grow up. You can say something along these lines:

> *Just as some people are better than others in solving math problems or playing sports, some people are already good at some of the skills we will be learning about, but everyone can learn some new things and improve their skills in this important area.*

These skills will help the class work together as a problem-solving team. Explain the idea in terms like these:

> *We are doing this because we all have times when we do not know what to do. Our social decision making lessons will help us understand our feelings and what we can do to solve problems and make good decisions.*

Tell the children where and when the lessons will take place. The days and times for skill instruction and skill-building activities can be posted as part of the regular schedule of events in the classroom.

2. Establish rules and agreements.

Tell the class that to work as a problem-solving team, they will first have to decide on some rules to follow so the meetings will go well. Ask the children to volunteer some rules that would help make everyone feel good about being a member of this team. Keep a list on the chalkboard or easel pad. Ask them to think about what would make them feel good about sharing their ideas and how they would like to be treated. Then ask:

> *What are some things that would make you not feel good about being part of this team?*

Rules should be brief, written down, and posted visibly for future reference. Here is a sample of some basic rules:

- Allow one person to talk at a time.
- Listen to the person who is speaking.
- Respect one another.
- No put-downs.

Talk with the class about what to call this list (for example: Class Rules, Problem-Solving Team Rules). The rules can be adjusted as the meetings proceed to pick up on cue phrases as you establish them; for example, "Allow one person to talk at a time" can be stated more simply as "Practice Speaker Power" once the students know what that means.

When making a poster or sign containing the group rules, work with the students to decide on a picture or symbols to accompany the words. Children often have good ideas for symbols and can sometimes do the drawing.

3. Introduce the Sharing Circle.

Explain that the first activity the class is going to learn is called a "Sharing Circle." Explain the ground rules for the Sharing Circle: Everyone (children, teachers, visitors in the room) in turn will at least say their name and then have a chance to answer a Sharing Circle question.

Go around the circle and give everyone an opportunity to share their name. You may wish to start out with your own name to demonstrate the process.

4. Introduce Speaker Power.

Select an object (magic wand, stuffed animal, scarf, ruler, pen . . .) that will be passed to the person speaking to designate a turn to talk.

A Speaker Power object helps remind us to respect the person who is speaking. Others are expected to listen quietly until Speaker Power reaches them.

Be sure to let students know that as the teacher, you always have a kind of invisible Speaker Power. You will ask for the object when it fits into the lesson to do so, but it's your job to speak whenever you regard it as necessary.

5. Complete a group exercise using Speaker Power.

Begin by asking a simple and nonthreatening question that will allow everyone in the group to have a turn. Let the students know that there are no right or wrong answers and they can share with the group anything that comes to mind as long as it addresses the question. During the initial Sharing Circle, it is a good idea to set the tone for further circles. Remind children that they are not being asked to agree with everything that is being said:

Remember that you can agree or disagree with someone's statement but still accept the person. Sometimes people think the same idea as others and that is OK. Other times someone might share an idea that is different from what you think, and that is OK, too.

Here are some sample first questions that we have found to be useful group builders:

- What is something that happened to you that made you feel happy?
- What is your favorite flavor ice cream?
- If you could be an animal for one day, what kind of animal would you be?

Compliment students when they respect Speaker Power. When necessary, remind them they may only speak if they are holding Speaker Power. If you begin to observe a loss of attention, ask if you can please have Speaker Power and say you will give it back in a minute.

Then ask the students how they think it went. What was easy or hard about remembering to use Speaker Power? How did it feel to have Speaker Power? Then begin again and continue to pause for feedback as needed.

As time permits, ask the children two or three additional questions that will gradually reveal something new about them to their classmates. After each question, have some children answer, then move on to the next question. The following questions have been found to be quite useful for an initial group-building exercise:

- What is your favorite food? (Why?)
- What is your favorite time of day? (Why?)
- If you were going to be the star of a television show, what show would you pick? (Why?)
- If you could spend one hour talking to anyone you wanted to, who would you pick? (Why?)

Additional Sharing Circle questions are provided as Worksheet 2.1.1.

6. Introduce a Reflective Summary.

As outlined in the Introduction, ask students to reflect on the question "What did you learn from today's lesson?" Reinforce key themes, then go over any follow-up work.

7. Follow up.

The following steps will help make sure that the students have a chance to continue working with the new concepts throughout the school day and at home.

Assignment

Help children prepare to contribute in the next lesson by providing them with the question you plan to use for the next Sharing Circle. Let them know that you will be using the cue words *Speaker Power* and *Sharing Circle* during other subjects and at other times in the day. Mention situations that the students suggested and encourage them to try using Speaker Power at those times.

Take-Home

Distribute a letter to parents or guardians like the one presented in the Introduction at this time (if it hasn't been sent earlier or distributed at Back to School Night) to introduce the SDM/SPS skill-building lessons to the students' families.

Also distribute the "Introduction to Sharing Circles" Take-Home (Worksheet 2.1.2) and tell students that the handout will explain what the class does in Sharing Circles and give their parents some suggestions about when they could use Speaker Power. Ask students to tell parents or guardians about it. Let students know that they might also need to help teach them about Sharing Circles and Speaker Power.

Plans to Promote Transfer and Generalization of Skill

Plan ahead to provide opportunities for students to practice a Sharing Circle and the use of a Speaker Power object as part of an academic lesson or class discussion.

For example:

- Before a health lesson or gym class exercise, ask, "What is your favorite sport or physical activity?"
- While reading a story, stop for a Sharing Circle and ask, "Who is your favorite person in the story so far? If you could say something to them or ask them a question, what would it be?" or "Who do you think has the biggest problem in this story? Why?"
- During a social studies lesson, stop and ask a Sharing Circle question to help students relate to the content in a personal way. For example, "If you could ask the people we are learning about a question, what would you ask?"

TIPS FOR TEACHERS

1. When getting started, it can be helpful to go first and model what is expected. Students often enjoy learning about their teachers—what makes the teacher feel happy or what kind of animal the

teacher would like to be—and this discovery helps begin an interest in what other people feel and think about a similar question.

2. Class size and maturity are important factors in determining how the Sharing Circle will best operate. Sharing Circle questions should allow for self-expression without calling for personal information considered confidential. Students may not be aware of these limits, so it is important to avoid questions that pull for such information, and to politely interrupt, support, and redirect any responses that are inappropriate for a classroom skill-building lesson. For example, you could say:

I can tell that you have strong feelings about this, and I want to hear about it. But it is better to talk about private things that happen at home privately, not in a large group. We can talk about this after we finish the lesson to respect the privacy of your family. Can you think of an example that happened to you at school or with your friends?

Be sure to follow up and refer to another professional if what students share is outside your area of professional training.

3. When introducing Sharing Circle, try to notice students who may need prompting to be drawn into the circle. Some teachers have been successful by allowing such students to pass and checking back later to see if they have thought of something to share. Seating, question choice, time to prepare, and many other ideas have been successful in engaging the quiet student.

Also, recognize the "talkers"—the children who may need time limits set. Many creative ideas have been used to solve these problems—for example, preparing ahead with limits such as one sentence or one minute (measured with a timer), or taking talkative students aside to compliment them for their willingness to express themselves and ask them to help the teacher encourage others who are less willing to share. While there is no magic answer for all students or groups, it is important to develop and consistently implement strategies to encourage participation from more withdrawn students. It is equally important to encourage students who need to set limits on how much they dominate the talk time to share Speaker Power equitably.

4. Many teachers we have worked with report that it becomes natural and automatic to include skill prompts and practice of SDM/SPS skills within academic subject areas throughout the course of the day once students have mastered the basic skills. At initial stages of implementation, however, it is helpful to think ahead each week and include activities for skill practice within the lesson plans. Thinking ahead to identify situations and subject content areas where the practice of SDM/SPS skills would fortify existing objectives is helpful. Documenting these plans and monitoring the degree to which opportunities for students to practice and gen-

eralize the skill they are learning to academic and real-life situations helps ensure that teaching practices remain true to the instructional design that led to research-validated outcomes. It also helps teachers—in their role as adult learners—integrate new skills within the complex repertoire of teaching skills needed.

5. Clear consequences should be established for disruption of the group by either aggressiveness or silliness. One strategy that has been successful for some students and groups is to first remind disruptive students about their agreement to keep the rules, such as respect one another, listen to one another, and attend to prompts for desired behavior. If this does not work, try having someone sit out for a few minutes, letting them know that you will be checking back in a few minutes to ask them if they are ready to come back and stick to the team agreements. This strategy is effective when the students enjoy the activities and don't want to be left out. As with any behavior management technique, it is important to find reinforcers and consequences that work for a particular child or group.

1. Do you think you have too many chores? If you could assign the chores in your house, which ones would you take for yourself?

2. If you could be invisible for a day, what would you do?

3. Would you like to have an identical twin? What about it would be best? Worst?

4. Imagine that your principal wanted to make school better and would change it in any way you suggested. What would you say to do?

5. What are you the most proud of having done? What would make you even more proud?

6. What was the luckiest thing that ever happened to you?

7. If this Saturday you could do absolutely anything you wanted, what would you do?

8. If you could be any animal for a day, which one would you be? Why?

9. What is the best costume you ever wore? Would you like getting dressed up in costumes once a week instead of just a few times a year?

10. If you could pick any one food and have as much of it as you wanted—but nothing else—during the next week, what would you pick?

11. If you could do one thing you are not allowed to do now because you are too young, what would you pick?

12. If you could be an adult for one week, what would you do during the week?

13. If you could have the ability to talk to one kind of animal, which would you choose and why? What would you talk about?

14. Would you rather have more brothers and sisters than you have now or fewer? What do you think is the best size for a family? Why?

15. If you had to pick a new first name for yourself, what would it be?

16. If you could take a friend home with you after school, what would you show your friend?

17. What is the best thing that could happen to you? The worst thing?

18. What do you think is the best thing about being a child? The worst thing?

19. If you could change one rule at school, which one would it be? At home?

20. What do you want to do for a living when you grow up? How would you prepare for that?

Sharing Circles

Dear Parents or Guardians:

A Sharing Circle is an opportunity for everyone to share their feelings and thoughts. Everyone agrees to respect and listen to what others have to say. In the classroom, having regular Sharing Circles helps us to get to know each other better, learn about our similarities and differences, and practice ways to listen and respect each other.

At home, you may want to develop and refine rules for conducting your own family Sharing Circle, and the following general guidelines may be helpful.

Sharing Circle Guidelines

1. Each member of the circle should have a chance to speak. It helps to pass around a Speaker Power object—a small, soft toy or something else that shows that the person talking is the one whose turn it is right now.

2. Members who would rather not speak at any point in the discussion should be permitted to pass the Speaker Power object along without saying anything.

3. The group should establish clear guidelines for responding to each member's remarks. Some prefer to reply to a remark as soon as it is made, while others would rather wait until after all members have spoken on a point.

To try out a Sharing Circle, pick something to use for a Speaker Power object. Then sit in a circle where you can all see each other and ask, "What is the best thing that happened to you today?" Pass the object around the circle, while each person responds to the question. Others listen carefully without interrupting. Ask your child to show the family how.

Your child may be asked in class to share what happened when you practiced this activity.

Thank you!

(Teacher signature)   *(Date)*

....

(Please sign and return this bottom section.)   **Sharing Circles   2.1.2**

Student _____ **Date** _____

We tried a Sharing Circle.   ❒ Yes   ❒ No

If you did, how did it go?

(Signature of parent or guardian)

2 Listening Position

OBJECTIVES	▪ To teach the components of good listening
	▪ To teach skills of Listening Position and paying attention
	▪ To provide practice for learning good listening skills and skill prompts to help promote use of these skills beyond these lessons
MATERIALS	Whole-class display of the steps in "Listening Position" (Worksheet 2.2.1)
	"Listening Activity Word Lists" (Worksheet 2.2.2)

INSTRUCTIONAL ACTIVITIES

1. Review the introduction.

With the students' help, review the main themes of Topic 1. Include the reasons for having these lessons, the meaning of Speaker Power, and other rules agreed upon during the first session to help the team work well together.

2. Conduct a Sharing Circle.

Use a question from the list provided or provide one of your own. As the Speaker Power object is passed around the circle, if students begin to appear distracted, ask if you can please have Speaker Power and let the next person know that they will have a turn in a minute. Stand behind a student who has already shared and ask the group:

Was anyone listening carefully when [name] had Speaker Power? Who can tell us what [name] had to share?

Reinforce good listening. If any details were not covered, ask if anyone can provide any other detail until the group accurately recalls details of what the person said. After everyone has had a chance to share, ask:

How did we do? Was it difficult to remember what people said? If so, what made it difficult? What did it feel like to have Speaker Power?

3. Establish the importance of listening.

Obtain the students' interest by asking them if they ever had a time when someone was not listening to them when they really wanted to say something. When someone agrees—and someone always will—ask:

How did it feel?

Can anyone think of a time when they should have been listening and they were not?

(Some teachers begin by sharing a story of their own to break the ice.)

What happened and how did it feel?

Ask the class when it is important to be a good listener. Some examples: when learning the rules of a game for the first time, when trying to understand the teacher's explanation of a difficult math problem, when trying to learn the words of a new song. . . .

4. Introduce Listening Position.

Explain that in this lesson the group is going to explore what listening is and how to go about doing it better. To be a good listener it is necessary to pay attention. Ask:

What is "paying attention?"

Can you act out the way a person looks who is not listening or paying attention? What are some behaviors that make you think someone is not listening or paying attention?

Generate a list of behaviors that show not listening. Then ask:

Can you act out the way someone looks when they are listening and paying attention?

How does it look when someone is listening carefully and paying attention?

Generate a list of behaviors that show that someone is listening and paying attention.

5. Establish the behavioral components of Listening Position.

Listening Position is quite remarkably consistent across cultures and age groups:

1. Sit or stand straight.

2. Face the speaker or source of sound.

3. Look toward the speaker or source of sound.

Tell the class that another important part of listening is paying attention. Ask them why it is important to pay attention. After accepting several responses, say:

Let's play a game that will help us learn about listening.

Ask the class to close their eyes.

Then ask the class to clap their hands only when they hear the word *cat* as you read the words from List 1. Read at about one word per second. Note both performance (clap on another word) and nonperformance (no clap on "cat") errors.

6. Have the children share their difficulties.

Ask the class to list some things people can do to listen more carefully and accurately. Be sure the list includes the following:

Listening Position: Sit or stand straight, face the speaker, look toward the speaker (or source of sound).

Pay attention (or concentrate): Do not interrupt or let anything distract you.

Model each of these behaviors for the children, and then have the children model all of them.

7. Conduct a practice activity.

Say:

Now let's practice our paying attention and listening skills again and try to remember the things that we just went over.

Repeat the clapping exercise. Be sure everyone is in a Listening Position before you start. Here are several variations that can be used with List 1:

- Clap on everything except cat.
- Clap on all animals only.
- Clap on all animals except cat.
- Clap only on words that are not names of animals.

8. Introduce a Reflective Summary.

As outlined in the Introduction, ask students to reflect on the question "What did you learn from today's lesson?" Reinforce key themes, then go over any follow-up work.

9. Follow up.

The following activity will help make sure that the students have a chance to continue working with the new concepts throughout the school day and at home.

Plans to Promote Transfer and Generalization of Skill

"Listening Position" is a skill that can be used often on a daily basis. As mentioned, when first implementing these lessons it is helpful to develop concrete plans for review and practice and record these activities within your weekly lesson plans.

For example, you can use "Listening Position" as a skill prompt after all transitions as a cue that a new activity is about to begin, as well as at key points within a lesson, such as right before beginning to read a story in language arts, before giving directions for a cooperative activity in social studies or health, or before giving instructions for an activity in gym, music, or art. At the beginning of the day and after recess are also times when a brief review and practice of Listening Position serves as a helpful management tool.

TIPS FOR TEACHERS

1. The list game has several variations that may serve your class better. These include having your students:

   - Clap and stamp feet.
   - Stand.
   - Walk around room and freeze on words.
   - Walk around room, freeze, and start again at the next word they are listening for.

2. If the class needs a review of listening skills, a different word list may reawaken their interest. Try List 2 or List 3 in that case.

Listening Position

1. Sit or stand straight.

2. Face the speaker or source of sound.

3. Look toward the speaker or source of sound.

From *Social Decision Making/Social Problem Solving: A Curriculum for Academic, Social, and Emotional Learning (Grades 2–3)*. Copyright © 2005 by Maurice J. Elias and Linda Bruene Butler. Research Press (800-519-2707; www.researchpress.com)

LIST 1

cuts	coat	horse	cut	dog	cow	cat
horse	cuts	cut	cow	cut	dog	cat
coat	cute	horse	dog	cute	cow	dog
cow	cut	cat	cat	dog	horse	cut

LIST 2

cat	shoes	pants	coat	cute	dress	cut
cute	cut	pants	shoes	dress	cat	shoes
coat	dress	pants	cut	dress	shoes	cut
coat	pants	cute	cat	coat	cut	shoes
cute	coat	cat	pants	cat	cute	dress

LIST 3

bush	leaf	true	tree	grass	tire	tear
tree	true	leaf	tear	bush	tree	leaf
bush	true	tire	tear	grass	tire	grass
true	tear	leaf	bush	grass	leaf	tear
tire	true	tree	tire	tree	grass	bush

From *Social Decision Making/Social Problem Solving: A Curriculum for Academic, Social, and Emotional Learning (Grades 2–3)*.
Copyright © 2005 by Maurice J. Elias and Linda Bruene Butler. Research Press (800-519-2707; www.researchpress.com)

3   Effective Listening

OBJECTIVE
- To learn to listen effectively to what is being communicated
- To establish *On-Topic* as shared language

NOTES   To the extent that a group is not cohesive, its members find it more difficult to learn the skills of social decision making and social problem solving, and it takes longer for them to feel confident and comfortable enough to try the skills in new situations.

The activities in this topic help foster a spirit of group cohesion, team building, and trust and are recommended even if the group already seems to be working cooperatively. One of the most important ways in which your class will come to feel like a problem-solving team is for the students to become comfortable working with one another in a group and to believe that they can say what is on their minds without being criticized or rejected.

It is important to use these group-building activities as an opportunity to observe group dynamics and take time to stop throughout to ask students to assess how well they are working as a group. Remind them to respect Speaker Power by not interrupting each other and to use Listening Position.

MATERIALS   None

INSTRUCTIONAL ACTIVITIES

1. Begin with a Sharing Circle as a group-building activity.

Review Sharing Circle rules. Ask the students how it feels to know their classmates are listening to them. Explain that last time they learned about Listening Position and today they are going to talk about the difference between listening carefully and not listening carefully.

2. Model an example of ineffective listening.

Have the class watch and listen carefully, and be prepared to discuss what they see and hear. The following is a sample conversation that can be rehearsed ahead of time with another adult or a child—or you can do it yourself in a pinch (rehearsing taking two roles—ideally moving from seat or place to place while modeling).

A: Hi, how are you?

B: OK, I guess—

A: Boy, I can't wait for school to be over today.

B: Yeah, well, I'm not looking forward to . . .

A: Did you see that new movie? I'm going later.

B: Lately, I haven't been able to . . .

A: Who's that over there? Hi, Billy!

Ask:

What did you observe?

What was A doing?

How would you feel if you were B?

List any behaviors mentioned. One aspect of this conversation that is valuable to highlight and label is that the things these two people are talking about are different. Introduce the label *On-Topic* to describe conversations where people are talking about the same thing.

3. Model an example of effective listening.

Once again, have the class watch and listen carefully, and be prepared to discuss what they see and hear.

Say:

Now we are going to listen again; let's try to see what is different from the first set of conversations.

A: Hi, how are you?

B: OK. How are you?

A: Pretty good. How about you?

B: OK, I guess . . .

A: What do you mean? What's going on?

B: Well, I have a lot of homework, and it's giving me trouble.

A: What are you having trouble with? Maybe I can help you.

Ask:

What did you observe?

What was A doing this time?

How would you feel if you were B?

4. Conduct a practice activity.

Begin by discussing what it means to stay On-Topic. Ask why is it important to stay On-Topic. Pair children up and give them a topic to talk about, using Listening Position and staying On-Topic.

Examples:

- Talk about what games they like to play after school.
- Talk about what they like best about recess.

Allow the students to practice and then have pairs present their example to the class. Reinforce and ask the class to notice any examples of Listening Position and On-Topic conversation.

5. Introduce a Reflective Summary.

As outlined in the Introduction, ask students to reflect on the question "What did you learn from today's lesson?" Reinforce key themes, then go over any follow-up work.

6. Follow up.

The following activity will help make sure that the students have a chance to continue working with the new concepts throughout the school day and at home.

Plans to Promote Transfer and Generalization of Skill

Use the prompt *On-Topic* or *Off-Topic* in response to each student's comments after one of their classmates speaks. If student discussion about a story begins to build on something silly one student mentioned rather than on the objective at hand, you can use one of these prompts:

- I am wondering if our discussion is On-Topic right now?
- What are we thinking about the story we are reading?
- Can anyone share an idea that will bring us back On-Topic?

T O P I C

4   Listening Power

OBJECTIVES
- To deepen and further develop listening skills
- To introduce and practice paying attention

MATERIALS AND
Whole-class display of the steps in "Listening Power" (Worksheet 2.4.1)

INSTRUCTIONAL ACTIVITIES

1. Begin by conducting a Sharing Circle.

Ask students if they had opportunities to practice Listening Position and staying On-Topic since the last lesson. Provide time for students to share some experiences. Also, have students share examples of situations in which they worked together as a team.

2. Go around the circle and talk about attentive listening.

Ask the children to address these questions:

- Who is someone that listens to you?
- What do they do to make you know they are listening?

Periodically, either after a student with Speaker Power has spoken or after everyone has answered, ask students to share in detail what other students had to say. This helps sharpen their listening abilities. Reinforce good listening skills and aspects of Listening Power observed.

3. Review the behavioral components of Listening Position.

Remind the class that Listening Position consists of three simple acts:

1. Sit or stand straight.

2. Face the speaker or source of sound.

3. Look toward the speaker or source of sound.

4. Introduce the new skill of Listening Power.

Explain that just hearing what someone is saying isn't enough. Use a narrative along these lines:

The new listening skill introduced today is a way to be sure that you understand what you have listened to. To be sure that you have paid attention and are right about what you heard, you can repeat what you think you heard. You might say, "I heard you say that . . ." and say back to the other person what you heard them say. And then you ask them if you are right by saying something like, "Did I understand you?"

To introduce Listening Power (sometimes referred to as "active listening"), emphasize the following points:

1. Use Listening Position.

2. Pay attention to what the other person is saying.

3. Repeat what the other person said.

4. Check to see if you are right.

5. Model the activity for the students.

Ask for a student volunteer to role-play with you.

Place two chairs in front of the room, facing each other, and remind your partner that both of you are going to use Listening Position and stay On-Topic. Then ask your partner a question. One question might be "What is your favorite thing to do after school?" Keep the response to 15–20 seconds by asking a question for more detail if the response is too brief or saying, "Thank you. Let me see if I understand what you have been saying so far" if it runs on too long.

Repeat back what the person said.

Ask if you are correct. ("Is that your favorite thing?")

6. Conduct a practice activity.

Pair two students and ask them to practice what they have seen in the examples.

Tell them that they will need to decide who will listen and who will talk first. (Give them a minute to decide.)

Explain that you will be giving them a question or topic to talk about. As the first person speaks, the other will use Listening Power and then repeat and check to see if they heard what the first speaker said. Then switch roles, and the person who talked first will be the listener and the person who listened first will be the speaker. Ask if there are any questions.

Stop after the first round and ask students what the activity was like for them.

Ask if the listener used Listening Position. Ask the speaker to tell the listener one thing they did that let the speaker know that they were listening.

> *Listener, did you check to see if you listened accurately? . . . What happened? . . . Did you get it right or did you forget something? . . . What was difficult or easy about listening?*
>
> *Speaker, how did it feel when someone repeated back what you said? . . . How does it feel when you know someone is listening to you?*

Repeat the activity with a new question as time permits. Switch partners for the next topic or question, if the logistics of group management and the group's maturity allow.

7. Introduce a Reflective Summary.

As outlined in the Introduction, ask students to reflect on the question "What did you learn from today's lesson?" Reinforce key themes, then go over any follow-up work.

8. Follow up.

The following steps will help make sure that the students have a chance to continue working with the new concepts throughout the school day and at home.

Assignment

Ask students if they can think of some times when it would be a good idea to check and be sure that they are listening accurately to what other people say. Generate a list of ideas.

Plans to Promote Transfer and Generalization of Skill

1. Ask students, "Who has used their Listening Power and can check back with me to be sure that you understand what you need to do tonight for homework?"

2. Stop after giving directions for an assignment in science, math, social studies, health, or another subject to assess students' understanding.

3. During a class discussion, stop intermittently and ask if someone was using their Listening Power and could summarize what another student just said.

TIPS FOR TEACHERS

1. Depending on the maturity of the class, move into having two students model Listening Power. Ask the group to notice any behaviors that demonstrate good listening skills.

2. If the class has an odd number of students, ask the student who volunteered for the first example to take a turn being the listener and you will be the speaker first this time. When the roles switch, you can either play the part of the listener again and have the student talk about the new question or topic, or you can ask your student partner to help you walk around and see how other groups are doing.

   The best choice depends upon whether or not the students manage the activity well on their own. If the class is up to it, it's generally preferable to have the volunteer help with overall class observation. Even if the student could benefit from more practice as the speaker, a variety of additional practice activities will be available in the upcoming weeks.

3. Additional practice topics or question recommendations:

   - What movie would you recommend to a friend? What movie is it and what is good about it?

   - Pick an animal that you think makes a good pet. What kind of animal is it and why do you think it makes a good pet?

   - If you could have the perfect playground, what would it look like? What would be there?

   - *Speaker:* If you could eat the perfect meal, what foods would you have? *Listener:* If your partner mentions foods that you do not know, you can ask for a description. *Speaker:* If your listener does not know about the food that you would like to have, describe two things to help them understand why you like that food instead of telling them about many things they have never eaten or know about.

Listening Power

1. Use Listening Position.

2. Pay attention to what the other person is saying.

3. Repeat what the other person said.

4. Check to see if you are right.

From *Social Decision Making/Social Problem Solving: A Curriculum for Academic, Social, and Emotional Learning (Grades 2–3)*.
Copyright © 2005 by Maurice J. Elias and Linda Bruene Butler. Research Press (800-519-2707; www.researchpress.com)

TOPIC

5 Strategies for Remembering

OBJECTIVES
- To review and practice good listening skills
- To identify various *Strategies for Remembering*
- To increase student awareness of these strategies and give them an opportunity to practice using them.

MATERIALS
Six to twelve common household or classroom items; a scarf or large sheet of paper to cover the items

Chalkboard or easel pad

Poster board and markers

NOTE
After the group has compiled a final list of Strategies for Remembering, write their ideas on a sheet of poster board and display the list in the classroom. (Students can help by adding drawings or decorating the poster.)

INSTRUCTIONAL ACTIVITIES

1. Review.

Go over good Listening Position and Listening Power skills and remind students of the importance of using Listening Position during this lesson.

2. Introduce topic by asking students when they need to remember things.

Ask for examples that relate to school and home. One important example is in the area of homework. Ask for all the different aspects of homework that need to be remembered. Examples include remembering to write the assignment in the assignment book; remembering to bring home all the necessary books, materials, and supplies; remembering how to do the assignment; remembering to put the completed assignment in the book-bag; remembering to bring materials to school.

Elicit from students the consequences of not remembering things that they are told. Again, ask for examples relating to school and to home.

3. Discuss strategies.

Have students describe any strategies that they already use to remember things.

4. Introduce the Invisible Items activity.

Tell the students that they are going to play a game called "Invisible Items" that will help them learn about remembering. Say that you have placed a number of items under a scarf or large piece of paper and point to the surface where the objects are hidden. Begin with a number that you feel will be fairly easy for your group to remember—say, three or four items. Remove the cover. Have the students look at the items for about thirty seconds. Then completely cover the items.

5. Run an independent memory exercise.

Have the students write or draw all the items that they can remember. Have students share their lists.

6. Have the students as a group brainstorm a list of all the ways they used to remember the items.

List students' ideas on the chalkboard or easel pad. Label the list "Strategies for Remembering." Some examples include:

- Counting the items
- Taking a picture in your head of the items
- Saying the names of the items over and over
- Grouping the items by color, size, or use
- Telling a story about or making personal associations with each of the items.

After the list is compiled, ask students if they have heard one of their classmates describe a memory strategy that they never thought of before. Would that strategy work for them?

7. Play the game again.

Add enough items to the total covered up to make the game challenging. Remind the students that this is just a game, so it's a good way to learn about new strategies and find out if they can work for them. Have the students look at the items for another thirty seconds, then discuss the memory strategies that they used this time. Add any new ideas to the list.

8. Run a subtraction exercise.

Have the students look at the all the items for another thirty seconds, and then have them cover their eyes. When they are not looking, remove one (or more) of the items. Then tell the students to open their eyes and figure out what is missing.

9. Discuss applications.

Elicit examples from students of different situations in which they can use the Strategies for Remembering (a term you can use as prompt and cue) that they brainstormed during the lesson. For example, they can use the strategies when they need to memorize their spelling words or math facts, or during homework assignments.

10. Introduce a Reflective Summary.

As outlined in the Introduction, ask students to reflect on the question "What did you learn from today's lesson?" Reinforce key themes, then go over any follow-up work.

11. Follow up.

The following steps will help make sure that the students have a chance to continue working with the new concepts throughout the school day and at home.

Assignment

Ask students to pick one time when they can use a strategy to help them remember and to write it down on their homework list. Tell them that at the start of the next session they will have a chance to share a time when they used a strategy to help them remember and how it worked.

Take-Home

1. Parents and guardians can help children improve their memory skills by giving them common household chores and discussing what Strategies for Remembering the child can use to accomplish these tasks. Consider sending a note home that describes this activity, along with some specific ideas. For example, make a grocery list and have your child try to memorize part or all of the items on the list. Bring the list to the store and see how many items your child can remember.

2. Another way to practice using remembering skills is doing a trip recall. After returning from a family trip or vacation, have the child write a story or draw pictures of the activities that you did. Have the child try to remember as many details as possible, such as the names of places or the order of the events that happened.

Plans to Promote Transfer and Generalization of Skill

Academic

Assign students or student groups the task of coming up with a strategy for remembering challenging spelling words, math facts, or information for upcoming tests in any academic area. Also ask students to come up with a strategy to help them remember what they need to do as homework.

Social Practice

As a group-building activity, especially at the beginning of the school year, play a name game to help students remember the names of their new classmates.

TIPS FOR TEACHERS

1. The Invisible Items game can be played at intervals throughout the year. Vary the number of items in the set based on the cognitive level of the students. Making the game easy initially will give the students greater confidence and will make it fun. The number of items should continually be increased until a number is reached that seems fairly challenging—in other words, when students can remember many but not all of the items. The goal of the activity is metacognitive; the students should be starting to think about how they think and remember.

2. One strategy that is often helpful to younger children is engaging their tactile sense. You might want to allow the students to touch the items, if they are able to do it in a way that doesn't distract their classmates, who are also trying to memorize the items.

3. This activity is also about different learning styles. Some students seem to have difficulty with memory skills. It is possible that they are using a strategy that is not complementing their learning style, and they can be encouraged to use a strategy that might better fit their learning style.

4. A cooperative storytelling game can be adapted to promote memory development: One student starts a story, and each student has to repeat what the student before them said and then add a little

more until everyone has participated. Pick a topic of interest to your class or choose from among these:

- A Haunted House
- Who Took the Money?
- A Trip to Mars
- A Day in the City
- Planning a Party
- What Our Town Is Really Like

6   Following Directions

OBJECTIVES
- To review and practice good listening skills
- To practice using different memory strategies
- To learn to follow directions

MATERIALS   Copies of the "Ovals Exercise" (Worksheet 2.6.1)
"Directions for Ovals Exercise" (Worksheet 2.6.2)

INSTRUCTIONAL ACTIVITIES

1. Review Topic 5.

Go over good listening skills and remind students of the importance of using Listening Position and Listening Power during this lesson.

Have the students discuss the various Strategies for Remembering that they discovered. Ask if anyone wants to tell about any time since the last lesson when they used a strategy for remembering, and how it went.

2. Discuss following directions.

Ask students what it means to follow directions. After a few answers, ask them to share some times when it is important for them to follow directions. Ask for examples that relate to school and home and extracurricular activities. Be sure to mention driving and safety issues. Elicit from students the consequences of not following directions.

3. Introduce the activity.

Tell the students that in order to follow directions they need to use their listening and remembering skills. Tell them they will be using strategies for following directions that are similar to the strategies they used for remembering.

4. Distribute the Ovals Exercise worksheet.

Give each student two copies of the worksheet. If students are unfamiliar with the terms *first, second, third,* and so on, take a moment to review ordinal numbers with them.

Read the directions from Worksheet 2.6.2 to the students, giving each direction only once, and then have the students fill in the worksheet. When the directions are complete, go over the answers with the students.

Refer to the list of Strategies for Remembering from Topic 5, and elicit from students which strategies they could apply to this activity. Ask students what other strategies they used for this activity and add them to the list.

5. Do the activity again with another set of blank ovals.

If all or most of the students were able to get the less difficult set of directions correct, use the more difficult list for the second set of ovals. If the students had difficulty, use the second set of directions geared to the lower level.

Again, have the students discuss the strategies that they used, adding any new ideas to the list.

6. Discuss uses of the technique.

Elicit examples from students of different situations in which they can use their new strategies for following directions. For example, they can use the strategies when they do classwork or homework, or during tests and activities.

7. Introduce a Reflective Summary.

As outlined in the Introduction, ask students to reflect on the question "What did you learn from today's lesson?" Reinforce key themes, then go over any follow-up work.

8. Follow up.

The following steps will help make sure that the students have a chance to continue working with the new concepts throughout the school day and at home.

Take-Home

Recommend that parents or guardians help children with following directions by playing games and doing activities with them. For example, they can give a series of directions, ranging in difficulty from one to six different actions the child could take in the house. One example would be to go to the window, describe the weather outside, go to the closet and get a sweater or coat, then go stand by the front door. Another example could be a scavenger or treasure hunt in which the child is told to go to various rooms in the house and do or get certain things.

Advise parents or guardians to praise and reward the child for being able to successfully follow the directions and to challenge the child to increase the level of difficulty by using strategies for remembering and following directions. Children can also follow directions by helping with a recipe and by following the directions to a friend or relative's home.

Plans to Promote Transfer and Generalization of Skill

Academic

Replace the list of ovals directions with a list that reviews academic concepts such as spelling, math facts, or any other subject area. The ovals are a great activity for test review.

Social Practice

1. Games such as Simon Says can be used in physical education or during recess to practice following directions.

2. Use the prompts "What strategy will you use to remember [things needed for a field trip, homework, academic assignment, facts]?" and "What strategy will you use to remember and follow the directions?" as ongoing cues for students to apply skills from this Topic to actual life situations.

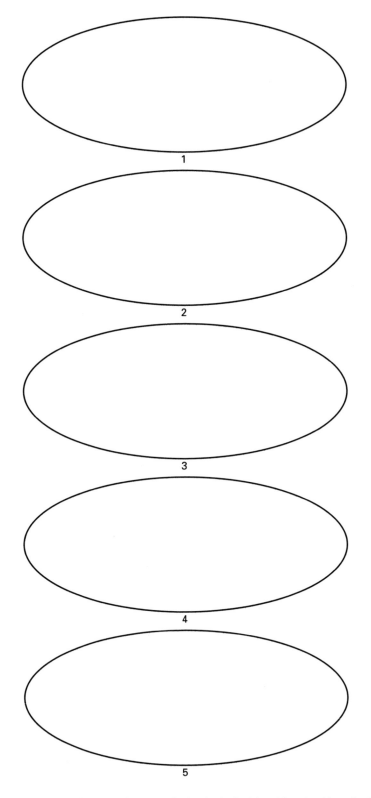

Less Difficult	**Less Difficult**
1. Color the first oval orange.	1. Color the first oval red.
2. Write an *X* in the second oval.	2. Write a *2* in the second oval.
3. Write a *3* in the third oval.	3. Draw a triangle in the third oval.
4. Draw a square in the fourth oval.	4. Write an *X* in the fourth oval.
5. Write a *5* in the fifth oval.	5. Color the fifth oval blue.
More Difficult	**More Difficult**
1. Make an orange *X* in the fifth oval.	1. Make a blue *X* in the fifth oval.
2. Color the fourth oval brown.	2. Color the first oval purple.
3. Draw a tree in the first oval.	3. Draw a house in the third oval.
4. Write your initials in the second oval.	4. Write your age in the second oval.
5. Write a *3* in the third oval.	5. Write a *9* in the fourth oval.

T O P I C

7

Be Your BEST: S = Speech (Say Something Nice)

OBJECTIVES
- To introduce the BEST concept as a whole
- To practice using the *S* component of BEST (Speech: Say something nice)
- To teach children the difference between passive, aggressive, and assertive ways to put a message into words

MATERIALS
Whole-class displays of "Be Your BEST" (Worksheet 2.7.1) and the "Be Your BEST Grid" (Worksheet 2.7.2)

A puppet or picture of a character that represents a mouse, a monster, and a "ME," as explained in the instructions

NOTE
A sample Be Your BEST Grid, including possible student responses, appears as Worksheet 2.7.3, at the end of this Topic. Your students may come up with other ideas.

INSTRUCTIONAL ACTIVITIES

1. Review Speaker Power and listening skills.

These were introduced in Topics 2–4.

2. Briefly introduce the components of BEST.

Tell the students that today the class will begin to work with a powerful new set of skills designed to help them be successful. A team is successful when all members of the team are their BEST. Point to each component on the display and explain the way being your BEST shows up in it:

B for Body Posture

E for Eye Contact

S for Speech (Say something nice.)

T for Tone of Voice

Say:

> *We'll begin with S, because what we say can make such a big difference to the people around us—and to the way they treat us.*

3. Explain that the class will be looking at three different ways people use words.

Introduce the three puppets or pictures and refer students to the BEST grid as you speak.

> *The Mouse: The mouse is very meek and almost always allows other people have their way. Mice don't stand up for themselves. They may be whiney and timid. We would call this behavior Passive (or Shrinking) behavior.*

Ask for examples of passive or mouselike words. List these on the grid.

> *The Monster: A monster can be scary or pushy and bossy. Monsters don't care what other people feel or want. Other words for monster are bully or blaster. We call what monsters do Aggressive (or Blasting) behavior.*

Ask for examples of aggressive words. List these on the grid.

> *The ME: Sit up tall, point to yourself, and say, "A ME is the best of both other ways to be. A ME thinks clearly, says how they feel, and respects others. A ME is considered Assertive (or BEST) behavior."*

Ask students to tell you some assertive words. List these on the grid.

4. Emphasize the importance of the words people use.

Ask:

> *How does it feel when someone talks to you using mouse words or passive words? How do you respond to someone when they use mouse words?*

> *What about monster words? How does it feel when someone talks to you aggressively?*

5. Conduct a practice activity.

Have students work in pairs. Have one student ask the other to return a pencil using mouse words, monster words, and then ME words. How did each feel? What was the outcome?

6. Introduce a Reflective Summary.

As outlined in the Introduction, ask students to reflect on the question "What did you learn from today's lesson?" Reinforce key themes, then go over any follow-up work.

7. Follow up.

The following steps will help make sure that the students have a chance to continue working with the new concepts throughout the school day and at home.

Plans to Promote Transfer and Generalization of Skill

Whenever showing a video to the class, use it as a time to reinforce BEST skills. For example, pause the video and ask students to respond to the words being said and decide whether they can be said in a nicer or friendlier way. If they say yes, ask how. Give them a chance to role-play as time allows. As students learn other BEST skills, add them to what you ask them to observe and respond to.

TIPS FOR TEACHERS

1. Depending on the class, you may have to generate a list of passive, aggressive, and assertive phrases and ask students what category to put them in.

2. This is a good place to highlight manners, such as saying please and thank you and practicing delivering these messages using nice words and an appropriate tone of voice.

3. Feel free to use whatever terms you like if you feel that *mouse* and *monster* or *shrink* and *blast* will not be effective with your students.

Be Your BEST

B   Body Posture

E   Eye Contact

S   Speech (Say something nice.)

T   Tone of Voice

From *Social Decision Making/Social Problem Solving: A Curriculum for Academic, Social, and Emotional Learning (Grades 2–3)*. Copyright © 2005 by Maurice J. Elias and Linda Bruene Butler. Research Press (800-519-2707; www.researchpress.com).

	AGGRESSIVE (Blast)	ASSERTIVE (BEST)	PASSIVE (Shrink)
Body Posture			
Eye Contact			
Speech			
Tone of Voice			

	AGGRESSIVE (Blast)	ASSERTIVE (BEST)	PASSIVE (Shrink)
Body Posture			
Eye Contact			
Speech	Insults Accusations Bossy, bad words	Clear Nice words Polite	Unclear Muttering Mumbling
Tone of Voice			

8

Be Your BEST: T = Tone of Voice

OBJECTIVES
- To teach children the *T* component of BEST (Tone of Voice)
- To teach children to distinguish between passive, aggressive, and assertive voice tones

MATERIALS
A whole-class display of the "Tone of Voice Thermometer" (Worksheet 2.8.1)

Chalkboard or easel pad

PREPARATION
Before conducting this lesson, prepare and practice several short role-plays, modeling the way the same thing can be said using three different voice tones—passive, aggressive, and assertive. We suggest using a greeting, a good-bye, and a way to interrupt.

INSTRUCTIONAL ACTIVITIES

1. Have a Sharing Circle as a warm-up and review.

Ask an On-Topic question such as "Did you see an example of someone's using nice words during the past week?"

Then ask students to talk about what they can remember about saying nice words.

2. Introduce Tone of Voice.

Ask students if they know what *Tone of Voice* means. Point out that tone of voice is as important to communication as the words themselves.

3. Illustrate the monster tone.

Ask the students to show you what a monster sounds like. This is an aggressive tone of voice. Ask students to describe the monster tone. Write the words students generate on the chalkboard or easel pad under:

- Monster
- Aggressive

4. Illustrate the mouse tone.

Next ask students to show you what a mouse would sound like. This is a passive tone of voice. Ask students to describe the mouse tone. Write words on the board under these headings:

- Mouse
- Passive

5. Illustrate the BEST tone.

Next ask students to show you what the BEST/ME tone of voice sounds like. Ask students to describe the BEST/ME tone. Write their ideas on the board or easel pad under:

- BEST
- ME

6. Show the Tone of Voice Thermometer.

Put up the Tone of Voice Thermometer and explain the way it works. Say:

When we are talking to someone, we want to aim for the middle of the thermometer.

7. Role-play or use puppets demonstrating each of the tones of voice.

Use these three examples or something similar:

- I would like to eat lunch now.
- Today we are going to talk about tone of voice.
- Excuse me. I have a question for you.

Ask students to identify whether the tone is passive, aggressive, or assertive and ask them how they feel in each instance.

8. Extend the practice.

Read a scenario and then call out how you want students to practice it, either Mouse, Monster, or ME. Have students take turns doing each one. End with at least two "ME" examples in a row. Use these scenarios or something similar:

- Can I join your group?
- It's my turn next.
- Where is my pencil?

9. Introduce a Reflective Summary.

As outlined in the Introduction, ask students to reflect on the question "What did you learn from today's lesson?" Reinforce key themes, then go over any follow-up work.

10. Follow up.

The following steps will help make sure that the students have a chance to continue working with the new concepts throughout the school day and at home.

Plans to Promote Transfer and Generalization of Skill

Post the Tone of Voice Thermometer where it can be used throughout the day to prompt for self-monitoring and self-regulating of the tone of voice a student or the group is using. First ask:

Where on the picture would you rate tone of voice right now?

Then say:

Now let me hear what a "Be Your BEST" tone of voice sounds like.

Reinforce any noticeable improvement.

TIPS FOR TEACHERS

1. It often helps to explicitly state that everyone uses mouse, monster, and ME behaviors and tones some of the time. We are not talking about different types of people but about different styles of behaving.

2. Over time, reduce reinforcement of the terms *mouse* and *monster.* Students may be influenced to act in these ways or point out these negative behaviors in others. Phase out these terms, stressing the "Be Your BEST" prompt.

Aggressive

**Assertive
BEST**

Passive

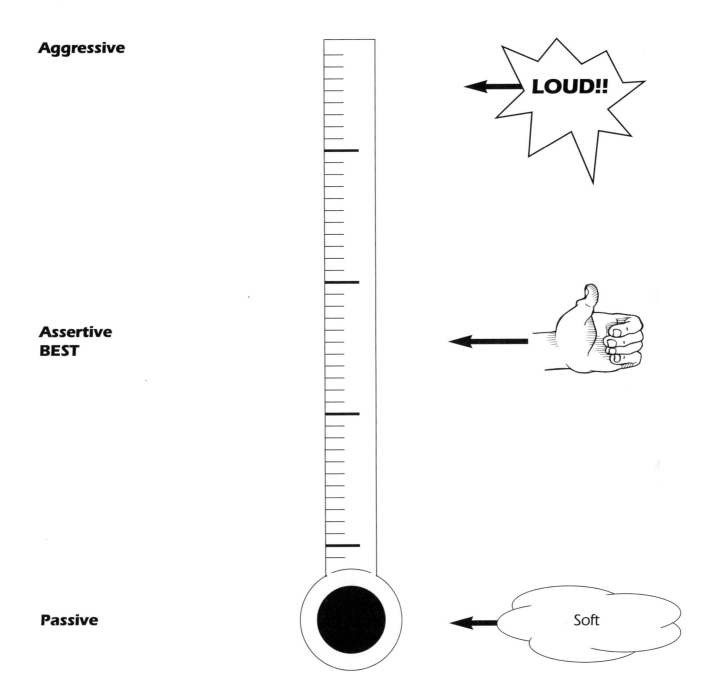

9

Be Your BEST: Putting S and T Together

OBJECTIVES
- To teach children to distinguish between passive, aggressive, and confident (assertive) styles of behavior
- To model and provide students with practice using assertive and confident behaviors as shown by their body posture, eye contact, speech (words used), and tone of voice
- To practice the *S* and *T* components of BEST behaviors in role-plays of simple teammate interactions such as greetings and saying good-bye

MATERIALS

Whole-class display of the "Be Your BEST Grid," including the responses students gave in Topic 7.

PREPARATION

Prepare and practice three short and simple role-plays to demonstrate different ways to say the same thing, using words and tone of voice (passive, aggressive, and assertive). We suggest using a greeting, a good-bye, and a way to interrupt.

NOTE

Worksheet 2.9.1 adds sample student responses for the "Tone" row of the grid. Your students' responses may vary.

INSTRUCTIONAL ACTIVITIES

1. Review.

Ask students what they remember from Topic 8. Provide some reminders to help them if necessary.

2. Ask students if they remember what Tone of Voice means.

Those who remember will reply with things like how your voice sounds; how loud, happy, mad, sad, or normal a voice sounds; it is like a note of a musical instrument, only it is your voice and words.

Conduct a Sharing Circle using Speaker Power. Ask children to say hello using an appropriate tone of voice for the classroom, which you can then refer to as "regular tone" or "your classroom voice." If anyone wants to share the equivalent of hello in another language, that would be fun, also.

3. Talk about being a team.

Explain that an important part of being a team is treating each other and ourselves with respect. Ask students what respect means. Refer back to Topic 1, when the group described how they like to be treated as a member of the team, and note that many of those things were summarized as being respectful of one another. Have students describe disrespectful behavior and what it does to the feelings of others.

Say:

> *An important part of being a team is respecting the rights of everyone to say what they think and feel so they can all participate and know they belong to the group. The way we talk to one another is the most important part. This year we are mostly working with the last two letters of BEST—Speech and Tone—that is, what you say and how it sounds when you say it. We'll talk a little about the first two—Body Posture and Eye Contact (the way you stand and whether you look the other person in the eye), but we won't have any separate lessons on them. You'll learn more about them in the third grade.*

4. Model someone coming into the classroom displaying three ways of self-presentation.

Continue by saying:

> *I would like to review three different ways a person could act when talking to another person or other people. Let's start at the beginning of our day. I am going to pretend that I am a second grader coming into the classroom. I am also going to pretend that one of my class teammates is standing right inside the door facing me and says hello to me. I want you to try to imagine how you would feel if you were that person.*
>
> *Here is one way I could do it. I could be aggressive or blast my teammate:*
>
> *What are you looking at, you jerk?*
>
> *You're an idiot; you're stupid!*

Explain how the *S* and *T* show up here:

> *Speech:* Strongly aggressive language (threats, put-downs, insults)
>
> *Tone of Voice:* Harsh, loud, and mean

Refer to the BEST Grid and ask students to describe what they observed. List their descriptions within the box on the grid designated speech and tone of voice. Then say:

> *Now I am going to pretend again and show you another way I could enter the classroom in the morning.*

Demonstrate passive behavior:

> *Speech:* Vague, indirect words (you could mumble something inaudible or whiney)
>
> *Tone of Voice:* Low or squeaky and hesitant

Refer to the "Passive" column of the BEST Grid and record behaviors the students observed related to the four components.

Let students know that one final time you are going to role-play how someone could enter the classroom in the morning. Because there is no one way to Be Your BEST, some teachers ask students for suggestions on what to say or do. Let them know that all of their appropriate suggestions would be good examples of BEST. Choose something to say from the group or use one of the suggestions given here.

Demonstrate assertive (BEST) behavior:

> *Speech:* Say nice, polite words: "Good morning. How are you today? or "Hi." "I hope you have a great day" as you continue into the room or "Hey, nice catch on the playground this morning." An alternative is to use a suggestion from the group or say whatever cheerful and friendly words are natural and comfortable for you.
>
> *Tone of Voice:* A calm, even tone of voice.

5. Review examples of behavior recorded on the BEST Grid.

Ask students if they would rather have passive, aggressive, or BEST behaviors from teammates:

> *Which way of acting would make you feel good about the team and ready to do good work?*

6. Conduct a practice activity.

Have students stand in a circle and ask them to think about what they would say as a morning greeting to a teammate. Ask them to remember to respect Speaker Power (without using the object) and then face the person on their right and greet them, using their BEST. Depending on the maturity of the group, students could pair up and each practice giving their partner a morning greeting.

Have students brainstorm ways that they could say good-bye to a teammate that would make the person feel good about being a part of the team. Give students time to pick something they would like to say and have students role-play saying good-bye around a circle or in pairs. Remind them to use their regular tone or classroom voice.

7. Introduce a Reflective Summary.

As outlined in the Introduction, ask students to reflect on the question "What did you learn from today's lesson?" Reinforce key themes, then go over any follow-up work.

8. Follow up.

The following steps will help make sure that the students have a chance to continue working with the new concepts throughout the school day and at home.

Assignment

Encourage students to use BEST and tell about it next time. Provide children with positive feedback for acting their BEST during the day. Be sure to ask for changes in specific behavior:

> *I can tell that you want to tell me something, but please start again and remember to use your BEST tone of voice.*

Be sure to thank the students or find other ways to reinforce any positive behavior change.

Plans to Promote Transfer and Generalization of Skill

1. Teachers can encourage students to use BEST and to help their teammates remember to use it, too. Having shared language and skill prompts can empower class teammates to help each other when these situations occur. We've heard children use these techniques; on the bus, for example, one boy told another who was getting teased that his voice was not strong enough and that he was not standing tall.

2. In classroom situations, assemblies, and other gatherings, use the prompts, "regular tone of voice" or "classroom voice" to keep children from getting too loud. This real-time coaching, teamwork, and camaraderie can be of significant help in giving youngsters the confidence and pride that they need to function in school as well as in peer, family, and, ultimately, job situations. Some teachers incorporate having students greet one another every morning as part of their classroom routine.

TIPS FOR TEACHERS

1. Remember that there are cultural and ethnic differences in what might be regarded as proper BEST behavior. For example, Latino children may be less likely to make eye contact with adult males, out of respect. This may be open to potential misinterpretation, as once occurred in an assessment case with which the authors

are familiar. Group leaders should keep in mind that behavior in the BEST areas strongly influences impressions in social interactions but that there are cultural differences in how and when certain of those behaviors should be displayed.

2. When students begin to role-play they should only be working to be their BEST. We have found no real value in having students engage in role-playing undesirable teammate behaviors. The objective is to demonstrate behaviors to clarify the concept of BEST by illustrating what it is rather than what it is not.

3. Depending on the maturity of the group, you might want to repeat the role-play several times asking that they only observe one or two of the behavioral components at a time.

4. This lesson is meant as a simple introduction to this skill as a general guideline and prompt for good teammate behaviors. This skill will be explored and practiced more extensively in the next lesson.

5. When first demonstrating aggressive behavior, we recommend speaking to an empty chair, not addressing a particular student. For many children, seeing their teacher act in an aggressive way can help to illustrate that people do have choices in how they treat others, but they may lack the sophistication to understand that you don't really mean what you're saying if you seem to be speaking directly to them. Pretending to be talking to an imaginary person helps avoid upsetting a child in a role-play of aggressive behavior.

6. These initial role-plays are used to clarify what BEST is and what it is not. Once students learn the distinctions, we recommend fading out the words *blast* and *shrink* and instead using the positive corrective prompt "Be Your BEST." This calls for the child to use the skill instead of placing the focus on what someone is doing wrong.

7. It has been helpful to explicitly state that everyone uses blast and shrink behavior some of the time and there are times when these behaviors are a good choice. Ask students for examples, such as yelling when someone is in danger or walking away from someone who is bullying. Emphasize that this lesson is not about different types of people but about different ways of behaving.

	AGGRESSIVE (Blast)	ASSERTIVE (BEST)	PASSIVE (Shrink)
Body Posture			
Eye Contact			
Speech	Insults Accusations Bossy, bad words	Clear Nice words Polite	Unclear Muttering Mumbling
Tone of Voice	Yelling Screaming Loud	Mostly calm Medium	Soft Low Whiny

10 How to Give Praise

OBJECTIVES
- To define the word *praise*
- To develop skills for giving praise using BEST
- To teach children to look for positive qualities in their peers

MATERIALS
Chalkboard or easel pad

Whole-class display of the steps in "Giving Praise" (Worksheet 2.10.1)

INSTRUCTIONAL ACTIVITIES

1. Introduce the general topic.

Tell the students:

Today we will be learning a very important skill. This skill is called Giving Praise.

2. Introduce the skill of Giving Praise.

Obtain students' interest by asking:

Did anyone ever tell you something that they liked about you or something that you did? Tell a story about a time when this happened to you.

After a few answers, ask the class what praise is. After a few responses, summarize and provide a definition. Ask:

How does it feel when someone praises you?

3. Present and model the behavioral components of Giving Praise.

Explain that there are three things to remember about Giving Praise:

1. Look for something you like about the other person. (This is a good place to ask the class to list some things you could like about a person—appearance, behavior, or accomplishments, for example.)

2. Be honest and don't try to praise someone for something that is not true.

3. Be simple—say clearly what you like.

4. Demonstrate the skill.

Model and discuss the following examples:

You have a friend you like to listen to music with. How could you praise your friend? (For example, you could say, "I like listening to music with you. It's fun.")

You like someone's new outfit. What could you say? (You could say, "That's a nice-looking shirt" or "You look good in that shirt.")

Now ask the class to role-play the following situations:

Someone comes in with new shoes and they look nice. What could you say? (You could say, "Hey, I like your shoes.")

You notice that someone is helping another classmate named Lee. (You could say, "You're a being a big help to Lee, there. That's nice of you.")

Someone takes the time to ask you, "How are you feeling? I know you felt sick yesterday." (You could say, "I'm feeling better today, and thank you for asking.")

5. Discuss why it is important to give praise.

Some examples:

- If you thank people when they do something for you, they are likely to do it again.
- If you compliment someone, that person is more likely to compliment you at another time.
- We all like to get compliments.
- If you thank and compliment people, they will enjoy being around you.

6. Conduct a practice activity.

Put students in pairs around the circle, and take a seat in the circle yourself. Model giving compliments by giving appropriate praise to the person on your right, and then on your left.

Have one student in each pair turn to the person on the right and praise them, then trade off.

Ask the class how it felt to give compliments and praise.

Teach them, "If you cannot think of something nice to say, say what you see." (For example, "Jamad, your shirt is so yellow" or "Maya, you are sitting up very straight.")

7. Introduce a Reflective Summary.

As outlined in the Introduction, ask students to reflect on the question "What did you learn from today's lesson?" Reinforce key themes, then go over any follow-up work.

8. Follow up.

The following steps will help make sure that the students have a chance to continue working with the new concepts throughout the school day and at home.

Assignment

Tell the class to practice giving praise to others. Ask children to think about how it felt to give compliments and praise. Tell them that in the next lesson you will be asking them to share a time when they were praised and how they felt.

Plans to Promote Transfer and Generalization of Skill

1. Inform the students that you will be listening for praise in the class. Use a positive reinforcement—stickers, charts, jellybeans in a jar, and so on—to encourage using praise. Listen for insults as well, and require children who use them to reword their insult so as to give a positive statement.

2. Make a bulletin board to use for reinforcement. Choose a shape such as a heart. Put a big heart on the board and write on it "Who gave praise today?" At the end of each day, ask for volunteers to nominate someone they heard praising another student. Put the student's name on the bulletin board, along with the date. Continue until everyone is listed or for a predetermined time.

3. Initiate a "Student of the Day" for being good at giving genuine praise.

4. As a way of starting the school day, have students think about a good characteristic of any classmate that they wish to compliment. Ask for volunteers to share their compliments. You may wish to model complimenting several children.

5. After a cooperative activity in language arts, gym, social studies, music, or any other subject, conduct a Sharing Circle and ask students to say one good thing about someone specific or to praise a way that students worked together as a team.

Giving Praise

1. Look for something you like about the other person.

2. Be honest. Don't try to praise someone for something that is not true.

3. Be simple. Say clearly what you like.

TOPIC

11 How to Receive Praise

OBJECTIVES
- To develop the ability to receive praise using BEST
- To practice giving and receiving praise using BEST

MATERIALS Whole-class display of the "Be Your BEST Grid," including the responses students gave in Topics 7 and 9

INSTRUCTIONAL ACTIVITIES

1. Review Topic 10.

Ask the class what they discussed in the last session. Useful follow-up questions:

- Who can tell me what praise is?
- What are some ways to give praise?
- What are some things to remember when we give praise?
- Why is it important to give praise?

2. Pick up from the preceding meeting.

As promised, ask if anyone would like to share a time when they were praised this week. Encourage the speaker to talk about how it felt to be praised.

3. Introduce the topic.

Tell students:

Today we will talk about how you act when someone praises you.

Ask them to think about the different ways they might act when they get praised.

What might you say or do? How?

Be sure to elicit both positive and negative ways that students react. Some examples: Say thank you, make some acknowledgment, smile, giggle, blush, avoid looking at the person, deny the praise, question it, ignore it, or argue about it.

4. Model examples of alternative ways to receive praise.

Ask the class to think about what they might say if you were to tell one of them, "Your reading out loud is very clear. Good work." Model some of the ways a student might respond:

- Glare and snap back, "No way. I made a lot of mistakes!"
- Giggle, look embarrassed, look down, mutter, "No I didn't."
- Look straight at the person, smile, and say, "Thank you."

Ask the class to label each example on the display of the BEST Grid.

5. Discuss receiving praise.

Talk about ways to accept praise that would show in the way you used your words and tone of voice.

What would you say that would be encouraging to person who was encouraging you?

What would your tone of voice be?

Ask:

Why is it important to use your BEST skills when someone praises you?

Some examples:

- To encourage (not discourage) people to continue to praise you
- To show you appreciate praise
- To show your respect for the other person's opinion
- To help you feel good about yourself

6. Conduct a practice activity.

Have pairs of students role-play some or all of the following situations, with one child giving praise and the other receiving. Encourage children to use *ST.* Assign the audience the task of looking at specific actors and for specific components of *ST.* Discuss each role-play upon completion.

Sample role-plays:

- Compliment a classmate on doing a project or assignment well.
- Thank a friend's parent for a ride home from school.
- Tell someone you like their new haircut.
- Thank a relative for cooking your favorite dinner.
- Thank a friend for helping with a homework assignment.
- Thank a teacher for helping with a class assignment.
- Compliment a teammate for playing well.

7. Introduce a Reflective Summary.

As outlined in the Introduction, ask students to reflect on the question "What did you learn from today's lesson?" Reinforce key themes, then go over any follow-up work.

8. Follow up.

The following assignment will help make sure that the students have a chance to continue working with the new concepts throughout the school day and at home.

Assignment

Tell the students to remember how they act when they are praised this week and be prepared to share it with the class. Remind students to give praise to one another as well.

TIPS FOR TEACHERS

1. In preceding lessons, students learned to recognize praise and began to give and receive some nice comments. Many students are not used to being praised, however. In our experience, well-meaning adults sometimes alienate students by offering praise that the students find uncomfortable to hear. It is important that students not deny praise they receive and that they encourage people to give them more praise by responding in a favorable way. Students' self-concepts can be built up by having them enter into positive cycles of responding to and giving genuine praise.

2. The reasons for students' discomfort with being praised may vary, but are probably linked to the sense of self-efficacy or identity. Some students become secure with an identity and a set of self-expectations that are negative. For them, the consistency of knowing that negative things will occur is, paradoxically, a source of comfort, security, and anxiety reduction. Praise disrupts that security and is therefore uncomfortable and usually rejected. Other students have cultural reasons to be uncomfortable with praise. Behaviors that might lead to praise are, by this logic, stopped. You can use the activities in this Topic to intrude gently into such children's negativity. If a student continues to be highly resistant to praise, consult school support personnel so that more comprehensive intervention can be considered.

TOPIC

12 Asking for Help and Giving Help to Others

OBJECTIVES
- To learn how to tell when it is appropriate to ask for and to give help
- To learn appropriate ways to ask for help using BEST
- To be aware of signs that others are needing help
- To learn ways to offer help using BEST
- To be aware of others' feelings when receiving help

MATERIALS
Filled-in version of the "Be Your BEST Grid"

A dictionary

INSTRUCTIONAL ACTIVITIES

1. Review Topic 11.

Ask the class what they discussed in the last session. Some of the same questions from the Topic 10 review may be useful again. Encourage them to talk about their experiences giving and receiving praise.

2. Introduce the basic topic.

Obtain students' interest by saying that today's topic will be giving and asking for help. Ask:

What does the word help *mean?*

After getting a few answers, take out a dictionary and read a definition.

3. Ask students to think about times others have helped them.

Ask for examples of a time when they asked someone to help them. "How do you feel when you ask for help?" Some answers may be *afraid, embarrassed, feel you should know it, uncomfortable,* or *comfortable.*

Discuss the fact that everyone needs help at some time and all people have strengths and weaknesses in some areas.

4. Introduce skill components.

Ask the class to think about ways people can ask for help once they decide they need it. Some answers may be raising hands or asking quietly, not by throwing pencils or ripping papers. Then ask whether there are times that are better than others to ask for help. (After you've tried to solve the problem on your own, not when someone is concentrating or busy with their own work, and not when the person is busy helping someone else.)

5. Conduct a practice activity.

Tell the students that they will role-play some situations where children are asking for help. Use the following situations or real classroom situations and have students show a positive (and negative) way of asking for help.

1. Student A is working on a really difficult word puzzle and cannot get the last two words. What should Student A do?

2. Student A and B are playing a game. Student C is too shy to ask to play. What should Student C do?

3. Student A is having trouble with the day's homework and decides to call Student B. How should Student A ask for help?

Remind the actors to use *ST* when they are role-playing. Refer them to the Be Your BEST Grid as needed.

6. Talk about giving help.

Continue by asking the students:

Has anyone ever helped someone? When?

How did you feel when you gave help?

The class is likely to reply with things like good, helpful, pleased to be asked, and to report learning material better themselves while helping someone.

Then ask:

What are some signals that show someone else needs help?

Some answers: Scratching their head, tapping their feet, chewing pencils, and similar behaviors.

What could you do if you noticed someone needed help?

Some answers: Using your *ST,* ask if you can help, and if they say yes, then help them.

Tell the class that they will role-play some situations where students are giving help. Using the following situations or real classroom situations, have students show a positive (and negative) way of giving help.

1. Student A notices that Student B is absent. Today's assignments are on the desk. How would Student A volunteer to take the work home?

2. Student A notices the teacher is putting up a new bulletin board. How would Student A offer to help?

3. Student A notices a friend is having trouble with a math problem. What should Student A do?

Remind the actors to use *ST* when they are role-playing. Ask different sections of the class to concentrate on specific components of *ST.*

7. Review the lesson.

Useful questions include:

- Is it OK to ask for help?
- Should you feel uncomfortable?
- Is it a compliment when someone asks you for help?
- What could you do if you needed help?
- Is there anyone who never needs any help?

8. Introduce a Reflective Summary.

As outlined in the Introduction, ask students to reflect on the question "What did you learn from today's lesson?" Reinforce key themes, then go over any follow-up work.

9. Follow up.

The following steps will help make sure that the students have a chance to continue working with the new concepts throughout the school day and at home.

Assignment

1. Encourage students to look for signals of those who need help. Also, encourage students to use an acceptable way and time to ask for help.

2. During language arts or art class, have students write or draw thank-you notes to other students, parents, or others for help they have given.

Plans to Promote Transfer and Generalization of Skill

1. There are many ways to extend the concepts into language arts and other subject areas. For students who have difficulty writing, for example, it can be useful to assign projects involving pictures, dioramas, and collages that focus on helping. Teachers have also posted a "Helping Hand" in the room, with words or pictures on each finger. Students generate different ways to seek help, of which five are selected and put on the fingers of the Helping Hand.

   The Helping Hand provides a reference and a prompt when students are stuck in trying to solve a problem and need ideas about how to get help. The Helping Hand idea is also good to use with parents and guardians at home-school conferences.

2. Peer tutoring is also useful to both parties. Pair children with weaker and stronger skills within grade level, or cross-grade. Encourage the tutors to find something the students they are helping do well and praise them for it. Encourage the students receiving help to let their tutors know what they liked about the help they gave.

TIPS FOR TEACHERS

Although many of us encourage our students to be independent and self-reliant, some students carry this a bit too far and develop an attitude that does not allow them to admit mistakes or acknowledge that they are having difficulty with something. In later years, this may show up as social withdrawal or isolation, a desire to appear to be perfect, or as an arrogant, know-it-all perspective. It is useful to be certain that students know when it is appropriate to ask for help and to give help to others. Part of being a genuine group involves being helpful to one another.

Topics 13–26

13 Selecting and Caring for Friends

OBJECTIVES
- To identify characteristics of a good friend (*Good Friendship Behaviors*)
- To identify undesirable characteristics of a friend (*Not-Good Friendship Behaviors*)
- To increase children's understanding of the importance of caring and being cared about

MATERIALS
Chalkboard or easel pad

Poster board and markers

Copies of "What Makes a Friend a Friend?" (Worksheet 2.13.1; *optional*)

NOTE
After the class has compiled a list of "Good Friendship/Not-Good Friendship Behaviors," write these behaviors in two columns on a sheet of poster board and display the poster in the classroom. (Students can help by adding drawings or decorating the poster.)

INSTRUCTIONAL ACTIVITIES

1. Review Topic 12.

Ask the class what they discussed in the last lesson. Did they ask for help or see someone who needed help?

2. Introduce the new topic.

Tell students that you would like them to do an activity that will help them learn about other people. Emphasize the point that an important rule of this activity is to describe what people do—and not to use any names. Repeat *no names, no names.*

Ask students to close their eyes and think of their best friend: someone they look forward to spending time with and someone they feel good being around.

3. Generate a list of what makes a friend a friend.

Help students define their ideas in terms of what a good friend does. Questions like these set the right tone:

- What kinds of things does a good friend say?
- What does the person do that is nice or good for a friend to do?

Make a list of the behaviors. When a list has been generated, write "Good Friendship Behaviors" on top.

Ask the class to describe some ways that friends show they care about one another. Add the answers to the list, and make sure it includes "give help," "give praise," and "listen when you are talking."

Continue the discussion by saying something like this:

> Now that we all know how a good friend behaves, what are some behaviors that we do not like in a friend? Are there things that a person might do that would make it not fun to be around them?

Have the class generate a list of characteristics they do not like. Label this list "Not-Good Friendship Behaviors."

4. Conduct a practice activity.

Read the following situations and ask children to be thinking about what they just learned about good friendship behavior.

Example 1

> Alex is playing with a ball when Rodney approaches him. Rodney is a friend of Alex's.
>
> Rodney approaches Alex and says, "Let me have that ball—I want to play with it!"
>
> What should Alex do, using good friendship behavior, since Rodney is supposed to be his friend? What could Rodney do instead to show that he is a good friend?

Example 2

> Shakia and Ramona are friends playing a game. Kimmara comes up and starts whispering to Ramona about Shakia. Ramona then tells Shakia that she does not want to play with her anymore and goes off to play with Kimmara.
>
> What should Shakia do? Is Ramona being a good friend? What should Ramona do? Could they have all played together?

Ask the class to generate ideas of what people should do when their friends show these negative signs. You can add other situations or additional activities to help make the point. For example, have the class fill out the "What Makes a Friend a Friend?" worksheet, or make

"Wanted" posters—like the ones seen in post offices but titled "A Cooperative Friend" and listing all the qualities the student can remember. They can then draw a picture of a cooperative friend to illustrate the poster.

5. Introduce a Reflective Summary.

As outlined in the Introduction, ask students to reflect on the question "What did you learn from today's lesson?" Reinforce key themes and review the list of good friendship behaviors, then go over any follow-up work.

6. Follow up.

The following steps will help make sure that the students have a chance to continue working with the new concepts throughout the school day and at home.

Plans to Promote Transfer and Generalization of Skill

1. Be on the lookout for good friendship behaviors in student interactions both inside and outside the classroom, and reinforce them with praise.

2. Have the class pick "Secret Friend" names. Tell the students they must do one thing each day that shows good friendship behaviors for their secret friends—while trying to make sure that the secret is not discovered. At the end of the week, have them discuss their experiences as giver and receiver of friendship acts.

TIPS FOR TEACHERS

1. Students' choice of friends is extremely influential in terms of how students develop, the kinds of situations they will encounter, and the skills they will use to cope with problems. This lesson is designed to help students think about their choice of friends.

2. Friendship has been linked to social support and adjustment. If children have difficulty making friends, or if they frequently enter into friendships in which they are used, taken advantage of, or influenced to do unsafe things, this is both unfortunate and understandable. The activities for this topic provide youngsters with some especially valuable tools to help them select and keep praiseworthy and caring friends. These activities are important for all students, but especially for any students with educational differences, who often find it hard to make positive friendships.

3. In addition to referring to the two lists of friendship behaviors, some teachers then use them as a way to begin monitoring behaviors in the classroom. When good friendship behaviors are observed, the teacher can tally them and later reward the group for exhibiting these skills. In addition, if not-good friendship behaviors are observed, a tally can promote awareness. If several marks are made after a particular behavior (such as saying something to put someone down), the teacher can call attention to the problem and develop a plan with the class to decrease that behavior.

4. Some teachers have used "Teammate Behavior" instead of "Friendship Behaviors" in the lists. Their idea is that friends are personal, but anyone can be a good teammate to anyone else.

5. Other teachers have noted the overlap between the concept of "kindness" and SDM/SPS lessons targeting friendship behaviors and giving help. By reading the book *Kids' Random Acts of Kindness* by Donna Markova (Conari Press, 1994), students are exposed to concrete examples and models of kindness by children of all ages.*

6. Some teachers have collected examples of kind acts, friendship behaviors, and giving help by having students write them on "Helping Hands" that are posted around the room or on decorations for the holidays or other visual displays.

*Additional classroom activities to promote acts of kindness are available through a free *Teachers' Guide to Random Acts of Kindness* by contacting Conari Press, 2550 Ninth Street, Suite 101, Berkeley, CA 94710 (800) 685-9595.

Student _____ Date _____

Things I like about my friends

1. _____

2. _____

3. _____

4. _____

5. _____

6. _____

7. _____

8. _____

9. _____

14 Packing Your SDM/SPS Toolbox

OBJECTIVES
- To provide students with an opportunity to review the social decision making and social problem solving skills they have learned to date
- To make a "toolbox" containing SDM/SPS skill symbols
- To provide teachers and students with an opportunity to assess skill gains

MATERIALS
Copies of the "Tools for the SDM/SPS Toolbox" (Worksheet 2.14.1)

Copies of the "How Am I Doing?" self-report form (Worksheet 2.14.2)

Large envelopes, crayons or markers, drawing paper, scissors

INSTRUCTIONAL ACTIVITIES

1. Review Good and Not-Good Friendship Behaviors.

Ask students to describe any situations in which they saw the different kinds of behavior.

2. Introduce the activity.

Let students know that today they are going to make a toolbox for all of the social decision making skills they have learned so far in the second grade.

The skills and concepts learned thus far, and the Topics in which they were introduced, are as follows:

- Sharing Circle (Topic 1)
- Listening Position (Topic 2)
- Listening Power (Topic 4)
- Strategies for Remembering (Topic 5)
- Following Directions (Topic 6)
- Be Your BEST (Speech, Tone of Voice) (Topic 7)
- Giving Praise (Topic 10)
- Receiving Praise (Topic 11)
- Asking for and Giving Help (Topic 12)
- Good Friendship/Not-Good Friendship Behaviors (Topic 13)

3. Conduct a Sharing Circle.

Here are some suggested Sharing Circle questions that would be On-Topic:

Let's think about all the SDM/SPS skills we have learned and practiced so far. What is your favorite skill?

Can you think of a time when you used a skill that you learned during our SDM/SPS lessons, and it helped you?

What is something that you like about our problem-solving team?

4. Talk about tools and toolboxes.

Introduce the concept of tools with a conversation like this:

Teacher: If we needed to put two pieces of wood together, which tool or tools would we use?

Student: Hammer and nails.

Teacher: Great. What if we needed to cut a piece of wood in half?

Student: Saw.

Teacher: Super. And what if I were going to put a hole in the wood?

Student: A drill.

Teacher: Excellent!

Reinforce students for knowing what tool to use when it was needed. Explain that social and emotional situations are the same. You need to know what the situation is and then which tool to use.

5. Distribute copies of the "Tools for the SDM/SPS Toolbox" worksheets and envelopes.

Explain that today the students are going to create their own Social Decision Making/Social Problem Solving toolboxes.

Tell them that their first job is to color the tools and cut them out. Then have them label their envelopes with their name, teacher's name, and "SDM/SPS Toolbox." They can also color or decorate their toolboxes any way they like. Let them know that they will be keeping the toolboxes in or on their desks for future use.

Tell the students that they have an extra tool, "Keep Calm," which they will be learning about soon (in Topic 21) to help them when they have very strong feelings to stay in control of their behavior. Have them color it and keep it in their toolbox with the other skills. (If no drawing is provided for a skill or concept students choose to include in their toolbox, they may draw and color their own.)

6. Conduct a practice activity.

After students are done, explain that you are going to give them a chance to see if they are as good at choosing the right tools for social decision making as they were at choosing what tools a carpenter might use to build something. Let them know that you will be reading descriptions of something that might happen to them, and they should hold up the tool they would use in that situation.

What tool would you use if . . . ?

The principal is standing in front of the school in the auditorium waiting to start a show. (Speaker Power and Listening Position)

Reinforce the idea that sometimes it's important to use more than one skill.

The fire alarm goes off. (Listening Power and Following Directions)

Ask the class how they would put the tools in this example to work.

You notice that a student who is new to our school is alone on the playground looking a little shy. (Be Your BEST, Giving Help)

Ask the class how they would put these tools to work.

You notice that someone did a great job coloring their SDM/SPS Toolbox. (Praise, Be Your BEST)

Ask the students how they would use these tools. Partner students to show their toolboxes to each other. Ask them to look for something they like about how their partner colored or decorated their toolbox. Remind them to give and receive praise, using their BEST. Be sure to allow time for both participants to give and receive praise.

7. Distribute copies of the "How Am I Doing?" self-report worksheet.

Let the students know that you are interested in hearing from them what tools they are using and what tools they have a difficult time remembering to use.

Tell the class that you are going to be asking them to show you what tool they could use when situations come up throughout the week. Tell them to have their toolboxes ready!

8. Introduce a Reflective Summary.

As outlined in the Introduction, ask students to reflect on the question "What did you learn from today's lesson?" Reinforce key themes, then go over any follow-up work.

9. Follow up.

The following steps will help make sure that the students have a chance to continue working with the new concepts throughout the school day and at home.

Assignment

Ask students to keep their toolboxes where they can see them as a reminder to use their skills. Tell them that you would be happy if they notice a time when an SDM/SPS skill tool could help in a situation and make that suggestion on the spot.

Plans to Promote Transfer and Generalization of Skill

1. Before activities that involve group work, movement to a new area, or attending an event, ask students to think about their tools and which ones they will use. Having the them take the tool out of the box (envelope) to identify and explain why the tool would be helpful is a concrete way to prepare students for behaviors that will be expected. Ask the class to bring their toolboxes with them. If people are forgetting to use their skills, a member of the group can volunteer to put their tool symbol in a place where it can remind people to use it.

2. Some students benefit from a visual reminder of a skill they are having trouble remembering to use. If you notice someone forgetting a tool, have them place the tool symbol on their desk where they can see it.

3. Scan ahead for situations characters face in language arts, social studies, health, or a movie or video when the use of social decision making skills would be beneficial.

4. Students can be asked to:

   ■ Think ahead about what tools a character might want to take out of their toolbox before heading into a situation.

   ■ Think about what tools a character used or could have used from their SDM/SPS Toolbox. (What happened as a result of using or not using the tools?)

TIPS FOR TEACHERS

1. This lesson is a great review and allows teachers to assess the skill gain of their students.

2. Skill gain requires time and practice. If teachers feel that their students need more practice and are not ready to proceed, then ear-

lier activities or whole Topics can be reviewed or repeated to enable students to further practice these skills.

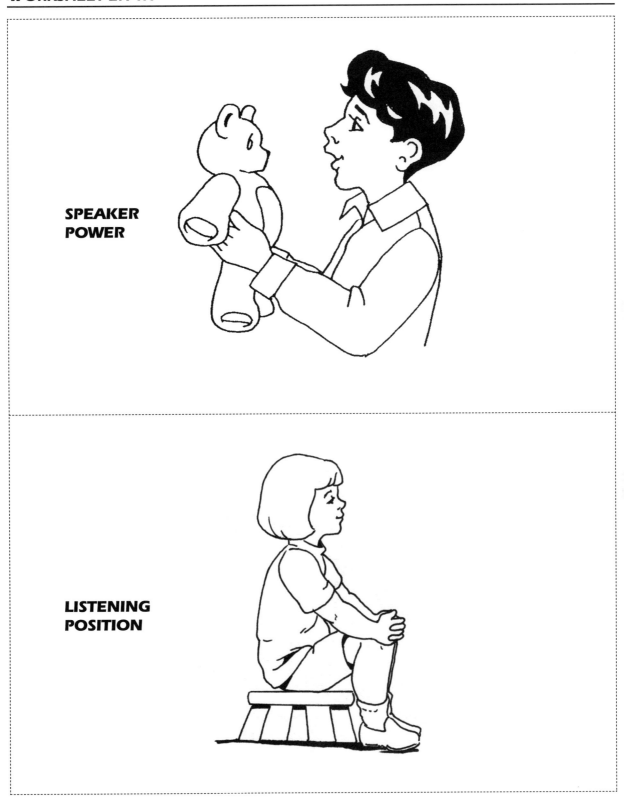

SPEAKER POWER

LISTENING POSITION

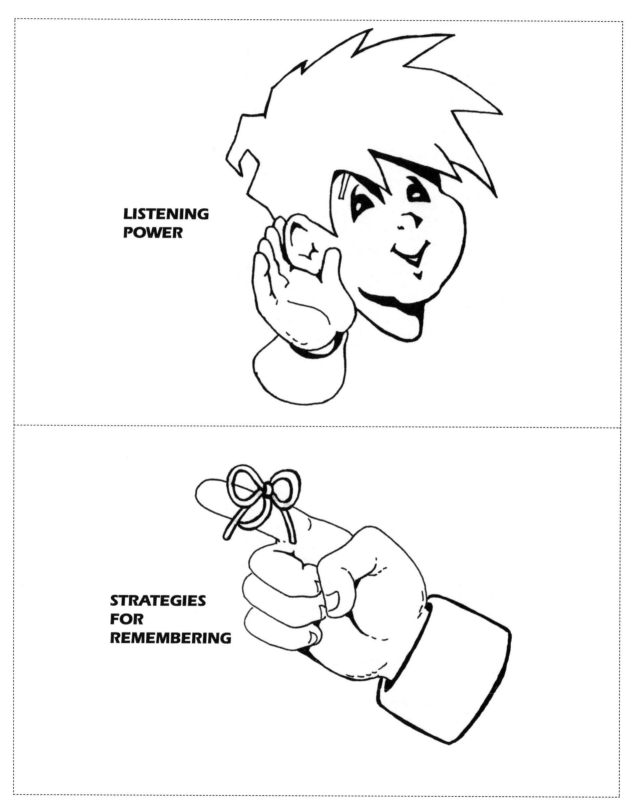

LISTENING
POWER

STRATEGIES
FOR
REMEMBERING

FOLLOW DIRECTIONS

BE YOUR BEST

GIVING PRAISE

GOOD FRIENDSHIP BEHAVIORS

KEEP CALM

HELP

Student _____ Date _____

1. I used Speaker Power.

2. I used Listening Position.

3. I used Listening Power.

4. I Followed Directions.

5. I Praised Others.

6. I was Helpful.

7. I used Calm, Nice Words.

T O P I C

15 Pull Your Class Together

OBJECTIVES
- To share and express feelings
- To build class cohesion

MATERIALS Chalkboard or easel pad

INSTRUCTIONAL ACTIVITIES

1. Review good listening skills.

Explain that good listening skills will be very important in the activities to follow.

2. Introduce the topic.

Obtain students' interest by explaining:

Today, we will be doing an activity to help us get to know one another better. As we get to know one another better, we will also learn how to work together better, the way a team does.

3. Start with a Sharing Circle.

Allow each student to answer a simple and interesting question like one of these:

- What is your favorite movie?
- What is your favorite indoor game?
- What sports do you enjoy?
- What is your favorite book?

After everyone has answered, ask students what they remember about what their classmates said.

4. Introduce the Smiling Faces activity.

Choose a student to start the activity. Explain that the task is to turn to the person on the right and say or do something that will make that person smile or laugh—make a funny face, give a compliment, tell a joke, or something else that doesn't involve getting up and moving around.

If the initial attempt is not successful, or if the student cannot think of something to do, turn the situation into a group problem by asking something along these lines:

What are some things that Ramon can do to make Debbie smile?

One or two class ideas can be tried. Whether successful or not, it will then be the recipient's turn to make the next child on the right smile. Continue as time allows. Encourage the class to help individuals who get stuck to complete the task.

5. Emphasize the value of knowing one another.

State how important it is for the class members to learn about one another and be kind to one another so that they can be a problem-solving team. Ask students to think about some things they would like to know about their classmates. Then brainstorm a list of their responses, recording them on the chalkboard or easel pad.

After that, ask each student to pick one thing to ask two classmates about. Give them a chance to do this, either by specifying how (turn to someone to the left or right; count off 1, 2, 3, 4 and have 1s talk to 2s and 3s talk to 4s) or by giving them free choice.

6. Introduce the Mirroring Activity.

Have the class break off into groups of three or four and stand in small circles. Choose one student from each group to go into the middle of the circle. Say that when you call out a certain feeling, you want the leader (the student in the center) to move as though he or she is having that feeling.

Encourage the leaders to use common body language to express feelings (facial expressions, body posture, arm movements, etc.), but also encourage students to add their own ideas and improvise. Start out with *happy.* As the leader shows happiness through body language, have the rest of the students mirror the leader exactly. Instruct the leaders to move deliberately and in slow motion so that the other students can follow along.

After a few seconds, call out another feeling, such as *tired.* Have the leader switch to this feeling. Then move through three or four other feelings, such as *sad, scared, proud,* and *confident.* Have the students rotate roles so each student gets a chance to act as leader. You can use the same sets of words or use new words, if you wish.

After all the students have participated as the leader, have them return to their seats, then ask the following questions:

- How did you keep track of what the leader was doing so you could mirror it?
- Did you find yourself feeling any of the feelings while you were mirroring them? If so, which ones?

Ask the students if any of them have ever heard the word *empathy*. If so, ask for their definitions. Make the point that empathy is when we feel what other people are feeling: Being a mirror helps us learn to be better at empathy and to know what our classmates or teammates are feeling.

7. Introduce a Reflective Summary.

As outlined in the Introduction, ask students to reflect on the question "What did you learn from today's lesson?" Reinforce key themes, then go over any follow-up work.

8. Follow up.

The following activity will help make sure that the students have a chance to continue working with the new concepts throughout the school day and beyond.

Plans to Promote Transfer and Generalization of Skill

As students read books in class, periodically ask them to think of questions they might ask about some of the characters. You can also have them practice mirroring by using that activity to show a character's changing feelings over the course of a paragraph, page, chapter, or book.

TIPS FOR TEACHERS

1. The activities for this topic serve two purposes. They were designed as a set of group-building experiences. Over the years, however, our observations have strongly suggested that many students have an impoverished vocabulary of feeling words and terms. They have difficulty recognizing or interpreting nuances of facial expression, posture, and vocal inflection. They lack sufficient labels to capture interpersonal experiences in a rich and varied manner. They seem to have difficulty grasping the meaning and implications of social situations and often seem to be left trying to fit feelings and events into a narrow "sad, glad, or mad" framework. This difficulty in sizing up situations has been shown to be an important contributor to students' adjustment difficulties. Not unexpectedly, these difficulties are greatest in children who experience behavioral or emotional problems.

2. One of the most important ways in which your class will come to feel like a problem-solving team is for them to become comfortable working with one another in a group and to believe that they can say what is on their minds without being criticized or rejected. The students are not being asked to agree with everything that is said. Rather, they will be helped to see that they can agree or disagree with someone's statement but still accept them as a person. For example, if a student makes a comment and another says, "You're stupid," this must be corrected to become "I don't agree with what you said" or "I don't think that's the best idea."

TOPIC

16 Identifying Personal Feelings

OBJECTIVES
- To identify internal feelings and share feelings with others
- To attend to signs of feelings in others
- To build class cohesion

MATERIALS
"Feelings Flashcards" (Worksheet 2.16.1)

Copies of the "Feelings Faces" (Worksheets 2.16.2–2.16.6)

Copies of the "Feelings Find" Take-Home (Worksheet 2.16.7)

"More Feelings Words" (Worksheet 2.16.8)

Crayons or markers

NOTE Worksheet 2.16.1 includes a page of blank flashcards. If you wish, create additional cards with different words (more words from which to choose are listed on Worksheet 2.16.8).

INSTRUCTIONAL ACTIVITIES

1. Review the SDM/SPS Toolbox.

Comment about some positive ways that students have been remembering to use their social decision making skills and SDM/SPS Toolbox.

Let children know that during this lesson the class will be playing some games that will help them learn about feelings. Asking the children, "What are feelings?" and "What are feelings for?" will help spark their interest.

2. Conduct a Sharing Circle.

Ask the class to take a minute and think of one feelings word that describes something they felt already today and share it with the class as Speaker Power is shared around the circle. Let them know that it is OK if their feeling is the same as or different from what others report.

3. Talk about feelings as an experience.

Comment that feelings are something that everyone has every day, and people can have many different feelings during each day, depending on what is going on. Share an example of your own—something along these lines:

> *I felt nervous this morning when I first woke up, and then I felt delighted when I heard one of my favorite songs on the radio on my way to work.*

Or:

> *I felt proud and excited about how well our class did at [mention an activity] yesterday, but later in the day I felt sad when I heard that a friend of mine was sick.*

It should be something you really felt; the class will be able to tell if you're just reading words.

4. Conduct the Feelings Flashbacks activity.

Let students know that the first activity is a game called "Feelings Flashbacks." This game will help the students learn about feelings by remembering some feelings they have had.

For this lesson, students will use a set of flash cards or index cards containing one "feelings word" each. Positive or mildly negative emotions are best at the beginning; the class doesn't need to use words like *angry* and *terrified*. (See the "Tips for Teachers" section at the end of this Topic.)

Prepare the class for the activity by discussing and modeling each feelings word flash card. (Possibly, this can be taught a day ahead of time.) Tell the students they will each be responsible for selecting at least one feelings card and then sharing a time when they felt this way with the class. They will be asked to share a specific time or situation.

Complete the Feelings Flashbacks activity by having students take turns picking a card. Ask them, "Can you tell about a time when you felt _____?" Have children volunteer their contributions. Continue with each feeling. Keep track and make sure that each student has contributed at least one feelings flashback.

5. Introduce a Reflective Summary.

As outlined in the Introduction, ask students to reflect on the question "What did you learn from today's lesson?" Reinforce key themes, then go over any follow-up work.

6. Follow up.

The following steps will help make sure that the students have a chance to continue working with the new concepts throughout the school day and at home.

Assignment

Ask students to find (or draw) pictures of feelings to bring to the next meeting. Supply old magazines and blank Feelings Faces and help children distribute and choose materials they might want to work with. Let them know that they can look for pictures in things that they have at home, too, but to be sure and ask a parent or guardian before they cut anything out of any books, magazines, or photographs at home.

Take-Home

Send the Feelings Find Take-Home to parents and guardians. Be sure to note when you want students to bring in their pictures. Review the pictures as part of an upcoming Sharing Circle or as a break in between other classroom activities.

Plans to Promote Transfer and Generalization of Skill

Language Arts

Teachers can scan ahead for feelings words in stories students will be reading and play Feelings Flashbacks as a way to introduce new vocabulary. It will also help students relate personally to the character who experiences the emotion in the book, video, or movie.

Social Studies

Students can be asked to imagine how a character would be feeling during a critical event being studied in history, current events in the news, or a discussion about a real-life "current event" that happened in the classroom or on the playground. Students can be asked to share a Feelings Flashback for the feelings words generated. Again, this helps them to better understand another's experience.

TIPS FOR TEACHERS

1. As noted previously, it is recommended that teachers use positive or mildly negative feelings words when first introducing the Feelings Flashbacks activity. This activity can be used on an ongoing basis for developing a vocabulary for feelings. The rationale for starting with feelings on the more positive end is to help students who are not comfortable or familiar with sharing their feelings begin with things that may be more fun to share. We have also

found that when offered a mixture of emotions, sometimes one student will wind up with *embarrassed,* for example, while another gets to share something they are proud of, a disparity that could be uncomfortable for some children.

2. If you have more student participants than flash cards, place the cards in a container and have students pick a card out of the container in turn. Keep the stack of flash cards that have been used outside the container, and shuffle and replace them until everyone has had a chance to share a Feelings Flashback. An alternative is to keep the unused flash cards in one pile and used cards in another. Once all of the cards are in the used stack, reshuffle and start again.

3. Some students benefit from beginning with a poster activity. Instead of flash cards, bring in a collection of pictures or cutouts from magazines that students can add to (see the Feelings Find Take-Home). Feelings illustrations can be numbered and students share based on the feeling that corresponds with the number they draw.

4. After students share their Feelings Find homework, the pictures or drawings can be used in a variety of ways:

   - Made into (or added to) a bulletin board or other display of feelings.

   - Arranged into groups that are the same or similar (for example, happy, excited, joyful, and proud might be in the same cluster).

   - Made into a notebook or dictionary of feelings for the class to use as a reference.

proud	**nervous**
angry	**afraid**
disappointed	**lonely**
excited	**sad**
surprised	**glad**
worried	**loving**

(page 2 of 2)

I am feeling _____

I am feeling _____

I am feeling _____

I am feeling _____

I am feeling _____

Feelings Find

Dear Parents or Guardians:

Your child has been asked to find or draw pictures that show different feelings. The assignment is

due on _____.

Ways You Can Help

1. Help your child decide what materials to use. Perhaps you have recent or old magazines or newspapers that can be cut up. You may have old photographs that your child can bring in.

2. Work with your child to find between five and ten pictures. For each picture or photo, ask your child, "Why did you choose that picture" and "What feeling does it show?"

3. If you like, either you or your child can write the feeling on the picture, on the back of the picture, or on a label you attach.

4. Help your child remember to bring all the pictures to school.

Your child may be asked in class to share what happened when you practiced this activity.

Thank you!

_____   _____

(Teacher signature)   *(Date)*

- -

(Please sign and return this bottom section.)   **Feelings Find   2.16.7**

Student _____ **Date** _____

We looked for pictures that show feelings.   ❐ Yes   ❐ No

If you did, how did it go?

_____

(Signature of parent or guardian)

SCARED	MAD	SAD	GLAD
Alarmed	Bothered	Unsure	Happy
Anxious	Annoyed	Disappointed	Cheerful
Cautious	Stressed	Hurt	Surprised
Concerned	Frustrated	Regretful	Joyful
Fearful	Outraged	Sympathetic	Ecstatic
Frightened	Enraged	Mixed Up	Lovestruck
Horrified	Disgusted	Depressed	Confident
Jittery	Troubled	Lost	Hopeful
Panicky	Overwhelmed	Confused	Encouraged
Shocked	Upset	Helpless	Enthusiastic
Shy	Aggravated	Guilty	Determined
Suspicious	Furious	Dismayed	Proud
Terrified			Amazed
Threatened			Content
Timid			Delighted
Uneasy			
Weak			
Worried			

17 Identifying Feelings in Others

OBJECTIVES
- To learn to recognize signs of feelings in others and demonstrate signs of different feelings in oneself
- To learn that feelings can vary in their degree of intensity

MATERIALS
Whole-class display or copies of "Feelings Can Be . . ." (Worksheet 2.17.1)

Copies of the "Feelings Faces" (Worksheets 2.16.2–2.16.6)

Crayons or markers

INSTRUCTIONAL ACTIVITIES

1. Begin with a Sharing Circle question about feelings.

An example of an On-Topic question is:

What is something you say or a noise you like to make when something happens that makes you feel great? How do you act when you say it?

Give one or two examples of something you do, such as say "Excellent!" or "Yahoo!" and use accompanying gestures.

2. Introduce the skill of looking for signs of different feelings.

Explain that good social decision makers and problem solvers learn to pay attention to the messages that other people send through the ways they look and act. People let you know how they are feeling in many more ways than just words.

Examples: Things people say, gestures, facial expressions, tone of voice, body posture, and so on. Be sure that the list includes aspects of nonverbal communication.

3. Conduct a practice activity.

Have students share their Feelings Find assignment (from Topic 16), in which they drew or found pictures of people showing their feelings.

Have students show a picture to the group, tell what feeling they think the person in the picture is having, and tell what they see that makes them think the person is feeling that way.

Depending on the maturity of the group, bring up the idea that in some pictures there might be more than one feeling word to describe what that person appears to be feeling. Ask the student and the rest of the group for any other feelings words that match what they see. Again, ask:

> *What do you see that makes you think that they are feeling that way?*

4. Introduce the idea that sometimes feelings can be very strong and sometimes they are not as strong.

Show students the whole-class version of the worksheet titled "Feelings Can Be . . ." or give a copy to each student. Let students know that the worksheet is a meter that they can use to rate feelings from 1 (Mild) through 5 (Very Strong). Tell them that you are going to read some little stories to them, and then you would like them to show if they think the feeling would be 1, 2, 3, 4, or 5 by the number of fingers they hold up.

Read the following situations to the class one at a time, pausing after each situation to ask the questions listed after the first one. Notice if some children differ in how strongly they feel about something. Let them know that this is what usually happens—people often have different levels of feelings about the same events.

- Someone took Pat's new bike for a ride without asking permission.

  How strong do you think the feelings would be on our rating scale or meter? Hold up your fingers to show the number you would rate the feeling.

  What feelings would the person in the story be having? How would you feel if the situation happened to you?

Other situations:

- You've just been chosen for an important part in the school play.
- Your best friend just told you about plans to move far away.
- Someone just cheated in a game you were playing.
- The teacher just yelled at you for not paying attention.
- Your friends won't let you play on their team.

It is often useful to go through the situations again and ask how the *other* people in each situation might be feeling.

5. Introduce a Reflective Summary.

As outlined in the Introduction, ask students to reflect on the question "What did you learn from today's lesson?" Reinforce key themes, then go over any follow-up work.

6. Follow up.

The following steps will help make sure that the students have a chance to continue working with the new concepts throughout the school day and at home.

Assignment

Ask students to pay attention to feelings they see when they watch television or movies, read a story, or work and play with teammates and friends in school and at home. They should note what people do to show their feelings.

Pass out blank Feelings Faces (Worksheets 2.16.2–2.16.6) and ask the students to fill in the name of a person they saw, draw the expression they saw on the person's face, and write the word for the feeling the drawing shows.

Plans to Promote Transfer and Generalization of Skill

1. Keep an ongoing collection of feelings words and pictures and "Feelings Can Be . . ." ratings on display and use them to help children express both what they feel and how strong the feeling is. Use the More Feelings Words list (Worksheet 2.16.8), if you need examples of some other words that students could use to expand their vocabulary for feelings.

2. Language arts, social studies, and health texts and topics provide ongoing opportunities for infusing practice of the identification of personal feelings and the feelings of others. The same questions used in this topic area can also be used daily within academic areas and real-life situations. For example:

   - How do you think [fill in character or person] might be feeling?
   - How strongly do you feel (or do you think they might feel) about this situation? (Use the "Feelings Can Be . . ." meter.)
   - Are there other feelings words that could help us understand what people are or might be feeling?

TIPS FOR TEACHERS

1. Teachers should expect that second graders will need ongoing prompts for skills related to feelings:

   - Using new words for feelings
   - Increasing the expression of feelings in daily communication or in writing
   - Recognizing and labeling the feelings of other people

2. When first getting started with this program, some teachers find it helpful to keep a list of questions to prompt feelings identification in plain sight as a reminder to use them. Some teachers have used thick paper and folded it like a tent with a list of new skill prompt questions on both sides. This tent card serves as a visual reminder to themselves and students, who can see the skill prompt questions written out on the teacher's desk at all times.

3. Scan ahead for academic content areas addressed during the week that lend themselves to infusing practice identifying feelings. Writing this activity into lesson plans as one of the objectives is also a helpful reminder. Topic 19 goes into more detail on ways to include the identification of feelings in the study of a story and also serves as useful practice for teachers and students of methods that can then be used in an ongoing way.

Feelings Can Be . . . .

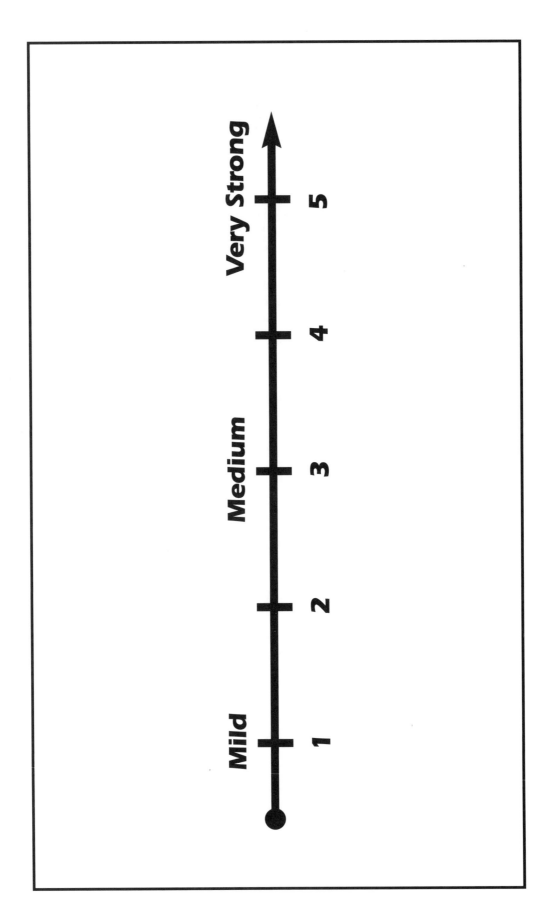

18 Identifying Personal Feelings and the Feelings of Others

OBJECTIVES
- To practice skills of identification and sharing of feelings and identifying feelings in others
- To increase a vocabulary for feelings

MATERIALS

Two sets of "Feelings Flashcards" (Worksheet 2.16.1). Recommended feelings words: *proud, disappointed, angry, excited, surprised, worried, nervous, afraid, lonely, sad, glad,* and *loving.*

INSTRUCTIONAL ACTIVITIES

1. Begin with a Sharing Circle about feelings.

For example, you might say:

Think about a feeling you had this week. Say the feeling and show us what that feeling looks like using your face and body posture.

Give students a minute to think about their answers and provide an example.

2. Have students work in groups of four.

Distribute a flashcard to each group from one of the sets of cards. Let students know that you will be asking them to look at the word on their card and then to share with their group a time when they felt that way. Demonstrate for the class before they begin by selecting a word, identifying or naming the feeling, and then telling about a time when you felt that way. Ask for any questions before telling the class to begin.

Once students have completed the first round, collect the flashcards and distribute a new card to each group. Repeat.

3. Teach students how to play the Feelings Match game.

Explain:

> *Class, today we are going to play a game called Feelings Match.
> The object of the game is to pick a card and then find another
> card that matches it. Every time you pick a card, tell about a
> time when you felt that way. Then pick another card. If the card
> you pick matches the one you just did, say, "Match" and you
> get to keep the two cards. Then another person gets to take a
> turn. Let me show you how to play the game.*

Demonstrate the game for the class. Place all of the flashcards (two
sets) face down on a desk or table, or tape or pin them to another surface. First, demonstrate the game as follows:

> *Hmm, now I think I will pick this card.*

Flip it over and show the class. Identify the feeling. For example:

> *Sad. I felt sad when my pet fish died.*

Select another card, saying what you're doing. Flip it over, show it to
the class, and demonstrate again. For example:

> *Lonely. I felt lonely when my friend was on vacation and I did
> not have anyone to talk to after school. No match!*

Flip both cards over and place back on the desk or surface. Remind
the class that if the second card had said *sad* you would have said,
"Match" and kept both cards.

Ask if anyone has any questions before they start the game.

4. Play the game.

Have students take turns coming up to the front of the room, flipping
over two cards, identifying the feeling and telling about a time when
they felt that way. If they make a match, they tell about another time
they felt that way and keep the cards. If they have trouble coming up
with a second example, after a few minutes of thinking time, ask them
if they would like to ask a classmate for help telling about a time when
someone had that feeling.

If time allows, continue with the game until all the matches are made.
If not, let the students know that it is time to stop the game. Reinforce
the students for learning the game and for sharing their feelings.

5. Introduce a Reflective Summary.

As outlined in the Introduction, ask students to reflect on the question "What did you learn from today's lesson?" Reinforce key themes,
then go over any follow-up work.

6. Follow up.

The following activity will help make sure that the students have a chance to continue working with the new concepts throughout the school day and at home.

Plans to Promote Transfer and Generalization of Skills

As students encounter feelings words in social studies, health, language arts, science, or other subjects, ask them to share a time when they experienced the same feeling. This simple exercise will let you assess the students' understanding of the words and promote empathy at the same time.

TIPS FOR TEACHERS

1. As suggested, this game can be used as a way to learn new feelings words as they appear in stories or reading in language arts, social studies, health, and other subject areas.

2. The game described in this topic is even more fun when the cards include pictures of faces with different emotions. You can work with students to create these game cards by having them bring in pictures of faces and having them help you sort, label, match, cut out, and mount the pictures to create the card sets.

19 Identifying Feelings in Stories

OBJECTIVE
- To practice identifying feelings of characters in the context of language arts

MATERIALS
A storybook of your choice

PREPARATION
Preview trade books and stories commonly used in the language arts curriculum for a book appropriate to the theme. Read the book and identify critical points when a character or characters encounter a situation that triggers emotion.

NOTE
The example used here is from *The Cat in the Hat,* by Dr. Seuss (Houghton Mifflin, 1957). Page numbers refer to this original edition.

INSTRUCTIONAL ACTIVITIES

1. Begin with a Sharing Circle.

Ask a question like this:

What is one of your favorite books or stories? It might be a book from school or a book that you read at home. It could even be a book you remember from when you were little.

2. Thank students for their answers and explain the purpose of this topic.

Comment that they have mentioned many wonderful stories that you love, too. Point out that reading stories is a great way to get to know about people and things that happen that they may never experience in their own lives.

Let the students know that this meeting will help them learn how to imagine how it would feel to be in the situation that the characters find themselves in. This helps them understand how other people feel in real life, too.

3. Introduce the chosen story.

For example:

Today we are going to read a story that was one of my favorite stories when I was in second grade. It is called The Cat in the Hat. *How many of you have read this story? We are going to use this story to practice our skills at using our imagination to think about what it would be like to be a person in a story. Let's start reading. Your job is to use Listening Power and your imagination and ask yourself, "How would I be feeling if I were the person in this story?"*

4. Read the story.

Stop at the critical points in the story that you identified earlier—the ones where characters encounter trigger situations. Ask children to look at illustrations of body posture and facial expressions and then to say how they think the characters are feeling. Then ask them what they see that makes them think that the person might be feeling that way. When applicable, ask them to show you (demonstrate) what the feeling looks like.

When a situation in the story has triggered emotions and some response may be called for, but has not yet occurred, stop and ask the following questions:

- If you were [character] how would you be feeling?
- Are there any more feeling words to describe what [character] might be feeling?
- Has anyone ever felt this way?
- What do you think [character] might be thinking right now?
- Let's keep reading and see what happens.

For example, suppose you're reading *The Cat and the Hat,* stopping to display the illustrations. On the first page of the book, you could point out the faces of the boy and the girl in the windows of their house and the bird in the tree outside. Ask questions such as these:

What do you think the boy and girl are feeling? What do you see that makes you think that? Show me what that looks like.

On the second page, when it describes that it was too wet to play and how they sat and did nothing at all, point out the body language of the two children. Also have the students look at the face and body language of the fish in the fishbowl. Ask:

What do you think the girl, the boy, and the fish are feeling? What do you see that makes you think that? Show me what that looks like.

On the third turn (to pages 4 and 5), there is a bump that makes them jump. Again, ask students to look at the body language and the faces of the boy and the girl and the fish and ask again:

What do you think they are feeling? What do you see that makes you think that they are feeling that way? Show me what that looks like.

Then read through the next three page turns. The Cat in the Hat enters the home and tells the children that he knows a lot of tricks to show them and good games to play that their mother will not mind at all. On the next page, their fish jumps out of its bowl to warn the children—"No! No!"—the cat should not be in the house, and they should not play when their mother is out.

This is an example of a critical point in a story when a situation may have triggered emotions and some response may be called for but has not yet occurred.

Ask students:

- If you were the boy or girl, how would you be feeling?
- Are there any more feeling words to describe what they might be feeling?
- Have you ever felt this way?
- What do you think the girl and boy might be thinking right now?
- What do you think might happen?
- Let's get back to the story and see what happens.

5. Continue reading and stop a few more times.

For example, on page 25 the fish confronts the cat with the children looking on, asking him to look at the consequences of his actions and to leave. The children's faces, the cat's body language and face, and the fish's body language and face all display different emotions.

Another possible critical point is on page 47, when the fish spots the mother coming home. Another critical point is on page 58, when the cat leaves the house with a tip of his hat. The cat, the fish, and the children all have faces and body language that are similar yet distinct in terms of feelings.

Finally, on page 61, the children are sitting back at their window seats and asking themselves if they should tell their mother about what went on that day. Ask students to remember the body language and faces of the children and the fish when they were in the very same position at the beginning of the story and think about what is similar and what is different. Ask students to identify the feelings of the children and the fish and then to anticipate what might happen. Ask them what they think the children will do. Then ask them, as the book does, what they would do if they were in that situation.

6. Introduce a Reflective Summary.

As outlined in the Introduction, ask students to reflect on the question "What did you learn from today's lesson?" Reinforce key themes, then go over any follow-up work.

7. Follow up.

The following steps will help make sure that the students have a chance to continue working with the new concepts throughout the school day and at home.

Assignment

Ask students to read an upcoming story and stop at an identified critical point in the story. As an assignment, ask them to list feeling words for what they imagine they would be feeling if they were in the same situation.

Plans to Promote Transfer and Generalization of Skill

1. Continue to use these procedures intermittently when reading stories in language arts.

2. Stop at critical points in social studies to consider the feelings of characters facing historical and current situations.

3. In health, develop hypothetical situations for health choices and ask students to imagine how someone would feel if faced with the choice.

TIPS FOR TEACHERS

1. When asking students to look at facial expressions and body language of characters illustrated in a book, it can be helpful to copy pages onto an overhead or another whole-class display so children can see the picture more easily and to save time in passing the book around.

2. Encourage students to come up with feeling words beyond *happy, sad, mad,* and *afraid.* As new feeling vocabulary words are introduced, keep a running list displayed for future reference.

20 Things That Bug You and How Your Body Responds

OBJECTIVES
- To help students become aware of situations that trigger or elicit strong emotions *(Trigger Situations)*
- To increase awareness of the unique way strong feelings make their presence known in the body *(Feelings Fingerprints)*
- To introduce the importance of taking responsibility for using Feelings Fingerprints as a sign that calming down is necessary before thinking and acting

MATERIALS
Whole-class display of the "Feelings Can Be . . ." meter (Worksheet 2.17.1)

Drawing paper and markers or crayons

Copies of "Things That Bug Me" (Worksheet 2.20.1) and "Feelings Fingerprints" (Worksheet 2.20.2)

NOTE
Some teachers have had students work in small groups to draw an outline of each team member's body on a large sheet of paper. Students work together to put their initials where a Feelings Fingerprint for each student in the group is located.

INSTRUCTIONAL ACTIVITIES

1. Open with a Sharing Circle.

Review Topic 19 by having students share the lists of feelings words that they did as their assignment.

2. Review vocabulary of feelings.

Introduce the lesson by asking students to review a list of feelings words (the one from Topic 16 or another that you have created or found). Ask students to find a word that they think would be a Number 5 on the "Feelings Can Be . . ." meter. They are looking for an emotion or feeling word that would be the highest rating (very strong). Let them know that it is fine to pick the same word as someone else.

Explain that during this lesson they will start to learn about strong, "Number 5" feelings. Tell them that everyone at one time or another has a problem that needs to be solved. These can be problems with parents, teachers, brothers, sisters, or friends.

Ask if any student who has brothers or sisters remembers a time that one or both of them had Number 5 feelings because of a problem that they were having.

Tell students that sometimes people jump right in and try to solve a problem before they are ready. If this happens, nothing gets accomplished because they are too upset and their feelings get in the way of being able to think clearly. Add:

> To make the BEST decision, we need to calm down our feelings so we can use our brains to think about what we can or want to do.

3. Introduce the idea of trigger situations.

Define *Trigger Situations* as events or situations that cause a Number 5—very strong—feeling.

Provide some examples–bullying, getting into an argument, and so on—and brainstorm some other common Trigger Situations with the group. Prompt children if needed to include emotions in categories other than anger, such as fear, nervousness, sadness, or being so excited that they cannot focus on their work or fall asleep at night.

Distribute the Things That Bug Me worksheet and have students write or draw a variety of Trigger Situations that happen to them. Tell students that they will be sharing at least one of their Trigger Situations with the class.

When students are done with their worksheets, have them share one of their Trigger Situations with the class.

4. Talk about physical signs of stress.

Explain that when someone is faced with a Number 5 trigger situation, they experience physical reactions. Tell students that people feel physical signs of these strong feelings in their bodies in different ways, and these are called *Feelings Fingerprints*.

You can help students brainstorm their Feelings Fingerprints, their personal physical signs of stress, by sharing your own experiences when faced with trigger situations. The list may include headache, rapid heartbeat, stomachache or butterflies, sweaty palms, tense shoulders, faster breathing, knees shaking—whatever you feel when going in for a job interview or doing something else that you find stressful.

This kind of openness may be tough, but students often respond well when teachers self-disclose an example (real or close to real) of their own Feelings Fingerprints. For example:

Once I was on my way to school and I got a flat tire. When I thought that I was going to be late and of you worrying about me, I got a tight feeling in my chest. That is my Feeling Fingerprint. When I get upset and worried, my chest gets tight and it's hard to breathe.

5. Distribute the Feelings Fingerprints worksheet.

Ask the children to draw on the worksheet where Feelings Fingerprints show up in their body. You may suggest that children close their eyes and try to remember how they felt in an upsetting situation. Ask them to try to visualize the experience and feel how their bodies felt at the time.

After students finish, ask them to share their pictures with a partner. Then ask the group for some volunteers to show and describe their personal Feelings Fingerprints.

6. Introduce a Reflective Summary.

As outlined in the Introduction, ask students to reflect on the question "What did you learn from today's lesson?" Reinforce key themes, then go over any follow-up work.

7. Follow up.

The following steps will help make sure that the students have a chance to continue working with the new concepts throughout the school day and at home.

Assignment

Ask students to try to remember any Trigger Situations that they experience. Also, ask them to remember the Feelings Fingerprints that they experience during the Trigger Situation. Tell students that you will be asking them to share one of their Trigger Situations and Feelings Fingerprints during the next meeting. Let students know that the next topic will be learning skills that help to calm down strong feelings so that they can think clearly and be their BEST.

Take-Home

Copies of the Things That Bug Me and the Feelings Fingerprints worksheets can be sent home so that parents and guardians can review these concepts with their children. Families can have a discussion about the various trigger situations and corresponding Feelings Fingerprints that arise both at home and at outside activities.

Plans to Promote Transfer and Generalization of Skill

1. Help students recognize any Trigger Situations and Feelings Fingerprints that occur throughout the week. Discuss situations that occur in the classroom, in the cafeteria, on the playground, and in the hallways.

2. Characters in stories often experience Trigger Situations and Feelings Fingerprints. Have students discuss this in the stories that you are reading in class. Also, have students share any Trigger Situations and Feelings Fingerprints that they see on television, in movies, and in stories that they are reading in their free time.

TIPS FOR TEACHERS

1. It can be helpful to explain to students that human bodies are equipped to respond to upsetting situations with a "fight or flight" reaction: What happens in a Trigger Situation is that the body makes a chemical called adrenaline, which causes physical reactions and provides a lot of energy. When strong feelings happen, it is a lot easier for someone to use fight or flight behavior than to think because another thing adrenaline does is make it hard to use the strongest part of the brain. It is important to be able to recognize times when it is difficult to "Be Your BEST" because of strong feelings—and know what to do about it.

2. Some children have a difficult time identifying their physical signs of stress or their Feelings Fingerprints. Think about stressful situations that you know your students have experienced—for example, being nervous performing in front of a large group or before a test—and ask students how they felt at that time. Many second graders have experienced nervousness and can explain how it feels. Then move into sadness; many have seen others cry and have cried themselves. Then move into anger and being scared.

3. Some students may need a real-life example of how their body goes through changes and sends out physical signs. Have students jog in place or do some other physical activity and then stop and describe their faster heartbeat, their quickening breath, and their face and body starting to turn red and feel hot.

Student _____ **Date** _____

```
┌─────────────────────────────────────────────────────────┐
│                                                         │
│                                                         │
│                                                         │
│                                                         │
│                                                         │
│                                                         │
│                                                         │
└─────────────────────────────────────────────────────────┘
```

```
┌─────────────────────────────────────────────────────────┐
│                                                         │
│                                                         │
│                                                         │
│                                                         │
│                                                         │
│                                                         │
│                                                         │
└─────────────────────────────────────────────────────────┘
```

```
┌─────────────────────────────────────────────────────────┐
│                                                         │
│                                                         │
│                                                         │
│                                                         │
│                                                         │
│                                                         │
│                                                         │
└─────────────────────────────────────────────────────────┘
```

Student _____ **Date** _____

21   A Strategy for Keeping Calm

OBJECTIVES
- To point out problematic situations in which students can use self-control to calm down before reacting
- To teach students a way to get calm and keep their self-control in a problematic situation

MATERIALS
Whole-class display of steps in "Keep Calm" (Worksheet 2.21.1)

"Keep Calm Reminder Cards" (Worksheet 2.21.2)

"Smell the Pizza Keep Calm Cards" (Worksheet 2.21.3; *optional*)

INSTRUCTIONAL ACTIVITIES

1. Begin with a Sharing Circle.

Review Topic 20 by having students share a Trigger Situation and that situation's Feelings Fingerprint.

2. Introduce the Keep Calm exercise.

Ask the class when it is important to be able to calm yourself down if you are upset. Explain that today's topic will be keeping calm—why it matters, and how to learn how to do it. Say:

It is possible to handle almost every type of problem or difficulty better if you are able to keep calm. To help us learn to keep calm, we are also going to learn about an exercise called "Keep Calm." This exercise can help you get through a problem situation without saying or doing something you later wish you hadn't.

Think about what happens when you lose your temper and yell or hit people or things. Today we are going to learn what you can do before you do something that could get you into trouble.

3. Explain the behavioral and cognitive components of the skill.

The key to keeping calm is to slow down your breathing.

Refer students to the whole-class display and introduce the four steps of Keep Calm:

1. Tell yourself to STOP!

2. Tell yourself to KEEP CALM.

3. Slow down your breathing with two long, deep breaths.

4. Praise yourself for a job well done.

At this point, it's useful to provide examples of people your students will relate to—sports figures or the heroes in stories you know they're following. Say:

> *Athletes, performers, and people in the martial arts have used methods like Keep Calm to help them achieve their best.*

4. Model the skill.

Model the skill by describing and demonstrating the steps to the class. First present a situation in which you could be irritated or nervous. Describe the situation, then say:

> *First, I would tell myself, "STOP!"*

> *Then I would tell myself, "Use Keep Calm to calm down."*

> *Then I would take two long, deep breaths. First, I would let out all the air in my lungs through my mouth. Then I would take a slow and smooth breath of air in through my nose to the count of five. I would hold that breath for the count of two and then slowly let the air out through my mouth to the count of five, while still saying to myself on the inside, "Keep Calm." Then I would do the breathing again.*

> *When I felt better, I would say to myself, "Good job." Using self-control can be hard work, and you need to praise yourself.*

Ask students to watch you demonstrate how to do it before they try it. Demonstrate the procedure counting with your fingers to five while taking a breath in and to two while holding your breath and again to five while breathing out. Then repeat the breath. Bring your hands down to your sides while you are releasing the breath through your mouth—indicating that you are saying, "Keep Calm." Smile after completing the breathing to indicate you are telling yourself, "Good job" on the inside.

Also show students how Keep Calm should *not* look (puffed out cheeks, breath holding, silliness).

5. Conduct a practice activity.

Have everyone try the procedure. Look for students who are doing the procedure correctly. Be specific in praising—"Nice, smooth breathing." If children need correction, state it positively, with information about what to do. For example, say, "Slow down your breathing" rather than "Don't go so fast."

Tell students that using Keep Calm does not need to be loud or obvious to others. Ask them for examples of when they could use "Keep Calm." After every example, have the whole group pretend that they are in the situation, and again practice doing the Keep Calm steps.

Generate situations when Keep Calm may be used. Most situations fall into three main categories:

- When you are nervous. (Before a test, up at bat, giving a speech, or other types of performance.)
- When you really need to concentrate. (Working on a test, working after recess, when you are distracted by noise in the room.)
- When you are angry or frustrated and about to lose your cool. (Beginning to yell during an argument or when you feel like you will do something that will get you into trouble.)

6. Conduct additional practice activities.

If time and interest permit (and it may be useful to apply this topic across two sessions), some additional practice activities often prove valuable:

- Have children write or draw situations where Keep Calm could be used. Keep papers on hand for future practice.
- Present children with situations by staging role-plays, acting out a situation yourself, or showing a video or pictures, and then have children add examples of their own to those presented. The following situations may be used:

  Feeling fidgety and talking in class

  Feeling nervous about a test or a report

  Being lost in a shopping center

  Going to a new school

  Competing in a sports event

- Introduce an object (a stuffed animal, a pen, a swatch of soft cloth like velvet or velour) called the "Keep Calm object." Make sure it is something quite different from the Speaker Power object. When an incident occurs in class and a student is upset, you can give them the object to hold to remind them to keep calm.
- Have the students draw a picture of someone before and after using the Keep Calm exercise.

7. Introduce a Reflective Summary.

As outlined in the Introduction, ask students to reflect on the question "What did you learn from today's lesson?" Reinforce key themes, then go over any follow-up work.

8. Follow up.

The following steps will help make sure that the students have a chance to continue working with the new concepts throughout the school day and at home.

Assignment

Encourage students to find a time when they can use Keep Calm and try it. Let them know that you will expect an example of how they used Keep Calm at the next meeting.

Take-Home

Instead of using the cards in Worksheet 2.21.1, students can create posters with the four Keep Calm steps, or a handout with the Keep Calm steps can be distributed to take home to parents and guardians. Parents and guardians should be encouraged to review the Keep Calm steps and hang the poster in a place when their child needs to remember to use Keep Calm, such as by the TV, in their room, on the refrigerator. Parents and guardians should also be encouraged to remind their child to use the Keep Calm technique.

Plans to Promote Transfer and Generalization of Skill

1. Make several posters of the four steps of Keep Calm and have students decorate them. Place them in areas of the room where they can best be used by students to guide them through the four steps while the skill is still new to them.
2. Use the Keep Calm skill prompts when a child is upset or is beginning to lose control:
   - Use your Keep Calm steps.
   - Stop and think about what's happening.
   - Let's use Keep Calm and get focused.
   - Let's take a look at what's going on—describe what is happening and how you are feeling.
   - Take a deep breath and use Keep Calm—then we can talk about it.
3. Try playing "ZZZZZZZZ: ZZZZZZ," a game developed by Marianne Torbert and described in her book *Follow Me: A Handbook of*

Movement Activities for Children (Prentice Hall, 1980), to help children develop social and emotional skills. Here's how it works:

The player pretends to be asleep. At the sound of a bell or timer they jump up and move quickly to another place, where they pretend to fall asleep again. This game was designed to develop the ability to relax quickly. Ask the children to use the Keep Calm steps when they pretend to fall asleep again.

4. In language arts, find characters that are experiencing strong emotion and could use the Keep Calm exercise. Ask students how the story could have changed if the character had used Keep Calm.

5. Remind students about Keep Calm before potentially stressful situations and changes in class such as art, music, physical education, lunch, and playground period. Encourage an upset child to use a Keep Calm object.

TIPS FOR TEACHERS

1. Some students may need a real-life example of what it's like to be nervous, antsy, or in danger of losing their temper. This can be illustrated in several ways. Use a mirror to show differences in physical appearances before and after using Keep Calm. Jogging in place to increase breathing can be used to show the contrast before and after Keep Calm.

2. Some students may have difficulty conceptualizing the breathing component of Keep Calm. Using the "Smell the Pizza" cards (Worksheet 2.21.2) is helpful for these children. They can pretend that they are holding a slice of pizza. They can breathe in to smell how good the fresh pizza smells, pause to enjoy it, and then they can blow on the hot, fresh pizza to cool it down. The concrete image of the pizza can help students with Keep Calm breathing even without the reminder cards.

3. Some students will learn to recognize their Feelings Fingerprints as a sign to use Keep Calm. Others will be prompted by Trigger Situations or other sets of cues. The skill will be learned to the extent that children can be prompted and reminded to use it in everyday situations, such as when moving from class to class, at recess, before a test, before an important meeting, when they are upset at home, or in performance situations, such as reading aloud, being in front of the class, being called on by the teacher, showing their work in music or art, or during sports activities.

4. The goal of Keep Calm is to have students begin to use the skill before they lose their self-control and not wait until after they are already very upset.

5. Regularly discuss and reinforce the use of Keep Calm, and find occasions to talk about the future use of Keep Calm. These discussions will promote future use of self-control. Students should be helped to use Keep Calm to prepare themselves for actual or possible trigger situations.

Keep Calm

1. Tell yourself to STOP.

2. Tell yourself to KEEP CALM.

3. Slow down your breathing with two long, deep breaths.

4. Praise yourself for a job well done.

From *Social Decision Making/Social Problem Solving: A Curriculum for Academic, Social, and Emotional Learning (Grades 2–3)*.
Copyright © 2005 by Maurice J. Elias and Linda Bruene Butler. Research Press (800-519-2707; www.researchpress.com).

KEEP CALM

1. Tell yourself to STOP.

2. Tell yourself to KEEP CALM.

3. Slow down your breathing with two long, deep breaths.

4. Praise yourself for a job well done.

KEEP CALM

1. Tell yourself to STOP.

2. Tell yourself to KEEP CALM.

3. Slow down your breathing with two long, deep breaths.

4. Praise yourself for a job well done.

KEEP CALM

1. Tell yourself to STOP.

2. Tell yourself to KEEP CALM.

3. Slow down your breathing with two long, deep breaths.

4. Praise yourself for a job well done.

KEEP CALM

1. Tell yourself to STOP.

2. Tell yourself to KEEP CALM.

3. Slow down your breathing with two long, deep breaths.

4. Praise yourself for a job well done.

SMELL THE PIZZA   KEEP CALM

SMELL THE PIZZA   KEEP CALM

SMELL THE PIZZA   KEEP CALM

SMELL THE PIZZA   KEEP CALM

22 Be Your BEST and Keep Calm

OBJECTIVES
- To review the Be Your BEST skill in the context of situations with strong emotions
- To understand how Keep Calm can be used to help students calm down and think at times they are at risk of falling back on aggressive or passive behavior
- To provide practice combining Keep Calm with Be Your BEST to respond to Trigger Situations

MATERIALS
Filled-in version of the "Be Your BEST Grid"

Whole-class display of the "Keep Calm" steps (Worksheet 2.21.1)

INSTRUCTIONAL ACTIVITIES

1. Review Topic 21 in a Sharing Circle.

Obtain students' interest by asking:

What do you do to calm yourself down when you are upset at a friend?

As students reply, ask them to show the class how they do it. This may be hard for some students, and if they are having a hard time, go on to another child. After a few have gone, make the point:

I notice that for a lot of you, calming yourself down means you calm your body down and then you try to solve the problem between you and your friend. This is very good! Today we are going to practice ways to calm your body and do some problem solving when trigger situations take place. We are going to practice Keep Calm and Be Your BEST.

(Ask for definitions of Trigger Situations before you proceed.)

2. Review behavioral components of Keep Calm and Be Your BEST skills.

Ask for volunteers who remember the steps of Keep Calm. Take a couple of answers and then summarize, pointing to the Keep Calm poster you have in your room.

Referring to the Be Your Best Grid, do the same, emphasizing the *S* and *T* and practicing how the two aspects of BEST look and sound different in aggressive, passive, and BEST (assertive) behaviors.

3. Practice combining the Skills of Keep Calm and Be Your BEST.

Ask students to think of times when they think it would be good to combine Keep Calm and BEST. Make a list.

Ask students to practice by reading the following scenario to them:

Alex Gets Teased

Alex is a boy in second grade. Alex likes to read and do puzzles in his free time. Several of the boys in Alex's class tease him and make fun of him because he does poorly at sports. When the teams are picked in gym, he is always picked last. The boys call him a loser and tell him that they don't want him on their team.

Have students repeat the story back to you to ensure understanding. Then ask:

Who wants to volunteer to be Alex? OK, pretend that you are playing sports and some students are teasing you and you are getting very upset. Show how you might use Keep Calm to calm yourself down.

Ask the class to provide feedback. Then have another child try the same thing; select a girl if the first was a boy, and vice versa. Give overall feedback.

Then say:

OK, pretend you are Alex and you are waiting to be picked for a team. No one picks you, and they tell you that you are a loser. Who wants to pretend to be Alex and show how you would use Keep Calm?

Repeat the procedure.

Divide students into four groups, assigning one aspect of BEST to each group. Have volunteers role-play the next step in each of the scenarios—first what Alex would say or do after being teased and then what Alex would say after being told he was a loser.

After each role-play, ask observers to give some praise for the skills they observed, focusing on *S* and *T.*

Ask students in the role-play and others if they have any suggestions that would make BEST even better. Ask students with suggestions to role-play their ideas.

Here are some additional Keep Calm and BEST practice situations:

- A group of girls in second grade were playing at recess, but they would not let Rosa play with them. Rosa walks away from the group and finds Alicia and they begin playing together. Then, the group of girls walks over to Alicia and says to her, "Why do you want to play with Rosa—don't you know that nobody likes her?"

■ Veronica is a new girl in class. She moved from a town in Canada. She is nice, but she speaks with an accent and uses words and phrases that the other kids in the class don't understand. A group of girls laugh and make fun of her by imitating her, and now they won't let her sit at the second-grade girls' lunch table.

■ Eli is a second grader, and he has difficulty learning math. He needs to go to the resource room teacher every day during math class. Several of the boys in his class call him "stupid" or "idiot." Every morning, they take the special math book that he uses and toss it to one another on the playground before school. They tease him about not knowing the answers to simple math problems.

4. Introduce a Reflective Summary.

As outlined in the Introduction, ask students to reflect on the question "What did you learn from today's lesson?" Reinforce key themes, then go over any follow-up work.

5. Follow up.

The following steps will help make sure that the students have a chance to continue working with the new concepts throughout the school day and at home.

Assignment

Encourage children to use Keep Calm and Be Your BEST during the week and to tell about it next time. Provide students with positive feedback for calming themselves, helping others calm themselves, or for being their BEST during the day. Be sure to ask for changes in behavior ("I can tell that you want to tell me something, but please start again and remember to use your BEST tone of voice"). Be sure to notice and specifically praise any behavior change.

TIPS FOR TEACHERS

1. Teachers should use Keep Calm and BEST skill prompts themselves but also encourage children to use these skill prompts with one another in pairs or group situations when they might be helpful. Having shared language and skill prompts can empower class teammates to help one another when these situations occur. This kind of peer-level interaction can be of significant help in giving youngsters the confidence and pride that they need to function in

school as well as in neighborhood, family, and, ultimately, job situations.

2. Some schools use a Keep Calm force of fourth- and fifth-grade students to remind students, especially younger ones, to use their Keep Calm and BEST skills at recess and at other unstructured times. (For further information, see www.umdnj.edu/spsweb.)

3. Praise students for any skill improvement you observe—for example, when children listen to feedback from the group or assess their own behavior and use their insights to improve their performance in a second role-play. Let them know that listening to the suggestions of teammates and coming up with their own ideas is a great way to improve their skills.

4. Remind the students that these are difficult skills because it is hard to think clearly and remember to Keep Calm when emotions are strong. Assure them that it is worth the effort to learn these skills now because the skills will help them for the rest of their lives. Point out that practice is how people get good at any skill, so starting now means these skills will be very strong by the time they grow up.

23 Introducing Problem Diaries in Our Lives

OBJECTIVES
- To establish the *Problem Diary* as a tool to keep track of Keep Calm and BEST skills in daily life and teamwork situations
- To learn how to use the Problem Diary to handle friendship problems
- To practice using the Problem Diary applied to real-life Trigger Situations

MATERIALS   Copies of the "Problem Diary" (Worksheet 2.23.1)

INSTRUCTIONAL ACTIVITIES

1. Review good listening skills.

Remind students of the importance of using Listening Position during this lesson.

2. Review the skills.

Ask students to remember the four steps of Keep Calm and the *ST* components of Be Your BEST. Tell students that during this lesson they will continue to learn ways to use Keep Calm and BEST in real-life situations.

3. Conduct a Sharing Circle.

Ask students to share a recent Trigger Situation or situation that bugs them.

4. Introduce the Problem Diary.

Give a copy of the *Problem Diary* to each student. Explain that the Problem Diary is something to use when there's no one around to help manage a Trigger Situation.

5. Conduct a practice activity.

Practice using Problem Diaries to help students handle difficulties with friends by having students fill out Problem Diaries describing a Trigger Situation that happened with a friend or classmate. It is important to tell the students that these will be shared with the class, so they should use no names, just describe the situation.

Ask students to share their Problem Diaries with the group. After they read the diary, ask students to role-play what they did to use Keep Calm and BEST. If they did not remember to use these skills, ask them to try role-playing how they could have used their skills in the situation.

Ask:

> *What is something else you could have done to handle the situation?*

Divide the class into four groups and have each group watch for a specific component of Keep Calm and BEST in the role-play. Have the class analyze the role-play and discuss whether the alternative solution that was tried could have worked. Have students create additional solutions that might work and then practice these role-plays. Remind students of friendship behaviors (Topic 13) and review some of the good friendship behaviors they brainstormed during that topic.

6. Introduce a Reflective Summary.

As outlined in the Introduction, ask students to reflect on the question "What did you learn from today's lesson?" Reinforce key themes, then go over any follow-up work.

7. Follow up.

The following steps will help make sure that the students have a chance to continue working with the new concepts throughout the school day and at home.

Assignment

Distribute new copies of the Problem Diary worksheet and have students complete them for homework, using a situation that arises during the upcoming week or using a character in a book, movie, or other media. Tell students that at the next session they will role-play the situations that seem most relevant. Emphasize that there is always more than one way to handle a difficult situation. Tell students that this activity is getting them ready for more advanced problem solving and decision making.

Take-Home

The Problem Diary is a tool that can be used to monitor various trigger situations, and it is a good review of all the previous program skills that have been taught. Parents can use this tool to help their children deal with trigger situations at home.

Plans to Promote Transfer and Generalization of Skill

Students have practiced using the Problem Diary in both academic and social settings. Students can continue skill building by completing Problem Diaries whenever they experience a trigger situation. All school staff should be made aware of the Problem Diary worksheet so that they can prompt the students to use them. Students can continue to complete Problem Diaries pretending that they are a character in a story, and this process can be repeated throughout the language arts curriculum.

TIPS FOR TEACHERS

1. Problem Diaries can be shared with parents during conferences or disciplinary meetings.

2. Support staff—such as cafeteria aides, classroom aides, and after-school care workers—can be trained to use the Problem Diary to prompt students to use this tool when problems arise.

Student _____ Date _____

What happened?

How did you feel?

**What did you want
to have happen?**

**What is something you
could have done to
make that happen?**

T O P I C

24 Problem Diaries and Literature

OBJECTIVE
- To practice using Problem Diaries applied to characters in literature

MATERIALS
Copies of the "Literature Problem Diary" (Worksheet 2.24.1)
A storybook of your choice

PREPARATION
Select a book appropriate to the theme. Read the book and identify critical points when the character encounters a Trigger Situation or problem.

INSTRUCTIONAL ACTIVITIES

1. Review Topic 23 in a Sharing Circle.

Have the students share the Problem Diaries that they completed for their assignment.

2. Distribute Literature Problem Diary worksheets.

Have students listen to a story in which characters experience a Trigger Situation or problem.

Stop reading the story at a critical point—after the character's problem is introduced, but before the character has begun any problem solving.

Have students complete the Problem Diary, inserting the name of the character(s) and answering the questions.

3. Have students role-play their situations.

Ask students to share their work with the class. Have students pretend that they are the characters in the story and have them role-play the situation and their ideas about how the characters could handle the situation and solve the problem.

Divide the class into groups and have each group watch for a specific component of Keep Calm and Be Your BEST in the role-play. Have the class analyze the role-play and talk about how well the positive alternative solutions that were tried would have worked. Allow several students to share their ideas. Then have students brainstorm additional solutions that might work.

Read the remainder of the story and summarize the lesson by discussing the similarities and differences between the students' ideas and the real story.

4. Introduce a Reflective Summary.

As outlined in the Introduction, ask students to reflect on the question "What did you learn from today's lesson?" Reinforce key themes, then go over any follow-up work.

5. Follow up.

The following steps will help make sure that the students have a chance to continue working with the new concepts throughout the school day and at home.

Assignment

Distribute a new copy of the Literature Problem Diary and have students complete one for homework using a character's problem situation in a story of their choosing. Tell students they will have an opportunity to share their diaries during the next lesson.

Plans to Promote Transfer and Generalization of Skill

1. Have students complete Literature Problem Diaries from the point of view of characters in literature or social studies, saying the idea is to assess how well the characters managed their emotions and how effectively they communicated. Have students compare their ideas of how to handle the problem or situation with the characters' solutions. Remind students that the characters' solutions may or may not be better than what they think of.

2. The use of Problem Diaries, introduced in Topic 23, and Literature Problem Diaries is mutually reinforcing. Have a stack of blank Problem Diaries available for use when Trigger Situations arise. Some teachers set up a Keep Calm corner where skill step posters are displayed as a place where students can reflect on their behavior, practice Keep Calm, and complete a Problem Diary.

3. Tell students that when they have a problem or Trigger Situation, they can complete a Problem Diary and file it in a private social decision making portfolio or notebook. Doing so will allow them to assess their own skill gains as they have time to practice their skills.

4. Leave a box for completed Problem Diaries to be turned in if students wish to do so, and use the worksheets as future hypothetical situations for social problem solving and social decision making role-plays.

5. Students can complete a Problem Diary and then ask their teachers to talk with them to help them solve their problems or prevent future difficulties.

6. Problem Diaries are also useful tools for guidance counselors, child study team members, and principals and vice principals to help students in dealing with difficult situations. Some schools have had success providing lunch and playground aides with Keep Calm areas and a stack of Problem Diaries. Young children benefit most from interventions that help them link reflection about their behavior to the immediate situation.

TIPS FOR TEACHERS

1. Problem Diaries are a powerful way for students to review and practice the self-control skills that they have learned. By using Literature Problem Diaries in academic situations, students can further practice and apply their skills.

2. Literature Problem Diaries can be shared with parents during conferences or disciplinary meetings.

Student _____ Date _____

Book or story you are reading _____

Characters you are writing about

_____

_____

1. **What happened?**

2. **How did _____ feel?**

3. **What did _____ want to have happen?**

4. **What is something _____ could have done to make that happen?**

TOPIC

25

Using Problem Solving to Reduce Tattling

OBJECTIVE
- To practice thinking about a common problem: tattling

MATERIALS
Chalkboard or easel pad

A whole-class display or copies of the "Problem Diary" (Worksheet 2.23.1)

Poster board and markers

NOTE
After the class has compiled final lists of situations that are "Important Reporting" versus "Tattling," write the lists on a sheet of poster board and display them in the classroom. Situations can be added to the list as they arise. (Students can help by adding drawings or decorating the poster.)

INSTRUCTIONAL ACTIVITIES

1. Begin with a Sharing Circle.

Ask:

What is something you like about how members of our class treat one another?

Emphasize how the things they mention help the class work together as a problem-solving team. Then ask who remembers what Problem Diaries are. Take some answers and then say:

Today, we are going to use our Problem Diaries to solve a problem that keeps teams and classes from being their BEST.

2. Introduce the specific topic.

Ask:

What is tattling?
How do we feel when we are tattled on?
How do we feel when we tattle?

Explain that you and the class will be creating two lists. The students will generate situations and problems that occur regularly, and you will decide which column the idea belongs in:

a. Important things that you (or other teachers) must know about

b. Situations that are not important and can be solved in ways other than reporting to you or other teachers

Point out that treating something in group (b) as though it belonged in group (a) is tattling. It is up to you to decide under which column the items will fall. The choice will depend on the age, population, and general makeup of the group.

Label list (a) "Important Reporting" and list (b) "Tattling."

Have students role-play how they could use Be Your BEST when they tell the teacher something important (use a situation from the class list).

Have observers give praise and suggestions for making BEST even better.

3. Discuss tattling.

Use a whole-class display or individual Problem Diaries to talk about a tattle from the list. Brainstorm different ways to solve the problem without telling the teacher.

Have students role-play how they could use their BEST when they put an idea into action to try to solve the problem on their own.

Have observers give praise and suggestions for making BEST even better.

Pick other tattles and continue the same format as time allows.

4. Introduce a Reflective Summary.

As outlined in the Introduction, ask students to reflect on the question "What did you learn from today's lesson?" Reinforce key themes, then go over any follow-up work.

5. Follow up.

The following steps will help make sure that the students have a chance to continue working with the new concepts throughout the school day and at home.

Assignment

Ask students to be on the lookout for tattling versus telling something important. They can help one another by saying, "Is that on the 'Important Reporting' list?"

Plans to Promote Transfer and Generalization of Skill

1. Post the lists generated and refer to them as a reminder. The lists can be modified and added to as situations arise.

2. Review the lists periodically before lunch and recess and remind children to check the lists before they come to you with a situation. When students come to you with a tattle, have them complete a Problem Diary to find another way to solve the problem.

3. You may find it useful to track the number of tattles from day to day or week to week and record reductions.

TIPS FOR TEACHERS

Sometimes it can be difficult to draw a clear line between tattling and appropriately telling an adult when a student, for example, witnesses bullying or teasing. One way to convey this is to say, "It is important to tell an adult if you see other students doing something that might hurt themselves or hurt someone else. That is not tattling."

26   Review SDM/SPS Tools and Celebrate Success

OBJECTIVES
- To provide students with an opportunity to review the social decision making and social problem solving skills they have learned
- To provide teachers and students with an opportunity to assess skill gains
- To anticipate and plan ways to use social decision making and social problem solving skills in the next grade

MATERIALS
Whole-class display of "Our SDM/SPS Tools: Grade 2" (Worksheet 2.26.1)

Copies of the following:

"How Am I Doing Now?" self-report form (Worksheet 2.26.2)

"Certificate of Achievement"(Worksheet 2.26.3)

"Student Progress Report" Take-Home (Worksheet 2.26.4)

"SDM/SPS Summary and Recommendations" (Worksheet 2.26.5)

Crayons or markers, drawing paper, scissors

Students' SDM/SPS Toolboxes (from Topic 14)

INSTRUCTIONAL ACTIVITIES

1. Review the difference between tattling and important reporting from the previous Topic.

Ask students to describe any examples of tattling or important reporting they may have experienced or seen. Repeat that it is appropriate to tell an adult about something that may hurt them or someone else.

2. Direct students' attention to the SDM/SPS Tools worksheet.

Explain that this lesson will give students a chance to think about all of the skills and ideas they have learned so far as a part of social decision making and social problem solving. Review the worksheet; encourage students to give their own definitions and descriptions of the tools. Ask:

What skills were the easiest for you to learn? What were the hardest?

What do you like most about our class as a problem-solving team?

The skills and concepts learned during Grade 2, and the Topics in which they were introduced, are as follows:

- Sharing Circle (Topic 1)
- Listening Position (Topic 2)
- Listening Power (Topic 4)
- Strategies for Remembering (Topic 5)
- Following Directions (Topic 6)
- Be Your BEST (Speech, Tone of Voice) (Topic 7)
- Giving Praise (Topic 10)
- Receiving Praise (Topic 11)
- Asking for and Giving Help (Topic 12)
- Good Friendship/Not-Good Friendship Behaviors (Topic 13)
- Things That Bug Me; Feelings Fingerprints (Topic 20)
- Keep Calm (Topic 21)
- Problem Diary (Topic 23)

3. Introduce and conduct the practice activity.

Distribute the paper, crayons or markers, and scissors. Instruct students to fold and cut the paper in half so they have four sheets. Ask students to think about which skills they use the most, and then pick four from the whole-class display. Invite them to draw a picture for each of the four skills.

Have students form small groups and take turns sharing their most useful skills and concepts by showing and explaining their drawings, one at a time, to the other group members. Each student should share a drawing, then invite someone else in the group to describe the skill. After that student has answered, the first student may ask other group members to offer feedback and corrections, then describe his or her own use of the skill.

Students should go around the group until everyone has had a chance to share at least two drawings—more if time allows. When they have finished, have them pack all of their drawings into their SDM/SPS Toolboxes.

4. Review progress.

Distribute the "How Am I Doing Now?" self-report and let the students know that you are interested in hearing from them what tools they are using and what tools they have a difficult time remembering to use. Have students complete the worksheet and turn it in.

5. Wrap up and celebrate the unit.

At the final meeting of the problem-solving team, praise students for their accomplishments. Ask students if they have any praise for the accomplishments of the team.

Conduct a final Sharing Circle, asking everyone to praise the person they pass the Speaker Power object to about some way that person was a good teammate.

Conduct a short ceremony where every member of the team is presented with a Certificate of Achievement. End with a round of applause for the great teamwork they have had.

6. Introduce a Reflective Summary.

As outlined in the Introduction, ask students to reflect on the question "What did you learn from today's lesson?" Reinforce key themes, then go over any follow-up work.

7. Follow up.

The following steps will help make sure that the students have a chance to continue working with the new concepts throughout the school day and at home.

Assignment

Have students take their SDM/SPS Toolboxes with them as a reminder to use their skills during the summer and into the next grade.

Plans to Promote Transfer and Generalization of Skill

1. Ask students how they feel about going into the third grade. Then brainstorm possible problems they might have. Using full or small groups, encourage students to come up with goals and plans for how they could cope with problems making the transition to a new grade. If possible, spend several discussion sessions on this subject.

2. An SDM/SPS Summary and Recommendations form, designed to provide information to teachers in the next grade about their incoming students, may be filled out for each student.

3. A Social Decision Making Progress Report is also included for sending parents a summary of students' skill gains and recommendations for helping their children celebrate their achievements and continue building skills.

4. Student portfolios can be sent home as a reminder of skills and record of all that was learned and achieved.

Our SDM/SPS Tools: Grade 2

1. Sharing Circle
2. Listening Position
3. Listening Power
4. Strategies for Remembering
5. Following Directions
6. Be Your BEST (Speech and Tone of Voice)
7. Giving and Receiving Praise
8. Asking for and Giving Help
9. Good Friendship/Not-Good Friendship Behaviors
10. Things That Bug Me
11. Keep Calm
12. Feelings Fingerprints
13. Problem Diary

From *Social Decision Making/Social Problem Solving: A Curriculum for Academic, Social, and Emotional Learning (Grades 2–3)*. Copyright © 2005 by Maurice J. Elias and Linda Bruene Butler. Research Press (800-519-2707; www.researchpress.com).

Worksheet 2.26.1

Student _____ Date _____

1. I used Speaker Power.

2. I used Listening Position.

3. I used Listening Power.

4. I Followed Directions.

5. I Praised Others.

6. I was Helpful.

7. I used Calm, Nice Words.

From *Social Decision Making/Social Problem Solving: A Curriculum for Academic, Social, and Emotional Learning (Grades 2–3).*
Copyright © 2005 by Maurice J. Elias and Linda Bruene Butler. Research Press (800-519-2707; www.researchpress.com)

(page 1 of 2)

8. I know my Feelings
   Fingerprints.

9. I notice how Others
   Are Feeling.

10. I think about how characters are
    Feeling when I read stories.

11. I use Keep Calm when
    I am upset.

12. I use the Problem Diary.

SDM/SPS
CERTIFICATE OF ACHIEVEMENT

_____
(Student)

Has successfully developed many Social Decision Making and Social Problem Solving skills

Sincerely,

_____   _____
(Teacher)   (Date)

Student Progress Report

Dear Parents or Guardians:

 I appreciate your support and partnership as we have worked this year to help your child develop social decision making and social problem solving abilities. As the school year comes to a close, I would like to share my assessment of your child's progress and make some recommendations to you about ways that you can help to continue the development of these skills through the summer months.

Skill improvement

_____

_____

_____

Suggestions to help you reinforce and continue skill development

_____

_____

_____

Additional comments

_____

_____

_____

Thank you!

_____

(Teacher signature)

(Please sign and return this bottom section.)   **Progress Report   2.26.4**

Student _____ **Date** _____

We received the report.   ☐ Yes   ☐ No

Comments:

_____

(Signature of parent or guardian)

From *Social Decision Making/Social Problem Solving: A Curriculum for Academic, Social, and Emotional Learning (Grades 2–3)*.
Copyright © 2005 by Maurice J. Elias and Linda Bruene Butler. Research Press (800-519-2707; www.researchpress.com)

Teacher _____ Date _____

Students in my class worked on a Social Decision Making and Social Problem Solving (SDM/SPS) team this past year to develop a variety of skills. I have noted below accomplishments and areas of focus for particular students.

1. **Students with general strengths in SDM/SPS:**

   _____   _____

   _____   _____

   _____   _____

2. **Students needing overall growth in SDM/SPS:**

   _____   _____

   _____   _____

   _____   _____

3. **Students with strengths in particular SDM/SPS areas:**

   Student   *Area*

   _____   _____

   _____   _____

   _____   _____

   _____   _____

4. **Students needing skill development in particular SDM/SPS areas:**

   Student   *Area*

   _____   _____

   _____   _____

   _____   _____

   _____   _____

SUPPLEMENTAL

Topics 27–29

27
Using Problem Diaries to Solve Playground Problems

OBJECTIVES
- To use the format introduced for Problem Diaries to prepare students with strategies for coping with common playground problems
- To introduce a procedure that students and teachers can continue to use to help students develop plans for coping with everyday problems they encounter on the playground or in other less structured school situations

MATERIALS
Chalkboard or easel pad

Whole-class display of the "Problem Diary" (Worksheet 2.23.1)

PREPARATION
Identify a common difficulty that students have on the playground. You can ask students to submit problems or simply wait until student reports cluster around a common theme. Some teachers choose a situation that has been a common problem for second graders they have worked with in the past and help students develop strategies for dealing with the situation before it becomes a problem. Turn the situation into a hypothetical story using fictitious names.

INSTRUCTIONAL ACTIVITIES

1. Begin with a Sharing Circle.

Use a playground-related question. For example:

What is your favorite thing about recess time? What do you like to do or what do you like the most about it?

2. Explain the purpose of the lesson.

Things sometimes happen at recess time that can keep students from enjoying their free time. Ask:

Why do we have recess time?

What is supposed to happen during recess time?

After several responses, validate the students' ideas and share goals from your point of view. For example:

These are all good ideas. What I want to have happen during recess is for all of you to have some fun and exercise and free time. The goal is to take a nice break from all the hard work we do in the morning. When you have fun for a while, it makes you better able to come back to class fresh and happy so we can get back to work.

3. Make a list of goals.

Ask students if they can all agree on goals for recess time. Let several students state a few of the main ideas and list them on the chalkboard or easel pad for further reference. For example: To have fun; take a break; come back in a good mood; come back ready to work.

Then ask:

What happens when there are fights or disagreements on the playground?

What are some feelings that students have when they have fights or disagreements during recess time?

When these things happen, are we reaching our goals?

4. Convene the class as a problem-solving team.

Explain that the students' job is to think about ways to handle some problems that can happen on the playground in a way that will help them enjoy their time outside and come back happy and ready to work. Let them know that you have picked an example of something that sometimes happens for them to work on together. Say:

Today I will show you how we can work together to solve a play-ground problem. Once we know how to do it, we can do it again if we have other problems to solve.

5. Present a hypothetical situation.

Display the whole-class version of the Problem Diary. Let students know that the same questions used on the Problem Diary can help guide the class as a team to solve problems that come up at any time.

Tell a story based on a real-life situation. For example:

There was a second-grade boy named Josh. He was swinging on the tire swing on our playground one day with his friend

Juan. Suddenly, one of their classmates, Max, came running up and jumped on the tire swing so hard that Josh fell out and scraped his elbow.

Or:

One day on the playground, Emily and Sasha got together with a group of girls from their class to play a game of soccer. They were having a lot of fun when Darrell, a boy from their class, came over and grabbed the ball while a group of girls were trying to chase it down. He held the ball over his head and ran off the field, saying, "The girls have had this ball long enough—now it's the boys' turn to play!"

For each story, ask questions like these, changing the names as needed:

- First, how do you think Josh would be feeling? Can you think of other feelings he would have?"
- How do you think Max would be feeling? Are there any other feelings he might have?
- What was the problem? Who can put the problem into words?
- What do you think Josh wants to have happen? Are there things that Josh does not want to have happen?
- What can Josh do to solve this problem? Let's think of all of the ideas we can. What else could he do?

Now call the class's attention to the list of goals. Review the list generated at the beginning of the lesson and any other goals generated by the class for the student in the story they're discussing. Ask:

Who thinks they have an idea about what the best thing is that Josh could do?

Does anyone else have an idea about what they would do if they were Josh?

For each of the suggested solutions, ask students if this is an idea that might help the students in the stories reach their own goals.

6. Conduct a practice activity.

Choose several solutions selected by students that are acceptable and lend themselves to role-play practice and to the use of Keep Calm and BEST. Tell the class that the next thing to do is to bring these good ideas to life.

Say, for example:

OK. If you were to go and ask the playground aide to help you take care of your elbow and talk to Max about not jumping on the swing because people get hurt, how would you do that? What would you do first? . . . What would you say? . . . How would you say it? . . . Who would like to pretend to be Josh and show what you would say and do? . . . I will pretend to be the playground aide. Let's try it and the rest of you watch carefully and watch for the way Josh uses Keep Calm and BEST.

Repeat for several other solutions, using the Emily/Darrell story as well as other stories, as time allows.

7. Introduce a Reflective Summary.

As outlined in the Introduction, ask students to reflect on the question "What did you learn from today's lesson?" Reinforce key themes, then go over any follow-up work.

8. Follow up.

The following steps will help make sure that the students have a chance to continue working with the new concepts throughout the school day and at home.

Assignment

If the problem you have been working on is one that students are currently facing, give them the assignment to try out their new ideas and be ready to report back how well their plans worked. Set up a time for follow-up and continue to solve any problems they encounter.

Plans to Promote Transfer and Generalization of Skill

1. Continue to collect examples of playground problems through personal records and notes by collecting information and situations from students (through a Playground Problem Box or survey), or from past experience. Conduct group problem-solving sessions as new situations emerge or as a prevention method for situations that you've observed occur commonly among second graders.

2. In language arts, read books that depict common playground problems. Stop at a critical point in the story—when a character is bullied, teased, or faced by another problem—and use the Problem Diary to guide students to a solution from the point of view of the character in the book.

TIPS FOR TEACHERS

Playground problems can often be solved in several different ways. By considering a variety of options—as long as they reach the goal of using Keep Calm and BEST, and are not against the school rules (fighting, saying mean things)—students learn that there are many ways to solve a problem and can then choose the one that works best for them.

28 Learning How to Use the Problem-Solving Corner

OBJECTIVE
- To model and teach students how to use Problem Diaries and other methods when they need to sit out to rethink their decisions about behavior

MATERIALS
Copies of the "Problem Diary" (Worksheet 2.23.1)

Copies of each "Feelings Face" (Worksheets 2.16.2–2.16.6)

Skill prompt posters (Worksheets 2.12.2, 2.4.1, 2.7.1, 2.10.1, and 2.21.1)

Pencils, crayons, and markers

PREPARATIONS
Choose a cubicle, desk, or other isolated corner or section of the classroom. Provide a chair, writing surface, and various items to promote "Keep Calm": stuffed animals, an hour glass (in which sand flows slowly from top to bottom), and other inspirational posters or pictures. Post the skill prompt posters where students can easily see them.

INSTRUCTIONAL ACTIVITIES

1. Begin with a Sharing Circle.

Use a question that calls attention to problem solving. For example:

What are some of the ways that our class works well together?

2. Introduce the Problem-Solving Corner.

Summarize positive aspects of the way the class functions that students shared and mention additional aspects they may have left out. Let the students know that the Problem-Solving Corner is a place to go when things are not going as well as they can. Let them know that the purpose of today's lesson is to learn what to do in the Problem-Solving Corner to help get back on track when things are not working out as well as they should.

3. Talk about sitting out.

Ask the students whether any of them have watched a basketball game. Then ask what the referee does when a player makes too many fouls. (Blows a whistle and the player sits out for a while). Let students know that taking some time out to stop and Keep Calm can help a player get back into the game, ready to perform in a better way. Many adults have learned that taking a little time away from a situation to get control and come up with a plan for how to handle things helps them make better decisions and be more successful.

4. Walk over to the Problem-Solving Corner and introduce the class to the space prepared.

For example, say:

> *This is going to be our Problem-Solving Corner and it is a place to go when you need a little time to stop, use Keep Calm, and come up with a plan to improve your performance or behavior.*

Explain that there will be times when you will ask students to take some time to think, in the Problem-Solving Corner. If you ask them to do so, you are acting as referee of the class team. Sending them to the Problem-Solving Corner is a way to teach them how to take time to stop and think of a different way to handle a situation or as a way to help them remember the rules and make a new plan to follow them.

5. Demonstrate use of the Problem-Solving Corner

Tell students that first you will pretend that you are going to the Problem-Solving Corner and show them an example of what to do there. For example:

> *Let's say that I am a second grader and my class is having a Sharing Circle. I like to use Speaker Power and most of the time I am good at Listening Power, too, but on this day, I keep forgetting to respect Speaker Power when other people are talking. This is now the third time that I called out and interrupted someone. At first my teacher tried to remind me, but I kept forgetting. What the teacher would say to me is "Please go to the Problem-Solving Corner and think about what it means to respect Speaker Power." Once I am here I can use a Problem Diary or a Feelings Face worksheet to draw or write how I am feeling. Then I can think about what I can do to help me remember to use Listening Power and to respect Speaker Power when someone else is talking. I know it is sometimes hard to do.*

Then go sit in the Problem-Solving Corner and fill out a Problem Diary, saying out loud what you might write:

I think I will use the Problem Diary to decide what to do. I am feeling . . . the problem is . . . what I want to have happen is . . . what I think I will try . . .

When you're finished, raise your hand and say:

I think I am ready to come back and use Listening Power.

Explain that sometimes you will check in with students to see if they are ready to come back into the game, but they can also let you know when they think they are ready to try out a plan.

6. Talk about using the Problem-Solving Corner.

Ask students for examples of times when it would help someone to get control and think of a way to improve. List the examples on the chalkboard or easel pad.

As time allows, have students role-play what they would do if they went to the Problem-Solving Corner, using some of the examples listed.

7. Introduce a Reflective Summary.

As outlined in the Introduction, ask students to reflect on the question "What did you learn from today's lesson?" Reinforce key themes, then go over any follow-up work.

8. Follow up.

The following steps will help make sure that the students have a chance to continue working with the new concepts throughout the school day and at home.

Plans to Promote Transfer and Generalization of Skills

Once students have been introduced to how to use the Problem-Solving Corner, begin to use it for minor incidents to help make it a common and familiar class procedure that everyone can benefit from. Go to the Problem-Solving Corner yourself and model using Keep Calm and taking time to think of a new plan when you encounter one of your own trigger situations in the classroom.

TIPS FOR TEACHERS

1. It is important to use the Problem-Solving Corner in a constructive and teaching way. This method is intended to stop action and provide a structure of prompting behavior change. The message

and tone should be one of encouragement and confidence that the student will come up with a good plan and just needs the time to get control and problem solve.

2. Some students benefit by having a peer tutor help them work through a Problem Diary.

3. A trip to the Problem-Solving Corner may not be effective if the student is already out of control. In this case, the goal is to first help the student gain control through Keep Calm or other methods to get emotions settled. Students are not able to access their problem-solving skills until their emotions are regulated, so worksheets and other methods to elicit problem solving should be done at a later time.

TOPIC

29 Using Technology to Practice Identifying Feelings and Develop a Vocabulary for Feelings

OBJECTIVE ▪ To integrate the use of technology to help students develop a vocabulary for feelings and the ability to identify feelings

MATERIALS Computer, digital camera, printer

Internet access

Software to create graphics that illustrate feelings *(optional)*

NOTE If you don't have the items listed, you can still do these activities with a conventional film camera and without the access to a computer.

INSTRUCTIONAL ACTIVITIES

1. Conduct a Sharing Circle as part of a regular technology or computer lesson.

Use an On-Topic question like this one:

What is something you enjoy or something you find difficult about working on the computer?

2. Introduce the idea of applying social decision making skills in a technology lesson.

Explain that during this lesson, students will be working on their social decision making skills while also learning about ways to use the computer. Depending upon the technology available, try some of these activities:

Use a Digital Camera to Develop Feelings Faces

Have each student pick a feelings word from a prepared set of Feelings Flashcards (see Worksheet 2.16.1) or chosen by students from the dictionary or from a list of vocabulary words. Have students work with a partner to take turns helping each other work out a facial expression that clearly illustrates the feeling on each of their cards (or their personal choices).

Using a digital camera, take a photograph of each student as they make a facial expression that depicts their assigned emotion.

Use these photos as a way to illustrate how digital photos can be stored and used to illustrate written text. Have students write several sentences that describe the feeling and what made the person feel that way; insert the photo on the page as an illustration.

Alternatively, print out the photographs, laminate them, and use them as Feelings Flashcards.

Use a Digital Camera to Create a Social Story

"Social stories" are a method that was developed for working with children with developmental difficulties such as autism or Asperger's Syndrome to help them learn appropriate ways to interact in social situations. This method can be adapted for use with all students.

Use a digital camera and computer to create illustrated short stories that depict daily interactions and how they make people feel. For example, digital photos can be taken to illustrate the following social story:

> *When the bell rings for recess to end, the teacher is happy to see all the children line up and walk to their classrooms. Many children are excited that they get to hear a story. The teacher is glad to see the children in Listening Position. After the story is finished, students use Speaker Power and have a Sharing Circle to talk about what they liked about the story. The students are curious to hear what their classmates have to say.*

Take photos to illustrate each step in the story, having students act as characters, demonstrating the feelings described. Help the students to create a written storybook that uses the photos to illustrate each step and the feelings. Print out the storybooks for students to read as a review of expected behaviors and related feelings.

Use computer software (such as "Smart Alex" or "Kid Pix") to teach students to create or use computer-generated graphics to illustrate a range of emotions for a character they are learning about in social studies or reading about in language arts.

Use Web-Based Applications

Web-based applications available through the Internet provide students with one-on-one or small-group practice in identifying feelings and developing their vocabulary for feelings. For example, a game called "About Face" can be found at the PBS Web site. The game allows players to click on one of several characters from the cartoon show *Arthur* to hear about a variety of social situations they encounter. After Arthur describes the situation (via audio for nonreaders), a series of feelings faces are displayed. Students click on the feelings face that they think shows what the character would be feeling. (You can find the game at www.pbskids.org/arthur/games/ or by searching the Web for "Arthur PBS Series.")

3. Introduce a Reflective Summary.

As outlined in the Introduction, ask students to reflect on the question "What did you learn from today's lesson?" Reinforce key themes, then go over any follow-up work.

4. Follow up.

The following steps will help make sure that the students have a chance to continue working with the new concepts throughout the school day and at home.

Take-Home

As you find additional Web-based applications that are helpful for practicing feelings identification, send a list home to parents and guardians, recommending the sites as sources of computer games children can play to further develop their skills.

Plans to Promote Transfer and Generalization of Skill

Students can create and read social stories to review procedures or behaviors being taught as often as needed to help them internalize the steps and perform independently.

TIPS FOR TEACHERS

Computer games and applications are helpful for students who seem to need more individualized practice with feedback to internalize skills than can be provided in the regular classroom sessions.

RECOMMENDED TOPICS FOR GRADE 3

Becoming a Problem-Solving Team

Feelings

Social Decision Making and Social Problem Solving

Supplemental

GRADE 3 WORKSHEETS

Becoming a Problem-Solving Team

Topics 1–13

1

Introduction to Social Decision Making/Social Problem Solving (SDM/SPS) Lessons

OBJECTIVES
- To introduce and orient students to SDM/SPS lessons
- To establish ground rules for SDM/SPS meetings
- To introduce and participate in a *Sharing Circle*
- To introduce and provide opportunities to practice Speaker Power, and to establish *Speaker Power* as shared language and a skill prompt
- To build a sense of group trust, belonging, and cohesiveness

MATERIALS
Speaker Power object

Chalkboard or easel pad

Poster board and markers

Copies of the "Sharing Circles" Take-Home (Worksheet 3.1.1)

NOTE
When the group has determined a final set of group rules, copy them on a sheet of poster board and display them in the classroom. Students can help by writing down the rules or illustrating the poster.

After this meeting, keep the Speaker Power object handy to use when needed.

PREPARATION
It is helpful to have a chairs in a circle for a Sharing Circle, or if this is not possible some arrangement that will allow the children to see one another. This format will eventually be used as a vehicle for working through the problem-solving steps during formal lessons and class problem-solving discussions. Determine the location and arrangement of the Sharing Circle and the procedure for having the children settle into it. Many teachers have found it successful to ask the students for ideas about efficient ways to move into a Sharing Circle.

INSTRUCTIONAL ACTIVITIES

1. Introduce lessons.

Begin by telling students that they will be having lessons that will help them learn skills for getting along with other people and making good decisions. Knowing how to make decisions that will help solve problems and get along with other people is important in third grade and will also help them to be successful and healthy as they grow up.

These skills will also help the class work together as a problem-solving team. Say:

> We are doing this because we all have times when we do not know what to do. Our social decision making meetings will help us understand our feelings and what we can do to solve problems and make good decisions.

Ask students if they remember having any lessons like this in the second grade. Take time to let them share their recollections so you will know what you have to build on.

Tell the students where and when the lessons will take place. The days and times for skill instruction and skill-building activities can be posted, as with other topic areas.

2. Establish rules and agreements.

Tell the class that to work as a problem-solving team they will first have to decide on some rules to follow so the meetings will go well. Ask the students to volunteer some rules that would help make everyone feel good about being a member of this team ("Good Teammate Behavior"). Record their responses on the chalkboard or easel pad. Then ask:

> What are some things that would make you not feel good about being a part of this team?

Create a list of "Not-Good Teammate Behavior." Tell students that during these meetings they will be learning more about good-teammate skills that will help them and the class be more successful in everything they do.

Usually, most of the student suggestions fall into general categories that overlap nicely with skills that will be covered during upcoming meetings and later given a label (or skill prompt). Therefore, at this point, team rules should be brief and positively stated, leaving room for more explicit phrasing to be added later.

Here are some common basic rules:

- Listen to each other without interrupting.
- Respect each other in words and actions.
- Remember that behavior outside the rules has consequences.

3. Introduce Sharing Circles.

Explain that the first activity is called a *Sharing Circle*. Some teachers refer to the Sharing Circle as a "Team Huddle" and a time to learn about, practice, and use skills needed to be a successful team.

Explain the procedure for the first Sharing Circle: Everyone (children, teachers, visitors in the room) in turn will say at least their name and answer a Sharing Circle question.

4. Introduce Speaker Power.

Select an object (magic wand, stuffed animal, scarf, ruler, pen . . .) that will be passed to the person speaking to designate a turn to talk. A *Speaker Power* object helps remind everyone to respect the person who is speaking and to remember that the job of the other team members at that time is to listen carefully without interrupting. Point out that this is a skill that will help the class keep to the rules about listening to each other and showing mutual respect. Everyone will have a chance to have Speaker Power—either by receiving the object as it gets passed around the group or by raising a hand to ask for it.

Remind students that as their teacher, you always have a kind of invisible Speaker Power. You will ask for the object when it fits into the lesson to do so, but it's your job to speak without asking for the object whenever you regard it as necessary.

5. Complete a group exercise using Speaker Power.

Begin by asking a simple and nonthreatening question that will allow everyone in the group to have a turn. Let students know that there are no right or wrong answers and they can share with the group anything that comes to mind as long as it addresses the question.

During the initial Sharing Circle, it would be a good idea to set the tone for further circles. Let children know that they are not being asked to agree with everything that is being said; they can disagree with someone's statement, but still accept the person. Point out that it is fine if people share the same idea, but it is also OK if they have different ideas about the question.

In the beginning, it can be helpful for you to go first and model what is expected. Students often enjoy learning things about their teachers, and this discovery helps spark an interest in what other people feel and think about a similar question.

Sample first questions:

- What has happened to you that made you feel proud?
- What is your favorite food to have for lunch?
- If you could live in the ocean for one whole day, what would you want to be?

Compliment students for respecting Speaker Power. When necessary, remind students that they may speak only if they are holding Speaker Power. If you begin to observe a loss of attention, ask if you can please have Speaker Power and say you will give it back in a minute.

Ask the students how they think the exercise went. Then ask:

> *What was easy or hard about remembering to use Speaker Power?*
>
> *How did it feel to have Speaker Power?*

Then begin again and continue to pause for feedback, as needed.

As time permits, ask the children two or three additional questions that will gradually reveal something new about them to their classmates. After each question, have four or five children answer, then move on to the next question. The following questions have been found to be quite useful for an initial group-building exercise:

- What is your favorite book? (Why?)
- What is your favorite season of the year? (Why?)
- If you were going to be the star of a television show, what show would you pick? (Why?)
- If you could meet anyone you wanted to, who would you pick? (Why?)

6. Introduce a Reflective Summary.

As outlined in the Introduction, ask students to reflect on the question "What did you learn from today's lesson?" Reinforce key themes, then go over any follow-up work.

You can do this with the whole group in a Sharing Circle format, by having students fill out index cards, or by using other formats, as you choose. We recommend that you have some variety in formats. After getting a sense of what the students learned, reinforce key themes mentioned and add perhaps one or two that you would like them to keep in mind.

7. Follow up.

The following steps will help make sure that the students have a chance to continue working with the new concepts.

Assignment

Ask the students to remember and relate why they will be having these lessons and what they will be learning from them. Let them know that during the next session they will continue to practice Speaker Power and learn some skills for listening. Remind children that they have learned a new skill: using Speaker Power. Ask them if they can think of any other times when it would be good to use Speaker Power. Point out that it is possible to use the skill without having an actual object to hold.

Help students come prepared to share during the next meeting by providing them with the question that you plan to use for the next Sharing Circle. Let them know that you will be using the cue words *Speaker Power* and *Sharing Circle* during other subjects and at other times in the day. Mention situations that the students suggested and encourage them to try using Speaker Power at those times.

Take-Home

Distribute a letter to parents or guardians like the one presented in the Introduction (if it hasn't been sent earlier or distributed at Back to School Night) to introduce the Social Decision Making/Social Problem Solving skill-building lessons to the students' families.

Also distribute the "Sharing Circle" Take-Home and tell students that the handout will explain what the class does in Sharing Circles and give their parents some suggestions about when they could use Speaker Power at home. Ask students to tell them about it also. Let students know that they might need to help teach their parents or guardians about Sharing Circles and Speaker Power. Remind students to return the tear-off section at the bottom of the worksheet.

Plans to Promote Transfer and Generalization of Skill

Plan ahead to provide opportunities for students to practice a Sharing Circle and the use of a Speaker Power object as part of an academic lesson or class discussion. For example:

1. Before a health lesson or physical education class exercise, conduct a Sharing Circle on the question "What is your favorite sport or physical activity?" While reading a story, stop for a Sharing Circle on the question "Who is your favorite person in the story so far? If you could say something to them or ask them a question, what would it be?" or "Who do you think has the biggest problem in this story? Why?"

2. While studying about an individual or group in social studies or current events, stop for a Sharing Circle on the question "If you could ask a question or say something to the people we're studying, what would you say?"

3. After group activities, stop for a Sharing Circle on the question "What did you learn about working together as a team during this activity?"

TIPS FOR TEACHERS

1. Class size and maturity are important factors in determining how the Sharing Circle will best operate.

2. Sharing Circle questions should allow for self-expression without calling for personal information considered confidential. Students may not be aware of these limits, so it is important for teachers to avoid questions that pull for such information and to politely interrupt, support, and redirect any responses that are inappropriate for a classroom skill-building lesson. For example:

   I can tell that you have strong feelings about this, and I want to hear about it. But it is better to talk about private things that happen at home privately, not in a large group. We can talk about this after we finish the lesson to respect the privacy of your family. Can you think of an example that happened to you at school or with your friends?

   Be sure to follow up and make a referral to another professional if what students share is outside your area of professional training.

   For a list of sample Sharing Circle questions, turn to Worksheet 2.1.1, in the Grade 2 curriculum.

3. When introducing Sharing Circle, try to notice children who may need prompting to be drawn into the circle. Some teachers have been successful by allowing such children to "pass" and checking back later to see if they have thought of something to share. Seating, question choice, time to prepare, and many other ideas have been successful in engaging the quiet student.

   Also, recognize the "talkers"—the children who may need time limits set. Many creative ideas have been used to solve this problem— for example, preparing ahead of time with a one-sentence or one-minute rule (measured with a timer) or taking talkative students aside to compliment them for their willingness to express themselves and ask them to help the teacher encourage others who are less willing to share.

4. When making a poster or sign of the group rules, it is often useful to have a picture or symbol accompany the words to help poor readers. Students often have good ideas for symbols and can sometimes do the drawing. In addition, having students build their own poster enhances their motivation to follow the rules.

5. Integrate skills as they are taught in your existing behavior management system. Many teachers we have trained report that it becomes natural and automatic to include skill prompts and practice of SDM/SPS skills within academic subject areas throughout the course of the day, once students have mastered the basic skills. At initial stages of implementation, however, it is helpful to

think ahead each week and include activities for skill practice within your lesson plans.

Think ahead to identify situations and subject content areas where the practice of SDM/SPS skills would fortify existing objectives. It is also useful to document these plans and monitor the degree to which opportunities for students to practice and generalize the skill to academic and real-life situations present themselves. This effort helps ensure that teaching practices remain true to the instructional design that led to research-validated outcomes. It also helps teachers—in their role as adult learners—integrate new skills within their complex repertoire of needed teaching skills.

6. Clear consequences should be established for disruption of the group by either aggressiveness or silliness. One strategy that has been successful for some students and groups is to first remind disruptive students about their agreement to keep to the rules to prompt desired behavior. If this does not work, try having such students sit out for a few minutes, letting them know that you will be checking back with them in a few minutes to see if they are ready to come back and follow the team agreements. This strategy is effective when the students enjoy the activities and don't want to be left out. As with any behavior management technique, it is important to find reinforcers and consequences that work for a particular student or group.

Sharing Circles

Sharing Circles are an opportunity for children to share their feelings and ideas. In the classroom, we encourage the use of an object that can be passed from person to person to maintain "Speaker Power." When someone has Speaker Power, they may not be interrupted before they pass the object on to another person.

The Magic of Car Time

Car time can be a good time to really listen to what another person is saying. It is also a time when a structured activity can promote safety. You might want to try practicing a Sharing Circle and listening to each other while someone is driving. In the car—or at home—you can:

1. Choose a Speaker Power Object.

2. Take turns passing Speaker Power and answering one of the following questions, or come up with a question together:

- What is a family memory (or any memory) that makes you feel happy?

- Do you think boys or girls have it easier? Why?

Ask your child how the people in this car would look different if they were using Speaker Power and practicing their listening skills.

Your child may be asked in class to share what happened when you practiced this activity.

Thank you!

(Teacher signature)   *(Date)*

(Please sign and return this bottom section.)   **Sharing Circles 3.1.1**

Student _____ **Date** _____

We tried a Sharing Circle.   ❒ Yes   ❒ No

If you did, how did it go?

(Signature of parent or guardian)

2 Learning to Listen Carefully and Accurately

OBJECTIVES
- To teach the components of good listening
- To teach the skills of *Listening Position* and paying attention
- To provide practice for learning good listening skills and skill prompts
- To help promote use of listening skills beyond these lessons

MATERIALS

Chalkboard or easel pad

Whole-class display of "Listening Position" (Worksheet 3.2.1)

"Listening Activity Word Lists" (Worksheet 3.2.2)

INSTRUCTIONAL ACTIVITIES

1. Review the introduction.

With the students' help, review the main themes of Topic 1. Include the reasons for having these meetings, the meaning of Speaker Power, and the rules agreed upon during the last session to help the team work well together.

2. Conduct a Sharing Circle.

Review the Sharing Circle question you assigned in the Topic 1 lesson. As the Speaker Power object is passed around the circle, if children begin to appear distracted, ask if you can please have Speaker Power and let the next person know that they will have a turn in a minute. Stand behind a student who has already shared and ask:

Was anyone listening carefully when [child's name] had Speaker Power?

Can you tell us what [child's name] had to share?

Reinforce good listening. If any details were not covered, ask if anyone else can recall any other detail until the group accurately recalls details of what the person said. After everyone has had a chance to share, ask:

How did we do?

Was it difficult to remember what people said? If so, what made it difficult?

What did it feel like to have Speaker Power?

3. Establish the importance of listening.

Draw students' interest by inviting them to share a time when someone they were talking to was not listening to them. Ask:

How did it feel?

How could you tell that the person was not listening to you?

Make the points that it is not hard for people to tell when you are not listening to them and that they usually don't like it.

4. Discuss times when listening is important.

Ask the class when it is important to be a good listener. Some examples: when learning the rules of a game for the first time, when trying to understand the teacher's explanation of a difficult math problem, and when trying to learn the words of a new song. Ask:

What happens when we are not good listeners?

5. Introduce Listening Position.

Explain that in this lesson the group is going to think carefully about what listening is and how to go about doing it better. To be a good listener, it is necessary to pay attention. Ask:

What is "paying attention"?

What are some behaviors that make you think someone is not listening or paying attention?

On the chalkboard or easel pad, generate a list of behaviors that show poor listening. Then ask:

Can you act out the way someone looks when they are listening and paying attention?

Generate a list of behaviors that show that someone is listening and paying attention.

Ask if any students have ever heard of *Listening Position*. If so, give them a chance to describe it.

Establish the behavioral components of Listening Position by showing the whole-class display of Listening Position:

1. Sit or stand straight.

2. Face the speaker or source of sound.

3. Look toward the speaker or source of sound.

6. Play the Listening game.

Ask students to close their eyes. Then read the words from List 1, about one word per second. Ask the children to clap their hands only when they hear the word *cat.* Note both performance (clap on another word) and nonperformance (no clap on "cat") errors.

7. Have students share their difficulties.

Ask students to discuss some things that they can do to listen more carefully and accurately. Be sure the list includes the following:

Listening Position: Sit or stand straight, face the speaker, look toward the speaker (or source of sound).

Pay Attention (or *Concentrate):* Do not interrupt or let anything distract you.

Model each of these behaviors for the children, and then have the children model all of them.

8. Conduct a practice activity.

Have students practice their paying attention and listening skills again by trying to remember the things that they have just learned.

Repeat the Listening game. Be sure everyone is in a Listening Position before you start. Here are several variations that can be used with List 1:

- Clap on everything except *cat.*
- Clap on names of animals only.
- Clap on all animals except *cat.*
- Clap only on words that are not names of animals.

Reinforce proper Listening Position, concentration, and other skills during the lesson and throughout the day. Repeat the activities at other points during the day if possible. List 2 and List 3 can be used similarly, and you can make up your own.

9. Provide further opportunity to practice.

Pair students up and give them a topic to talk about for no more than a minute, using Listening Position.

For example:

- Best games to play after school
- Best things about recess

One student speaks to the other. Then the second student summarizes the main things the first one said. They switch roles. Then have pairs present their example to the class. Reinforce and ask the class to notice any examples of Listening Position and things students did to help them pay attention.

10. Introduce a Reflective Summary.

As outlined in the Introduction, ask students to reflect on the question "What did you learn from today's lesson?" Reinforce key themes, then go over any follow-up work.

11. Follow up.

The following steps will help make sure that the students have a chance to continue working with the new concepts.

Assignment

Ask students when they think it would be good to use Listening Position at other times during school or at home. Tell students to practice Listening Position and be prepared to share a time when they used it or should have used it.

Plans to Promote Transfer and Generalization of Skill

Listening Position is a skill prompt that can be used often on a daily basis. As mentioned, when first implementing these lessons it is helpful to develop concrete plans for review and practice and record these activities within your weekly lesson plans.

For example, you can use *Listening Position* as a skill prompt after all transitions as a cue that a new activity is about to begin. At the beginning of the day and after recess are times when brief review and practice serve as a helpful management tool.

TIPS FOR TEACHERS

1. Initially, conscious effort is needed to identify teachable moments when skill prompts provide a positive corrective management technique. For example, if one student is squirming and making

tapping noises while you are reading something to the class, stop reading and prompt:

I will continue when everyone is in Listening Position.

Some teachers have found it useful to introduce "On-Topic" as an additional prompt to bring students back to a main topic of discussion. If student discussion begins to build on something silly that one student has mentioned, rather than the objective at hand, prompt with,

I am wondering if our discussion is On-Topic right now. What are we thinking about the story we are reading? Can anyone share an idea that will bring us back on the topic?

2. The Listening game has several variations, and one of them may serve your class better than just clapping. You can have your students:

- Clap and stamp their feet.
- Stand up.
- Walk around the room and freeze on the word.
- Walk around the room, freeze, and start again at the next word they are listening for.

3. If students need extra help with the concept of listening, use the following additional practice activity.

Model examples of ineffective and effective listening by doing the following role-play. Have the class watch and listen carefully to discuss what they see and hear. Following are sample conversations that can be rehearsed with adults or students before the meeting.

Ineffective Listening

A: Hi, how are you?

B: OK, I guess . . .

A: Boy, I can't wait for school to be over today.

B: Yeah, well, I'm not looking forward to . . .

A: Did you see that new movie? I'm going later.

B: Lately, I haven't been able to . . .

A: Who's that over there? Hi, Billy!

Ask:

What did you observe?

What was A doing?

How would you feel if you were B?

List any behaviors the class mentions. One aspect of this conversation that is valuable to highlight and label is that these two people are talking to each other about different things. This can be labeled as not being "On-Topic."

Effective Listening

A: Hi, how are you?

B: OK, How are you?

A: Pretty good. How about you?

B: OK, I guess . . .

A: What do you mean? What's going on?

B: Well, I have a lot of homework, and it's giving me trouble.

A: What are you having trouble with? Maybe I can help you.

Ask:

What did you observe?

What was A doing that showed listening and paying attention?

How would you feel if you were B?

List the behaviors the class mentions and link behavioral components to Listening Position when appropriate.

Listening Position

1. Sit or stand straight.

2. Face the speaker or source of sound.

3. Look toward the speaker or source of sound.

From *Social Decision Making/Social Problem Solving: A Curriculum for Academic, Social, and Emotional Learning* (Grades 2–3).
Copyright © 2005 by Maurice J. Elias and Linda Bruene Butler. Research Press (800-519-2707; www.researchpress.com)

LIST 1

cuts	coat	horse	cut	dog	cow	cat
horse	cuts	cut	cow	cut	dog	cat
coat	cute	horse	dog	cute	cow	dog
cow	cut	cat	cat	dog	horse	cut

LIST 2

cat	shoes	pants	coat	cute	dress	cut
cute	cut	pants	shoes	dress	cat	shoes
coat	dress	pants	cut	dress	shoes	cut
coat	pants	cute	cat	coat	cut	shoes
cute	coat	cat	pants	cat	cute	dress

LIST 3

bush	leaf	true	tree	grass	tire	tear
tree	true	leaf	tear	bush	tree	leaf
bush	true	tire	tear	grass	tire	grass
true	tear	leaf	bush	grass	leaf	tear
tire	true	tree	tire	tree	grass	bush

TOPIC

3 Exercises to Pull Your Team Together

OBJECTIVES
- To build class cohesion
- To provide team-building activities as an opportunity to practice and obtain feedback on how well the group works as a team
- To provide opportunities to practice using Speaker Power, Listening Position, and Paying Attention in the context of team-building activities

MATERIALS   Copies of "People Find" (Worksheet 3.3.1)

INSTRUCTIONAL ACTIVITIES

1. Review good listening skills and team rules.

Explain that good listening skills will be very important in this meeting. Have students share a time when they used Listening Position. If students do not remember using it, have them tell about a time when they could have or should have used it.

2. Introduce the topic.

Draw students' interest by explaining that today they will be doing activities to help them get to know one another better. As they do so, they will also learn how to work with one another better, the way a good sports team works together.

3. Conduct a Sharing Circle.

Use a cooperative storytelling game as the format: One child holds Speaker Power and starts a story, then passes Speaker Power to another child, who adds a little more, until everyone has participated. Pick a topic of interest to your class or choose from among these:

- A Haunted House

- Who Took the Money?
- A Trip to Mars
- A Day in the City
- Planning a Party

This activity can be repeated, depending on time and student engagement. Reinforce how much more interesting and fun stories can be with everyone working together.

4. Lead the Smiling Faces activity.

The following activity will help students learn, individually or as a team, how to make others smile. Choose a student to start the activity and explain that the task is to turn to the person on the right and say or do something that will make that person smile or laugh—make a funny face, give a compliment, tell a joke, or do something else that doesn't involve getting up and moving around. If the initial attempt is not successful, or if the student cannot think of something to do, turn the situation into a group problem by asking something along these lines:

What are some things that Bobby can do to make Carmen smile?

One or two class ideas can be tried. Whether successful or not, it will then be the recipient's turn to make the next child on the right smile. Continue as time allows. Encourage the class to help individuals who get stuck to complete the task.

5. Distribute the People Find worksheet.

Read the directions and have students move around the room to find someone who possesses the attribute they are looking for. After the group is finished, ask how the activity went for them.

6. Introduce a Reflective Summary.

As outlined in the Introduction, ask students to reflect on the question "What did you learn from today's lesson?" Reinforce key themes, then go over any follow-up work.

7. Follow up.

The following activity will help make sure that the students have a chance to continue working with the new concepts.

Assignment

Have students think of ways that they can help others feel comfortable working together as a class team. Have them share their ideas in a Sharing Circle or write their ideas in their journals.

TIPS FOR TEACHERS

1. One of the most important ways in which your class will come to feel like a problem-solving team is for the students to become comfortable working with each other in a group and to believe that they can say what is on their minds without being criticized or rejected.

   To the extent that a group is not cohesive, it is more difficult for students to learn the skills of social decision making and problem solving, and it takes longer for the members to feel confident and comfortable enough to try the skills in new situations.

   The activities in this topic help foster a spirit of group cohesion, team building, and trust, and are recommended even if the group already seems to be working cooperatively.

   It is important to use these group-building activities as an opportunity to observe group dynamics and take time to stop throughout to ask students to assess how well they are working as a group. Remind them to respect Speaker Power by not interrupting each other and to use Listening Position.

2. Marianne Torbert has written extensively about the value of games for teaching children social and emotional competencies. She has given us her permission to include the following game from her book *Follow Me: A Handbook of Movement Activities for Children*. Many more activities are available in this book or from her Web site, www.temple.edu/leonardgordoninstitute.

   Here's a modified example that provides practice in listening.

Cows and Ducks

Depending on the size and maturity of your group, you might want to add a few other animals to Cows and Ducks, such as Cat and Dog or Horse. Let children know that they have to decide what kind of animal they want to be for this game—a cow or a duck (or a horse or whatever other animal is on the list). They cannot change their minds once the game has started.

All children begin moving around the room, making the sound of their chosen animal. All those making the same animal sound try to find each other. Once the small groups have formed, they can remain standing and have a short Sharing Circle, telling the others one reason why they picked the animal they did.

Student _____ Date _____

Find someone who can say yes to any one of these statements. Have them sign their name. Find someone different for each line.

1. **Can swim** _____

2. **Likes to read** _____

3. **Has freckles** _____

4. **Is wearing blue** _____

5. **Plays baseball** _____

6. **Can whistle** _____

7. **Loves science** _____

8. **Has a birthday in the summer** _____

T O P I C

4   Listening Power

OBJECTIVES
- To deepen and further develop listening skills
- To introduce and practice *Listening Power*

MATERIALS
Whole-class display of "Listening Power" (Worksheet 3.4.1)
Two facing chairs
Copies of the "Listening" Take-Home (Worksheet 3.4.2)

INSTRUCTIONAL ACTIVITIES

1. Conduct a Sharing Circle.

Ask students if they had opportunities to practice Listening Position since the last meeting. Provide time for students to share some experiences. Also, have students share examples of situations in which they worked together as a team.

2. Introduce the new skill of Listening Power.

Ask the students if they know what a *detective* is. After a couple of answers, make the point that detectives learn how to *detect*, or find out, the truth when someone commits a crime. Tell students that they are going to learn one thing all detectives need to know how to do. They will learn to *be sure they understand* what they have heard. Ask them how they can be sure that they have understood what others say.

Some answers: You can repeat what you think you heard. You might say, "I heard you say that . . .," and say back to the other person what you heard them say. And then you ask them if you are right.

Display the whole-class version of the components of *Listening Power:*

1. Use Listening Position.

2. Pay attention to what the person is saying.

3. Repeat what the other person said.

4. Check to see if you are right.

3. Model the activity for the students.

Invite a student volunteer to role-play with you at the front of the room.

Sit in the facing chairs and remind your partner that both of you are going to use Listening Position and pay attention. Then ask your partner, "What is your favorite thing to do after school?" Expand the student's response to a minute by asking a question for more detail if the response is too brief or say, "Thank you. Let me see if I understand what you have been saying so far" if it runs on too long.

Repeat back what the person said.

Ask if you are correct: "Is that your favorite?"

Depending on the maturity of the class, move into having two students model Listening Power. Ask the group to notice any behaviors that demonstrate good listening skills.

4. Conduct a practice activity.

Pair two students and ask them to practice with each other what they have seen in the previous examples. Tell them that they will need to decide who will listen and who will talk first. (Give them a minute to decide.)

Explain that you will be giving them a question or topic to talk about. As the first person speaks, the other will use Listening Position, pay attention, and then repeat and check to see if they heard what the first speaker said. The partners will then switch roles, and the person who talked first will be the listener and the person who listened first will be the speaker. Ask if there are any questions.

If you have an odd number of students in the class, ask the student who volunteered to role-play during the first example with you to take the role of listening while you speak.

Here are some additional practice questions:

- What movie would you recommend to a friend? What is good about it?
- Pick an animal that you think makes a good pet. What kind of animal is it, and why do you think it makes a good pet?
- If you could eat the perfect meal, what foods would you have?
- If you could have the perfect playground, what would it look like? What would be there?

Stop after the first round and ask students what the experience was like for them. Did the listener use Listening Position? Ask the speaker to describe one thing the listener did that let the speaker know that they were listening. Then ask:

Listener, did you check to see if you listened accurately? . . .
What happened? . . . Did you get it right or did you forget some-
thing? . . . What was difficult or easy about listening?

Speaker, how did it feel when someone repeated back what you
said? . . . How does it feel when you know someone is listen-
ing to you?

If you have time, repeat the activity with a new question. Switch partners for the next topic or question if logistics, group management, and
maturity permit.

5. Introduce a Reflective Summary.

As outlined in the Introduction, ask students to reflect on the question "What did you learn from today's lesson?" Reinforce key themes,
then go over any follow-up work.

6. Follow up.

The following steps will help make sure that the students have a
chance to continue working with the new concepts.

Assignment

Ask students if they can think of certain times when it would be a good
idea to check and be sure that they are hearing accurately what other
people say. Generate a list of ideas, such as when someone is explaining something to do, when someone is explaining why they think
doing something is a good or bad idea, and when getting instructions
or reminders of homework. Have students pick one of these ideas to
try, and have them write it in their assignment books or on their
homework lists. Let them know that they will have time to talk about
how well they listened during the next meeting.

Take-Home

Distribute the take-home page describing Listening Position and
Listening Power, with suggestions for times when parents or guardians
can prompt children to use these skills and activities for practicing listening skills at home.

Plans to Promote Transfer and Generalization of Skill

1. Conduct a workshop or plan for informal information sharing of
   the skills children are learning and suggestions about how the skill
   prompts can be used by special-subject teachers, administrators,
   and parents or guardians.

2. Continue using all skills prompts throughout the day.

TIPS FOR TEACHERS

Listening Power refers to behaviors and words that make it clear when someone is listening and understanding what a speaker is saying. This skill has been targeted as a foundation skill for resolving conflicts. Listening Position, asking questions for clarification, and concentration are all subsets of Listening Power skills. Listening Power helps students learn to paraphrase or summarize what has been said to be sure that they understand.

Listening Power

1. Use Listening Position.

2. Pay attention to what the other person is saying.

3. Repeat what the other person said.

4. Check to see if you are right.

From *Social Decision Making/Social Problem Solving: A Curriculum for Academic, Social, and Emotional Learning* (*Grades 2–3*).
Copyright © 2005 by Maurice J. Elias and Linda Bruene Butler. Research Press (800-519-2707; www.researchpress.com)

Worksheet 3.4.1

Listening

Your child has been learning two skills to become a better listener: Listening Position and Listening Power.

LISTENING POSITION

1. Sit or stand straight.
2. Face the speaker.
3. Look toward the speaker or source of sound.

LISTENING POWER

Listening Power means listening, accurately hearing and remembering what another person has said, and checking to be sure you have understood.

Which one of these children is in good LISTENING POSITION?

Instant Replay

To help children become more sensitive to the things they hear, try using Instant Replay at home. This activity involves stopping the action and asking what your child just heard.

You can use TV dialogue, commercials, videos or DVDs, recorded music, or a story that you're reading aloud. For example, you might ask your child to tell you the lyrics of a favorite song or dialogue from a favorite book after reading a section of it together.

Prerecorded information works best because you can actually replay the example to find out exactly what was said by whom. The idea is to engage your child in becoming a better listener, not to catch errors.

Your child may be asked in class to share what happened when you practiced this activity.

Thank you!

_____   _____

(Teacher signature)   *(Date)*

(Please sign and return this bottom section.)   **Listening   3.4.2**

Student _____ **Date** _____

We tried Instant Replay.   ☐ Yes   ☐ No

If you did, how did it go?

_____

(Signature of parent or guardian)

T O P I C

5 Strategies for Remembering

OBJECTIVES
- To review and practice good listening skills
- To discover various strategies for remembering
- To increase student awareness of *Strategies for Remembering* and give them an opportunity to practice using such strategies

MATERIALS
Six to twelve common household or classroom items and a large scarf or sheet of paper to cover them

Writing and drawing materials

Chalkboard or easel pad

Poster board and markers

NOTE
When the group has determined a final set of strategies, copy them on a sheet of poster board and display them in the classroom. Students can help by writing down the strategies or illustrating the poster.

INSTRUCTIONAL ACTIVITIES

1. Review Topic 4.

Go over Listening Position and Listening Power skills and remind students of the importance of using Listening Position during this lesson. Ask students when they have used their Listening Power.

2. Introduce the importance of memory.

Ask students when they need to remember things. Suggest they come up with examples that relate to school and home.

One important example is in the area of homework. Ask for all the different aspects of homework that need to be remembered. For example: remembering to write the assignment in the assignment book; remembering to bring home all the necessary books, materials, and supplies; remembering how to do the assignment; remembering to put the completed assignment in the book bag; remembering to bring materials to school.

Elicit from students the consequences of not remembering homework-related things. Have students describe any strategies that they already use to remember homework tasks.

3. Introduce the Invisible Items game.

Tell the students that they are going to play a game called "Invisible Items" that will help them learn about remembering.

Explain that you have placed a number of items under a scarf or large piece of paper and point to the surface where the objects are hidden. Begin with a number that you feel will be fairly easy for your group to remember—say, five or six items. Remove the cover. Have the students look at the items for about thirty seconds. Then completely cover the items.

4. Run an independent memory exercise.

Have the students write or draw all the items that they can remember. Have students share their lists.

5. Have the students, as a group, brainstorm a list of all the ways they used to remember the items.

Some examples include counting the items, taking a mental picture of the items; saying the names of the items over and over; grouping the items by color, size, or use; or telling a story or making personal associations with each of the items. Record the students' responses as they give them, and label the list "Strategies for Remembering."

After the list is compiled, ask students if they have heard one of their classmates describe a memory strategy that they never thought of before. Would that strategy work for them?

6. Play the game again.

Add items to make the game more challenging. Ask students to share a new strategy and when they might use it. Encourage students to try any new ideas they would like to try. Remind the class that this is just a game and a good way to learn new strategies and find out if the strategies can work for them. Have the students look at the items for another thirty seconds.

Have the students discuss the memory strategies that they used this time. Add any new ideas to the list.

7. Run a subtraction exercise.

Have the students look at all the items for another thirty seconds, and then have them cover their eyes. When they are not looking, remove one or more of the items. Then tell the students to open their eyes and figure out what is missing.

STRATEGIES FOR REMEMBERING   239

8. Discuss applications.

Elicit examples from students of different situations in which they can use the Strategies for Remembering they brainstormed during the lesson. For example, they can use the strategies when they need to memorize their spelling words, remember their math facts, or follow directions for homework assignments.

9. Introduce a Reflective Summary.

As outlined in the Introduction, ask students to reflect on the question "What did you learn from today's lesson?" Reinforce key themes, then go over any follow-up work.

10. Follow up.

The following steps will help make sure that the students have a chance to continue working with the new concepts.

Assignment

Ask students to pick one idea of a time when they can use a strategy to help them remember and to write it down in their assignment books or on their homework lists. Tell them that, at the start of the next lesson, they will have a chance to share a time when they used a strategy to help them remember and how it worked.

Take-Home

Parents and guardians can help children improve their memory skills by giving them common household chores and discussing what Strategies for Remembering the child can use to accomplish the task. If the opportunity arises, share these ideas with parents: Make a grocery list and have your child try to memorize some or all of the items on the list. Bring the list to the store and see how many items your child can remember. Another way to practice using memory skills is doing a trip recall. After returning from a family trip or vacation, have the child write a story or draw pictures of the activities you did. Have the child try to remember as many details as possible, such as the names of places or the order of the events that happened.

Plans to Promote Transfer and Generalization of Skill

Academic

Assign students or student groups the task of coming up with a strategy for remembering challenging spelling words, math facts, or information for upcoming tests in any academic area. Also, ask students to create a strategy to help them remember what they need to do as homework.

Social Practice

As a group-building activity, especially at the beginning of the school year, play a name game to help students remember the names of their new classmates. For example, after a Sharing Circle, ask for a volunteer to name one other person in the class. Then ask someone to name two different people, then three, four, and so on as time allows. This exercise can also be done as a written activity, challenging students to create and add more names to a list until they know (and can write the name of) everyone in the class. Always ask about students' remembering strategies.

TIPS FOR TEACHERS

1. In the game, you can vary the number of items according to the cognitive level of the students. Making the game easy initially will give the students greater confidence and will make it fun. Keep adding items until you reach a number that seems fairly challenging—when students can remember many but not all of the items. The goal of the activity is metacognitive. In other words, the students should be starting to think about how they think and remember.

2. This activity is also about different learning styles. Some students seem to have difficulty with memory skills. It is possible that they are using a strategy that is not complementing their learning style, and they can be encouraged to use a strategy that might be a better fit.

3. A cooperative storytelling game can be adapted to promote memory development: One student starts a story, and each student has to repeat what the student before said, then add a little more until everyone has participated. Pick a topic of interest to your class or choose from among these:

   ■ A Haunted House
   ■ Who Took the Money?
   ■ A Trip to Mars
   ■ A Day in the City
   ■ Planning a Party
   ■ What Our Town Is Really Like

   Stop midway and ask students to share the strategies they have been using to help them remember what other classmates have been saying. This activity can be used as a creative writing task.

6   Following Directions

OBJECTIVES
- To review and practice good listening skills
- To practice using different Strategies for Remembering
- To learn to follow directions

MATERIALS
Copies of the Ovals Exercise (Worksheet 3.6.1)
Directions for the Ovals Exercise (Worksheet 3.6.2)

INSTRUCTIONAL ACTIVITIES

1. Review Topic 5.

Go over good listening skills and remind students of the importance of using Listening Power during this lesson.

Review the preceding Topic and have students discuss the various Strategies for Remembering that they discovered. Ask for volunteers to describe any times since the last lesson they used a strategy for remembering, and how it went.

2. Discuss following directions.

Ask students when they need to follow directions in school and at home, as well as in extracurricular activities. Be sure to include safety and school routine situations. Elicit from students the consequences of not following directions.

Ask students to share what they do that helps them remember to follow directions.

3. Introduce the day's activity.

Tell the students that in order to follow directions, they need to use both their listening and remembering skills. Tell them they will be using strategies for following directions that are similar to the strategies they used for remembering.

4. Distribute the Ovals Exercise.

Hand out the worksheet containing ten ovals.

Read the directions to the students from the first list in Worksheet 3.6.2. Read each direction only once, and then have the students fill in the worksheet. When the directions are complete, go over the answers with the students. Refer to the list of Strategies for Remembering that students generated in Topic 5, as appropriate.

Elicit from students which strategies they could apply to this activity. Ask students what other strategies they used for this activity and add them to the list.

5. Do the activity again with another set of blank ovals.

If all or most of the students were able to get the first set of directions correct, use the harder list for a second set of ovals. If the students had difficulty, use the second set of directions geared to the lower level.

Again, have the students discuss the strategies that they used, adding any new ideas to the list.

6. Discuss the skill.

Elicit examples from students of different situations in which they can use their new strategies for following directions. For example, they can use the strategies when they do classwork or homework, or during tests and activities.

7. Introduce a Reflective Summary.

As outlined in the Introduction, ask students to reflect on the question "What did you learn from today's lesson?" Reinforce key themes, then go over any follow-up work.

8. Follow up.

The following steps will help make sure that the students have a chance to continue working with the new concepts.

Assignment

1. Encourage students to choose one of the strategies to help them remember and follow directions on their homework assignments. If students have difficulty in this area, have them try different strategies until they find some that really work for them.

2. Have students choose one or more strategies to use when they study their spelling words, number facts, or multiplication tables.

Encourage them to try different strategies to see which work best for them.

Take-Home

Parents and guardians can help their child follow directions by playing games and doing activities with them. Send home the following ideas as time allows:

- Give the child a series of directions, ranging from one to six different activities that the child can do in the house. One example would be to go to the window, describe the weather outside, go to the closet and get a sweater or coat, then go stand by the front door.

- Have a scavenger or treasure hunt in which the child is told to go to various rooms in the house and do or get certain things. Advise the parents or guardians to praise and reward the child for being able to follow the directions and to challenge the child to increase the level of difficulty by using their Strategies for Remembering and Following Directions.

- The children can also follow directions by helping with a recipe or following the directions to a friend or relative's home.

Plans to Promote Transfer and Generalization of Skill

Academic

Replace the list of ovals directions with a list that reviews academic concepts such as spelling, math facts, geography, or any other subject area. The ovals are a great activity for test review.

Social Practice

1. Games such as Simon Says can be played in physical education or during recess to practice following directions.

2. Have students work in teams to list the specific steps needed to do a common classroom activity. Encourage them to generate as accurate a list as they can. Have them trade lists and see if another team can follow their directions. Encourage the second team to do only what is written. All should discuss problems after this activity.

TIPS FOR TEACHERS

1. Follow-up activities are strongly suggested. There are many commercial programs to aid memory and encourage following directions (including audiotape programs, computer programs, and games). Find time during the week to use such activities.

2. The activities for this topic are diagnostic for the teacher and enjoyable for students, and they provide a vehicle for helping students identify and improve their memory strategies. Most teachers find that, after completing the lesson, doing any one of the activities on a daily basis takes little time and leads to gradual improvement in children's skills.

3. Use the prompt "What strategy will you use to help you remember?" when students have an assignment that involves remembering or following directions.

4. When first integrating a new skill prompt with students, it is often helpful to come up with your own strategy to remember to use the skill prompts as you begin to integrate these methods into your teaching repertoire. Posting and highlighting new prompts in prominent places throughout the room, scanning weekly lesson plans to consider times skill practice could be helpful, and asking students to help you remember are just a few suggestions that have been successful. What strategy will you use to remember to use skill prompts?

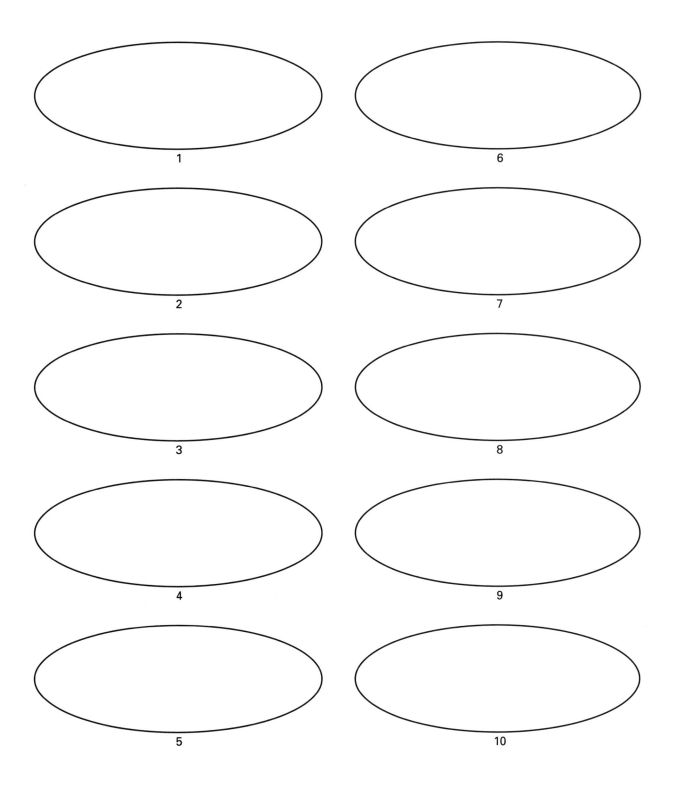

1

6

2

7

3

8

4

9

5

10

Less Difficult

1. Color the first oval orange.
2. Write an *X* in the second oval.
3. Write a *3* in the third oval.
4. Draw a square in the fourth oval.
5. Write a *5* in the fifth oval.
6. Write a letter of the alphabet in the sixth oval.
7. Draw a triangle in the seventh oval.
8. Color the eighth oval blue.
9. Draw a circle in the ninth oval.
10. Color the tenth oval green.

Less Difficult

1. Color the first oval red.
2. Write a *2* in the second oval.
3. Draw a triangle in the third oval.
4. Write an *X* in the fourth oval.
5. Color the fifth oval blue.
6. Write a *6* in the sixth oval.
7. Write the letter *G* in the seventh oval.
8. Draw a circle in the eighth oval.
9. Color the ninth oval yellow.
10. Draw a square in the tenth oval.

More Difficult

1. Make an orange X in the fifth oval.
2. Color the ninth oval brown.
3. Draw a tree in the first oval.
4. Write your initials in the tenth oval.
5. Write a *3* in the third oval.
6. Make a capital *B* in the eighth oval.
7. Draw a blue triangle in the second oval.
8. Color the fourth oval black.
9. Write your age in the sixth oval.
10. Make a red question mark in the seventh oval.

More Difficult

1. Make a blue *X* in the fifth oval.
2. Color the first oval purple.
3. Draw a house in the third oval.
4. Write your age in the tenth oval.
5. Write a *9* in the ninth oval.
6. Make a capital *Q* in the eighth oval.
7. Draw a red square in the second oval.
8. Color the fourth oval green.
9. Write your initials in the sixth oval.
10. Make an orange exclamation point in the seventh oval.

T O P I C

7 Learning to Role-Play

OBJECTIVES
- To teach students how to role-play
- To understand reasons and needs for role-playing
- To understand responsibilities of the audience

MATERIALS   None

PREPARATION   Review the "Role-Playing, Rehearsal, and Practice" section in the Introduction.

INSTRUCTIONAL ACTIVITIES

1. Review good listening and following directions skills from previous topics.

Have students share a time when they used a remembering and following-directions strategy.

Explain that these skills will be very important in today's topic because today the group will be learning to act out skills that they are learning by role-playing.

2. Introduce and define the skill of role-playing.

Brainstorm some ideas about what role-playing is. Ask if any of the students can remember doing role-playing in earlier lessons. Explain that role-playing is acting out situations, and the class will do this often in SDM/SPS lessons. Continue by saying that everyone has an important part in role-playing. The actors must use their following-directions skills, and the audience must use their listening skills. Stress that sometimes the role-plays may seem funny, but there is a serious objective behind each role-play.

3. Begin with pantomime.

Pantomime is a good way of easing students into role-playing. For each of the following situations, or similar ones that you may choose, whisper the role to a student, who will then play the part. Sample pantomimes:

- Shopping
- Driving a car
- Reading a book
- Waking up from a nap
- Brushing your teeth
- Eating dinner
- Getting dressed
- Talking on the phone
- Exercising in gym class
- Running and jumping for joy

Explain to the class that it's their job to try to guess what is being pantomimed.

4. Practice with speaking parts.

Next ask students to role-play some situations with multiple parts (for example, writing and mailing a letter, making a sandwich, choosing an outfit to wear to a very dressy occasion, picking and eating a ripe apple from a fruit stand).

In each case, be sure students don't leave out steps. For example, before writing a letter they will need to get paper, envelope, stamp, and a writing instrument. They will also need to get the address and return address and arrange either to mail the letter or to make sure that someone else will mail it. By adding these types of details to role-plays, students build critical thinking and analytical skills.

Ask students if they want to add to a given role-play, and give one or two a chance as time allows.

5. Introduce a Reflective Summary.

As outlined in the Introduction, ask students to reflect on the question "What did you learn from today's lesson?" Reinforce key themes, then go over any follow-up work.

6. Follow up.

The following steps will help make sure that the students have a chance to continue working with the new concepts.

Take-Home

When you have occasion to talk with them, encourage parents and guardians to use role-playing as they try to help their children create ways to deal with everyday problems and issues. (Games like charades are similar to the pantomime activities.)

Plans to Promote Transfer and Generalization of Skill

1. Continue to use skill prompts and cues throughout the day.

2. Look for opportunities to incorporate role-playing in other lessons, such as language arts or current events. You can ask students to act out parts of a book, try it in different ways, or act out something they read about or watched on TV related to current events.

3. Incorporate the use of short role-plays within your behavior management methods. Rather than simply asking students what they could do to improve their behavior, say:

   What would that look like? Please show me a role-play of what you will do.

OBJECTIVES
- To teach students to distinguish between passive, aggressive, and confident (assertive) styles of behavior
- To model and provide students with practice using assertive (BEST) behaviors as shown by their body posture, eye contact, spoken words, and tone of voice
- To practice BEST behaviors in role-plays of simple teammate interactions such as greetings and saying good-bye

MATERIALS

Whole-class display of "Be Your BEST" (Worksheet 3.8.1)

Whole-class display and copies of the "Be Your BEST Grid" (Worksheet 3.8.2)

Copies of the "Be Your BEST" Take-Home (Worksheet 3.8.4)

NOTE

Worksheet 3.8.3 shows a BEST grid filled in with sample student responses.

PREPARATION

To prepare for this lesson it is important to practice several short and simple role-plays for use in Step 5. The goal is to model three different ways you can say the same thing. For Step 8, recruit an adult partner to work with you outside of class and develop a role-play that will unfold naturally in front of the group.

INSTRUCTIONAL ACTIVITIES

1. Review Topic 7.

Go over the role-playing topic and inform students that they will be using their role-playing skills during the next several meetings.

2. Conduct a Sharing Circle.

Begin by asking students if they know what "tone of voice" means.

Common responses include how your voice sounds and how loud, happy, mad, sad, or normal a voice sounds; it is like a note of a musical instrument, only it is your voice and words.

Then go around the circle, using Speaker Power. Ask children to say hello using "an appropriate tone of voice for the classroom." If anyone wants to share the word *hello* in another language, that would be fun, too.

3. Review the idea of respect.

Explain that an important part of being a team is treating ourselves and each other with respect. Ask students what *respect* means. Refer back to Topic 1, when the group described how they like to be treated as a member of the team and note that many of those things could be summarized as "Respect each other in words and actions." Have students describe disrespectful behavior and how it affects the feelings of others.

4. Display the BEST Grid.

Explain that today's lesson will cover a very powerful new skill that will help the team be successful. A team is successful when all members of the team are their BEST. Point to each letter on the whole-class display and explain:

The way to Be your BEST shows in . . .

B *for Body Posture*

E *for Eye Contact*

S *for Speech—Say Something Nice*

T *for Tone of Voice*

Say:

An important part of being a team is respecting the rights of each person to say what they think and feel so everyone can participate and feel like a part of the group. The way we talk to each other is the most important part.

Give students a copy of the BEST Grid.

5. Role-play three ways of self-presentation.

Say:

I would like to go over three different ways a person could act when talking to another person or a group of people. Let's start at the beginning of our day. I am going to pretend that I am a third grader coming into the classroom. I am also going to pretend that one of my class teammates is standing right inside the door facing me and says hello to me. I want you to try to imagine how you would feel if you were that person.

Here is one way I could do it.

Proceed to demonstrate the aggressive approach:

- *Body posture:* Tense, tightened muscles, stiff back, lean forward, fists clenched, stomp.
- *Eye contact:* Glare, piercing stare.
- *Speech:* Strong, aggressive language (threats, put-downs, insults).
- *Tone of voice:* Harsh, loud, mean.

For example, you could say, "I hate this class" or "What are you looking at, you jerk?" or "You're an idiot; you're stupid!"

Ask students to describe what they observed. List their descriptions within the box on the grid designated for each of the four components in the "Aggressive" column. Then say:

*Now I am going to pretend again and show you another way
I could enter the classroom in the morning.*

Proceed to demonstrate the passive approach:

- *Body posture:* Slouched, rounded shoulders, head down, feet shuffling.
- *Eye contact:* Look down, look away, make eye contact briefly and then look away.
- *Speech:* Use vague, indirect words (mumble something inaudible).
- *Tone of voice:* Low or squeaky, hesitant.

Ask students to describe what they observed. List their descriptions within the box on the grid designated for each of the four components in the "Passive" column.

Let students know that one final time you are going to role-play how someone could enter the classroom in the morning. Because there is no one way to Be your BEST, some teachers tell the students that this time you are going to Be your BEST and ask them for some suggestions for what you could say. Let them know that all of their appropriate suggestions would be good examples of BEST. Choose something to say from the group or use one of the following suggestions.

Proceed to demonstrate an assertive or BEST approach:

- *Body posture:* Walk tall, a slight bounce in your step, pause slightly as you pass to make authentic contact, face the other person with a relaxed stance, don't slump, keep a friendly and relaxed look on face.
- *Eye contact:* Direct gaze, friendly and happy eyes.
- *Speech:* Use nice, polite words: "Good morning. How are you today?" or "I hope you have a great day" as you continue into the room or "Hey, nice catch on the playground this morning." An alternative is to use a suggestion from the group or say whatever pleasant thing that seems most natural and comfortable to you.

- *Tone of voice:* Calm, even.

Ask students to describe what they observed. List their descriptions within the box on the grid designated for each of the four components in the "BEST" column.

6. Review examples of behavior recorded on the BEST Grid.

Ask students how each of the three ways of presenting yourself would make them feel. Ask students if they would rather have aggressive, passive, or BEST behaviors from teammates.

Which way of acting would make you feel good about the team and ready to do good work?

7. Conduct a practice activity.

Have students stand in a circle and ask them to think about what they would say as a morning greeting to a teammate. Ask them to remember to respect Speaker Power (without using the object) and take turns facing the person on their right and greeting them, using their BEST. Depending on the maturity of the group, students could pair up and each practice giving their partner a morning greeting.

Have students brainstorm ways that they could say good-bye to a teammate that would make the person feel good about being a part of the team. Give students time to pick something they would like to say and have them role-play saying good-bye by taking turns around a circle or in pairs.

8. Role-play a scene.

Perform an everyday interaction to show the class how the BEST Grid elements play out in real life. As noted in "Preparation," it's useful to practice with the other person away from the class, to ensure that the class is unaware of how the role-plays are going to look.

One suggestion is to pretend that you are the main character and you are inviting a friend over to your house to watch a new television show that you really enjoy. The other person in the role-play will pretend that they do not like the show and that they do not want to watch it. The focus of the role-plays will be on the main character; the other person should respond in a normal and appropriate way.

For the first role-play, the main character (you) will act aggressively. For example, when the other person says that they do not want to watch your new favorite show, you will react by standing up, getting into the person's face and space, glaring at them, and yelling at them using words that are mean, nasty put-downs. After the first role-play, have the students guess which type of communication style you used. Have them explain how they know this by reviewing the four components of BEST and filling out their copy of the grid. Repeat the process using a passive communication style and then the BEST style.

9. Introduce a Reflective Summary.

As outlined in the Introduction, ask students to reflect on the question "What did you learn from today's lesson?" Reinforce key themes, then go over any follow-up work.

10. Follow up.

The following steps will help make sure that the students have a chance to continue working with the new concepts.

Assignment

Encourage children to use BEST and tell about it next time. Provide children with positive feedback for acting their BEST during the day. Be sure to ask for changes in behavior—for example, say:

> *I can tell that you want to tell me something, but please start again and remember to use your BEST tone of voice.*

Be sure to use thanks or praise to reinforce any positive behavior change.

Take-Home

If the opportunity arises, suggest that parents or guardians have a discussion with their child regarding the assertive, aggressive, and passive behaviors they see in the movies, videos, and television programs that they watch together. Also recommend that they discuss the impact of one character's assertive, aggressive, or passive behaviors on the other characters in the show.

Send the "BEST Take-Home" handout to parents or guardians and follow up as appropriate.

Plans to Promote Transfer and Generalization of Skill

1. Teachers can encourage students to use BEST and to help their teammates remember to use it, too. Having shared language and skill prompts can empower classmates to help each other when these situations occur. For example, one boy on a school bus told another (who was being teased) that his voice was not strong enough and that he was not standing tall.

2. This real-time coaching, teamwork, and camaraderie can be of significant help in giving youngsters the confidence and pride that

they need to function in school as well as in peer, family, and, ultimately, work situations.

3. Have children write, tell, or draw a story about a situation where they could have used BEST.

4. Find magazine pictures of people using aggressive, passive, and BEST behavior. Have children describe the behaviors that led to their decision. Using these pictures, categorize the three types of communication.

TIPS FOR TEACHERS

1. When students begin to role-play, they should only be working to be their BEST. We have found no real value in having students engage in role-playing anything but good teammate behaviors. The objective is to demonstrate behaviors to clarify the concept of BEST, focusing on what it is and not on what it is not.

2. Depending on the maturity of the group, you might want to repeat the role-play in Step 8 several times, asking that they observe only one or two of the behavioral components at a time.

3. It should be noted that various cultural and ethnic groups differ in what might be regarded as proper BEST behavior. For example, students from Latino backgrounds may be less likely to make eye contact with adult males, out of respect. This and other cultural differences of various groups may be open to misinterpretation. Teachers should keep in mind that behaviors in BEST areas strongly influence impressions in social interactions but that cultural differences exist in how and when certain of those behaviors should be displayed.

4. This lesson is meant as a simple introduction to this skill as a general guideline and prompt or good teammate behavior. This skill will be explored and practiced more extensively in the next lesson.

5. When you first demonstrate aggressive behavior, we recommend speaking to an empty chair, not addressing a particular student. For many students, seeing their teacher act in an aggressive way can help to illustrate that people do have choices in how they treat others, but they may lack the sophistication to understand that you don't really mean what you're saying if you seem to be speaking directly to them. Pretending to be talking to an imaginary person helps avoid upsetting a student in a role-play of aggressive behavior.

6. Students who took part in SDM/SPS activities in second grade may have learned the terms *mouse, monster,* and *ME* in association with passive, aggressive, and assertive behavior. They may also associate *shrink* with passive behavior, *blast* with aggressive behavior, and *BEST* with assertive behavior. You may wish to continue

using these terms, but the goal is to fade them and replace them with the positive corrective prompt "Be Your Best." This calls for the child to use the skill instead of placing the focus on what someone is doing wrong.

7. It has been helpful to explicitly state that everyone uses aggressive and passive behavior some of the time and there are times when these behaviors are a good decision. Ask children for examples: Possibilities include when someone is in danger or when someone uses bullying behaviors. It helps to emphasize that you are not talking about different types of people but about different styles of behaving.

8. Putting up posters of BEST (and other SDM/SPS skill prompts) in the classroom and elsewhere in the school and referring to them often is important in helping students internalize and generalize their skills.

Be Your BEST

B   Body Posture

E   Eye Contact

S   Speech (Say something nice.)

T   Tone of Voice

From *Social Decision Making/Social Problem Solving: A Curriculum for Academic, Social, and Emotional Learning* (Grades 2–3). Copyright © 2005 by Maurice J. Elias and Linda Bruene Butler. Research Press (800-519-2707; www.researchpress.com)

	AGGRESSIVE	**ASSERTIVE (BEST)**	**PASSIVE**
Body Posture			
Eye Contact			
Speech			
Tone of Voice			

	AGGRESSIVE	ASSERTIVE (BEST)	PASSIVE
Body Posture	Fists clenched "In your face" Tense Too close Grab, hit, slam Pound, push	Listening Position Relaxed Standing tall Straight	Slumping shoulders Shuffling feet Head down
Eye Contact	Glaring Staring	Direct Good eye contact	Looking down Looking away No eye contact
Speech	Insults Put-downs Bossy, bad words Mean words	Clear Nice words Polite	Unclear Muttering Mumbling
Tone of Voice	Yelling Screaming	Mostly calm Medium	Soft Low Whiny

Be Your BEST

Your child has been learning how important it is to show respect to others by using behaviors called called **Be Your BEST**.

BEST refers to:

BEST

B – <u>B</u>ody Posture

E – <u>E</u>ye Contact

S – <u>S</u>peech (Say something nice)

T – <u>T</u>one of Voice

Is this girl being her **BEST**?

Be Your BEST at Home

- Help your child learn to monitor personal behavior. When you see your child forgetting to use Be Your BEST, ask what the child could have done differently, and help role-play the BEST way to handle the situation.

- Help your child think of ways to stick up for himself or herself, instead of going along with the crowd because it is easier. Initially, children should practice being assertive in simple situations. This builds skills for the times when tougher issues arise.

Your child may be asked in class to share what happened when you practiced this activity.

Thank you!

_____   _____

(Teacher signature)   *(Date)*

- -

(Please sign and return this bottom section.)   **Be Your BEST   3.8.4**

Student _____ **Date** _____

We tried Be Your BEST.   ❏ Yes   ❏ No

If you did, how did it go?

_____

(Signature of parent or guardian)

TOPIC

9

Using Your BEST to Stop Bullying and Teasing

OBJECTIVES
- To review the Be Your BEST skill in the context of situations with strong emotions, such as those evoked by bullying and teasing
- To practice Be Your BEST in role-play situations

MATERIALS Whole-class display and copies of the "BEST Grid" (Worksheet 3.8.2)

PREPARATION Prepare a role-play with another adult in advance for Step 3.

INSTRUCTIONAL ACTIVITIES

1. Review Topic 8.

Ask students when they used their BEST communication skills and invite them to share their experiences.

2. Reinforce the concept.

Explain to students that it is important to practice ways to keep control and "Be Your BEST." BEST refers to a way of talking to someone without losing your cool or pushing them into losing their cool.

Distribute blank copies of the BEST grid and review the behavioral components of the Be Your BEST skill. Point out that using Be Your BEST can help make all students better social problem solvers.

Point to each letter on the BEST grid and review:

B for body posture

E for eye contact

S for speech

T for tone of voice

Have students model and describe how all four aspects of BEST look and sound different in aggressive, passive, and BEST behaviors.

3. Role-play a scene.

Perform an everyday interaction to show the class how the BEST Grid elements play out in real life. One suggestion is to pretend that you are the main character and you are with a friend and want to see a new movie that you are really looking forward to. The other person in the role-play will pretend that they do not want to see that movie or any movie. The focus of the role-plays will be on the main character, but the other person will respond in a normal and appropriate way.

For the first role-play, the main character will act aggressively and the other person could respond in an aggressive or passive way. For example, when the other person says that they do not want to go to the movies, you (the main character) will react by standing up, getting into their face and space, glaring at them, and threatening them, using words that are meant to bully them into going with you. The other person could respond by also acting this way, or they could be passive and back off.

After the first role-play, have the students guess which type of communication style you used. Have students explain how they know this by reviewing the four components of BEST and filling out their copy of the grid. Ask how the BEST style would be different.

Repeat the process using a passive communication style and then the BEST style.

4. Have students practice their BEST skills to handle a peer-pressure situation.

Students need to practice the BEST style of communication when they face peer pressure, instead of being passive or aggressive. The following role-play situation can be used for practice:

> *A group of girls in third grade are playing at recess, but they will not let Rosa play with them. Rosa walks away from the group and finds Alicia, and they begin playing together. Then the group of girls walks over to Alicia and say to her, "Why do you want to play with Rosa? Don't you know that nobody likes her?"*

Ask the students to focus on the person playing the role of Alicia, both when Rosa comes over to her and when she is pressured by the group of girls. Have the class brainstorm how the role-play will look and what the characters will say and do.

Divide students observing the role-play into four groups, assigning each group to watch "Alicia" and report on one aspect of BEST.

After each role-play, ask observers to give praise for aspects of the skill they observed.

Ask students in the role-play and others if they have any suggestions that would make Alicia's BEST even better. Ask students with suggestions to role-play their ideas. If time allows, repeat the scenario with a group of boys.

5. Have *students practice their BEST skills to handle a teasing and bullying situation.*

Ask students how it feels when someone teases them. Ask them how they feel when they are bullied by another student.

Introduce the following practice situations as ways to help students use their BEST when they are teased or bullied.

Veronica is a new girl in class. She moved from a town in Canada. She is nice, but she speaks with an accent, and she uses words and phrases that the other kids in the class don't understand. A group of girls laugh and make fun of her by imitating her, and now they won't let her sit at the third-grade girls' lunch table.

Han is a third grader, and he has difficulty learning math. He needs to go to the resource room teacher every day during math class. Several of the boys in his class call him "stupid" or "idiot." Every morning before school, they take the special math book that he uses and toss it to each other on the playground. They tease him about not knowing the answers to simple math problems.

Alex is a boy in third grade. Alex likes to read and do puzzles in his free time. Several of the boys in Alex's class tease him and make fun of him because he does poorly at sports. When the teams are picked in gym, he is always picked last. The boys call him a loser and tell him that they don't want him on their team.

Ask students to role-play what they would suggest Veronica, Han, and Alex do in these situations, using BEST. Begin with students' taking turns role-playing in front of the class. Move to pairing and then sharing if the students seem ready for it.

6. Reinforce the lesson.

Praise students for any skill improvement you observed when someone listened to feedback from the group or assessed their own behavior and used it to improve their performance in a second role-play. Let them know that listening to the suggestions of teammates and coming up with their own ideas about how to do their BEST is a great way to improve their skills.

Remind the children that these are difficult skills because it is hard to think clearly when emotions are strong. Assure them that it is worth the effort to learn these skills now because these skills will help them for the rest of their lives. Point out that practice is how people get good at any skill, so starting now means these skills will be very strong by the time they grow up.

7. Introduce a Reflective Summary.

As outlined in the Introduction, ask students to reflect on the question "What did you learn from today's lesson?" Reinforce key themes, then go over any follow-up work.

8. Follow up.

The following steps will help make sure that the students have a chance to continue working with the new concepts.

Assignment

Encourage students to use BEST and tell about it next time. Have students think about times when they did not remember to use their BEST and discuss what happened next. Provide children with positive feedback for acting their BEST during the day. Be sure to ask for changes in behavior:

> *I can tell that you want to tell me something, but please start again and remember to use your BEST tone of voice.*

Be sure to use thanks or praise to reinforce any positive behavior change.

Take-Home

Suggest to parents and guardians that they help their children think of ways to stick up for themselves instead of going along with the crowd because it is easier. Recommend that they use the prompt *Be your BEST* to help guide their children to practice ways of handling these kinds of situations.

Plans to Promote Transfer and Generalization of Skill

Have students write about a time when they used their BEST skills. If students cannot think of a time, have them write about a time they could have or should have used their BEST skills. Have them write about what happened when they forgot to be their BEST.

Have students choose a character in a story who did not act assertively when being teased, bullied, or picked on and then rewrite the story, using words or pictures that include the character's using BEST communication skills.

TIPS FOR TEACHERS

1. Sometimes it can be difficult to draw a clear line between tattling and appropriately telling an adult when a student, for example, witnesses bullying or teasing. One way to convey this is to say, "It is important to tell an adult if you see other students doing something that might hurt themselves or hurt someone else. That is *not* tattling."

2. Teachers have found that, with younger students, extending the BEST framework to include some standard procedures for what to say in certain situations can be helpful. The most common example occurs during teasing situations on the bus, at lunch, during gym, at recess, and in the hallways. Prompting students to use BEST seems to be quite effective in making them less fun to tease, but it is also useful to provide specific verbal strategies for responding to teasing and for appropriate assertive behavior. Teachers with whom we have worked have taught students to use the following sequence when faced with persistent teasing:

   - First, ignore the teasers.
   - Second, say, "Please stop."
   - Third, say, "Please stop; what you're doing is bothering me."
   - Fourth, say, "If you don't stop, I am going to tell the teacher [or the aide, bus driver, or other adult nearby] what you are doing."
   - Fifth, tell the teacher [or other adult], and use BEST as you tell what happened.

3. A related strategy that teachers have used with more immature students is to keep ongoing listings of "helpful things you've said when you've been teased" or faced other common Trigger Situations on a poster or computer and refer children to these listings.

10 Using Your BEST to Give and Receive Praise

OBJECTIVES
- To develop the ability to receive praise using BEST
- To practice giving and receiving praise using BEST

MATERIALS
Chalkboard or easel pad *(optional)*

Copies of the "Giving and Receiving Praise" Take-Home (Worksheet 3.10.1)

INSTRUCTIONAL ACTIVITIES

1. Review BEST Topics.

Ask the class to recall what they've been discussing about Be Your BEST.

2. Introduce the new skill.

Ask:

Who can tell me what praise *is? . . . What are some ways to give praise? . . . What are some things to remember when we give praise? . . . Why is it important to give praise?*

Ask if anyone would like to share a time when they were praised this week.

How did you feel when you were praised?

Tell students:

Today, we will discuss the skill of receiving praise. What are some positive and negative ways that you can act when someone praises you?

Some examples: Say thank you, make some acknowledgment, smile, giggle, blush, avoid looking at the speaker, deny the praise, question it, ignore it, or argue about it.

3. Model examples of alternative ways to receive praise.

Ask the class to imagine that you've told someone that their handwriting on a paper is very neat—good work. What are some ways they could respond? Model the following samples:

- (Glare back and bark) "Yuck, this is sloppy for me!"
- (Giggle, look embarrassed, look down) "No it's not."
- (Look straight at the person, smile) "Thank you."

Ask the class which way to accept praise would show using your BEST.

- What body posture would you use?
- What eye contact would you use?
- What would you say that would be encouraging to the teammate who was encouraging you?
- What would your tone of voice be?

4. Emphasize the importance of the skill.

Ask why it is important to receive praise correctly. Some examples:

- To encourage (not discourage) people to continue to praise you
- To show you appreciate praise
- To show your respect for the other person's opinion
- To let you feel good about yourself

5. Conduct a practice activity.

Have students role-play the following situations in pairs, with one student giving and the other receiving praise. Encourage children to use BEST. Assign the audience the task of looking at specific actors and specific components of BEST. Discuss each role-play upon completion. Suggested role-play situations:

- Compliment a classmate on doing a project or assignment well.
- Thank a friend's relative for a ride home from school.
- Tell someone you like their new haircut.
- Thank a relative for cooking your favorite dinner.
- Thank a friend for helping you with a homework assignment.
- Thank a teacher for helping you with a class assignment.
- Compliment a teammate for playing well.

6. Introduce a Reflective Summary.

As outlined in the Introduction, ask students to reflect on the question "What did you learn from today's lesson?" Reinforce key themes, then go over any follow-up work.

7. Follow up.

The following steps will help make sure that the students have a chance to continue working with the new concepts.

Assignment

Tell the students to concentrate on how they use BEST when they are praised this week and be prepared to share the situation at the next meeting.

Take-Home

Send the "Giving and Receiving Praise" Take-Home to parents and guardians and follow up as best you can.

TIPS FOR TEACHERS

1. The beginning of the lesson reviews students' ability to recognize praise and to give and receive some nice comments. Many students are not used to being praised, however. In our experience, well-meaning adults sometimes alienate children by offering praise that the students find uncomfortable to hear. It is important that students not deny praise they receive and that they encourage people to give them more praise by responding in a favorable way. Students' self-concepts can be built up by having them enter into positive cycles of responding to and giving praise.

2. The reasons for students' discomfort with being praised may vary, but they are probably linked to the sense of self-efficacy or identity. Some students become secure with an identity and a set of self-expectations that are negative. For them, the consistency of knowing that negative things will occur is, paradoxically, a source of comfort, security, and anxiety reduction. Praise disrupts that security and is therefore uncomfortable and usually rejected. There are also some cultural factors that may be operating for some students.

3. Behaviors that might lead to praise are, by this logic, stopped. You can use the activities in this Topic to intrude gently into the students' negativity. If a student continues to be highly resistant to praise, consult school support personnel so that more comprehensive intervention can be considered.

Giving and Receiving Praise

Your child has been learning to give and receive praise. Often, children tend to think of praising someone's clothing or a new toy. Encourage your child to praise others for personal qualities, such as, "You really make me laugh. I love spending time with you." Sometimes people feel embarrassed when they are praised; however, encourage your child to receive compliments in a positive way by simply saying, "Thank you."

You can help children practice the skills of giving and receiving praise by doing the following activities.

Compliment Heart

Draw and cut out a large heart shape and hang it in a visible place in your home. At the end of each day, ask everyone to talk about how they gave or received a compliment from another family member and take time to give each other praise. Write the compliments on the heart. Continue each day until the heart is filled, and then start another.

Making Compliments Stick

Some children do not feel praiseworthy, so they do not let compliments "stick." You can help your child by trying to praise when the child is calm, perhaps just before bedtime. Praise your child and then gently indicate that you would like a smile or a thank-you to let you know your words were heard.

Your child may be asked in class to share what happened when you practiced this activity.

Thank you!

_____   _____

(Teacher signature)   *(Date)*

(Please sign and return this bottom section.)   **Giving and Receiving Praise   3.10.1**

Student _____ **Date** _____

We tried Giving and Receiving Praise.   ❏ Yes   ❏ No

If you did, how did it go?

_____

(Signature of parent or guardian)

11

Using Your BEST to Give and Receive Help

OBJECTIVES
- To know when it is appropriate to ask for and to give help
- To learn appropriate ways to ask for help using BEST
- To be aware of signs from others who need help
- To learn ways to offer help using BEST
- To be aware of others' feelings when receiving help

MATERIALS   Chalkboard or easel pad

INSTRUCTIONAL ACTIVITIES

1. Review Topic 10.

Ask students to share times when they gave and received praise. Have students talk about how this felt.

2. Introduce the new skill.

Tell the group that today you will be talking about giving and asking for help.

Ask the students what *help* means to them. Ask them for some examples of how others have helped them. Ask for examples of a time when they asked someone to help them. How did asking for help make them feel? Some answers you may hear: Afraid, embarrassed, feel they should know it, uncomfortable, or even comfortable.

Discuss the fact that everyone needs help at some time and all people have strengths and weaknesses in some areas. Part of being a class or a team is to use your strengths to help those who may need help in those areas. Give an example from the class, such as arts and crafts, music, or physical education.

3. Talk about receiving help.

Ask:

Who could you ask for help, and how could you ask for help after you decide what your problem is?

Some answers may include raising hands or asking quietly—not by throwing pencils or ripping papers. Then ask:

Are there some times that are better than others to ask for help?

Some answers: After you've tried to solve the problem on your own, not when someone is concentrating or busy with their own work, and not when they're busy helping someone else.

Ask:

What can you say after someone has offered help to you?

Answers might include things like these:

- Saying, "Thank you."
- Using BEST.
- Giving them a compliment.

Also ask students to describe things that they should not do when someone is trying to help them (for example, being rude to, ignoring, or making nasty comments to the helper).

This is a good time to suggest that some students like to try to solve a problem on their own before seeking help and that if they are approached with an offer of help, they can politely decline or ask the helper to come back in a little while.

4. Conduct a practice activity.

Tell the class that they will role-play some situations where students are asking for help. Use the following situations or real classroom situations and have children show a positive way of asking and receiving help.

- Student A is working on a really difficult word puzzle and cannot get the last two words. What should Student A do?
- Students A and B are playing a game. Student C is too shy to ask to play. What should Student C do?
- Student A is having trouble with the day's homework and decides to call Student B. How should Student A ask for help?

Remind the actors to use BEST when they are role-playing. Encourage the rest of the class to share and practice ways to make asking for help even better.

5. Talk about giving help.

Continue by asking the students if they have ever given help to others, and, if so, when? How did they feel when they gave help? Some answers may include *good, helpful,* or *pleased* because someone chose me to help. Students may also say they learned the material better when they helped someone.

Ask what kinds of behavior would be signals that show someone else needs help. Look for signs like head scratching, foot tapping, pencil chewing, and so on. Say:

What could you do if you noticed someone needed help?

Some answers may be using your BEST; asking if you can help; if they say yes, then helping them.

6. Conduct another practice activity.

Tell the class that they will role-play some situations in which students are giving help. Using the following situations or real classroom situations, have students show a positive way of giving help. Also have students receive the help in positive ways.

- Student A notices that Student B is absent. Today's assignments are on the teacher's desk. How would Student A volunteer to take the work home to Student B? How would the teacher react?
- Student A notices the teacher is putting up a new bulletin board. How would Student A offer to help? How would the teacher react?
- Student A notices a friend having trouble with a math problem. What should Student A do? How would the friend react?

Remind the actors to use BEST when they are role-playing. Refer to the display of BEST components and ask different sections of the group to concentrate on specific components of BEST. Ask role-playing students and assigned group members for any suggestions for how the students doing the role-playing could make their BEST even better.

7. Introduce a Reflective Summary.

As outlined in the Introduction, ask students to reflect on the question "What did you learn from today's lesson?" Reinforce key themes, then go over any follow-up work.

8. Follow up.

The following steps will help make sure that the students have a chance to continue working with the new concepts.

Assignment

Encourage students to look for signals of those who need help. Also encourage students to use an acceptable way and time to ask for help.

Take-Home

Send a written or e-mail note to parents and guardians explaining that you are working with the class on helping, and suggest that they ask their children to list, while watching television with the family, examples of people helping each other. For example, how did the detectives crack the case against the suspect? What is an assist in sports like hockey, basketball, and baseball? How many examples of helping did you see? What were some signs that the characters needed help?

Plans to Promote Transfer and Generalization of Skill

1. For children who have difficulty writing, try assigning pictures, dioramas, and collages involving helping. Teachers have also posted a "Helping Hand" in the room, with words or pictures on each finger. Children generate different ways to seek help, five of which are selected and put on the poster.

2. Peer tutoring is often effective. Pair students with weaker and stronger skills within grade level or cross-grade. Encourage the tutor to find something the student they are helping does well and praise them for it. Encourage the person who receives help to let the person know what they liked about the help they gave. This is especially useful for building reading skills.

3. In language arts, ask students to take out a piece of paper and write about a time when they needed help. Have them include what they needed help with, how they felt, how they tried to get help, and what happened.

4. Have the students each write about a time when they were helpful to someone else in the class or school. Have students include how they knew the other person needed help. What were some signs they picked up on? How did they feel afterward? What did the other person say or do?

5. In art class, students may illustrate a situation in which students or others are giving each other help.

6. Prompt students to write thank-you notes to other students, parents, or anyone else after receiving their help.

TIPS FOR TEACHERS

Although many of us encourage our children to be independent and self-reliant, some children carry this a bit too far, developing an attitude that does not allow them to admit mistakes or acknowledge that they are having difficulty with something. In later years, this may show up as social withdrawal or isolation, a desire to appear perfect, or an arrogant, know-it-all perspective. It is useful to be certain that children know when it is appropriate to ask for help and give help to others. Part of being in a genuine group involves being helpful to other members when they need it.

T O P I C

12 What Makes a Friend a Friend?

OBJECTIVES
- To identify desirable characteristics in a friend *(Good Friendship Behaviors)*
- To identify undesirable characteristics in a friend *(Not-Good Friendship Behaviors)*
- To increase children's understanding about the importance of caring and being cared about

MATERIALS
Chalkboard or easel pad

Poster board and markers

Copies of "What Makes a Friend a Friend?" (Worksheet 3.12.1; *optional)*

NOTE
After the group has compiled final lists of "Good Friendship Behaviors" and "Not-Good Friendship Behaviors," write or have students write them on a sheet of poster board and display the poster in the classroom. (Students can add drawings or decorate the poster if you wish.) The poster will come in handy in Topic 21, "Using Problem Diaries in Our Lives: Part 2."

INSTRUCTIONAL ACTIVITIES

1. Review Topic 11.

Ask the class to talk about times when students gave and received help.

2. Introduce the new skill.

Tell students that you would like them to do an activity that will help them learn about friendship. Ask them what the word *friend* means. List their responses on the chalkboard or easel pad.

Ask students to close their eyes and think of one of their best friends: someone they look forward to spending time with, and someone they feel good to be around. Inform students that an important rule of this activity is to describe what people do—and not to use any names. Repeat, *no names, no names.*

Ask the students to draw or write a description of what the person does that makes it feel good to be with them.

3. Generate a list of what makes a friend a friend.

Have students share what a person does that is a good friendship behavior. Say:

What does the person do that is nice or good? What we are trying to do is make a list of specific things that a person can do if they want to be a good friend.

Make a list of the behaviors on the chalkboard or easel pad. When a list has been generated, write "Good Friendship Behaviors" across the top.

Ask the class to describe some ways that friends show they care about one another. Add the answers to the list, and make sure it includes "give help," "give praise," and "listen when you are talking."

Continue the discussion by saying something like this:

Now that we all know how a good friend behaves, what are some behaviors that we do not like in a friend?

Are there things that a person might do that would make it not fun to be around them?

Have the children generate a list of characteristics they do not like. Label this list "Not-Good Friendship Behaviors."

4. Conduct a practice activity.

Read the following situations and ask students what kinds of friendship behaviors the characters are using or could use.

Example 1

Student A is playing with a game (puzzle, ball) when he is approached by Student B. Student B is a friend of Student A. Student B approaches Student A and says, "Let me have that game (puzzle, ball). I want to play with it!"

What should Student A do, using the good friendship behaviors on our list, since Student B is supposed to be his friend? What could Student B do instead to show that he is a good friend?

Example 2

Student A and Student B are friends and are playing a game. Student C comes up and starts whispering to Student B about Student A. Student B then goes off with Student C, saying it's no fun playing with Student A anymore.

What should Student A do? Is Student B being a good friend? What should Student B do? Could they have all played together?

Help the class generate ideas about what to do when friends behave in these negative ways. You can add other situations or additional activities to help make the point. For example, have the class fill out the "What Makes a Friend a Friend?" worksheet, or make "Wanted" posters—like the ones seen in post offices, but titled "A Cooperative Friend" and listing all the qualities the student can think of. They can also draw a picture of a cooperative friend to illustrate the poster.

5. Introduce a Reflective Summary.

As outlined in the Introduction, ask students to reflect on the question "What did you learn from today's lesson?" Reinforce key themes, then go over any follow-up work.

6. Follow up.

The following steps will help make sure that the students have a chance to continue working with the new concepts.

Assignment

Have students choose a behavior that they are going to try to use often. Next, have students choose a behavior from the "Not-Good Friendship Behaviors" list that they are going to try to do less often.

Ask students to draw a picture that shows what they plan to do to show good friendship behavior. Have them bring it to the next session to share.

Take-Home

The "Good Friendship Behaviors" list is really a list of ways people can treat each other kindly. The list can be typed and sent home, and parents or guardians can discuss how their children can use these behaviors with their siblings, cousins, neighborhood children, and teammates in extracurricular activities.

Plans to Promote Transfer and Generalization of Skill

1. Be on the lookout for good friendship behaviors in student interactions in the classroom, the schoolyard, and elsewhere. Reinforce with praise.

2. Keep the lists of friendship behaviors (good and not good) posted and refer to them when students have conflicts with each other.

3. Have the class pick "Secret Friend" names. Tell the students they must do one thing each day that shows good friendship behaviors for their secret friends—while trying to make sure that the secret is not discovered. At the end of the week, have them discuss their experiences as giver and receiver of good friendship acts.

4. Establish a "Kindness Box" and ask students to submit a written description of examples they observe of people using good friendship behavior and kindness with each other.

TIPS FOR TEACHERS

1. This is an important lesson for children who are having difficulty making or keeping friends. Often these students do not know how they should or should not be behaving. This is the reason for creating lists of specific behaviors or actions. A student can select something from the list to show good friendship behaviors. Conversely, students can look at the other list to see if they are doing things that annoy or bother others.

2. Teachers can use these lists to help students who continually make poor friendship choices and who do not know what to do instead.

Name _____ Date _____

Things I like about my friends

1. _____

2. _____

3. _____

4. _____

5. _____

6. _____

7. _____

8. _____

9. _____

13 Packing Your SDM/SPS Toolbox

OBJECTIVES
- To provide students with an opportunity to review the social decision making and social problem solving skills they have learned to date
- To make a "toolbox" containing SDM/SPS tool symbols
- To provide teachers and students with an opportunity to assess skill gains

MATERIALS

Copies of the "Tools for the SDM/SPS Toolbox" (Worksheet 3.13.1)

Copies of the "How Am I Doing?" self-report form (Worksheet 3.13.2)

Large envelopes, crayons or markers, drawing paper, scissors

INSTRUCTIONAL ACTIVITIES

1. Review Topic 12.

Have the students read aloud the Good and Not-Good Friendship Behavior lists. Use paired and group reading to get many students involved.

2. Introduce the activity.

Let students know that today they are going to learn a way to keep track of all of the social decision making skills they have learned so far in the third grade.

The skills and concepts learned thus far, and the Topics in which they were introduced, are as follows:

- Sharing Circle, Speaker Power (Topic 1)
- Listening Position (Topic 2)
- Listening Power (Topic 4)
- Strategies for Remembering (Topic 5)
- Following Directions (Topic 6)
- Learning to Role-Play (Topic 7)
- Be Your BEST (Topic 8)
- Giving and Receiving Praise (Topic 10)

- Giving and Receiving Help (Topic 11)
- Good Friendship/Not-Good Friendship Behaviors (Topic 12)

3. Conduct a Sharing Circle.

Here are some suggested Sharing Circle questions that would be On-Topic for today's discussion:

Let's think about all the SDM/SPS skills we have learned and practiced so far. What is your favorite skill?

Can you think of a time when you used a skill that you learned during our SDM/SPS lessons, and it helped you?

Please share something that you like about our problem-solving team.

4. Talk about tools and toolboxes.

Say:

Imagine that our class is a team of people who have been hired to build a house. Before heading out to the job site, let's pretend that we are putting a toolbox together. Your toolbox is filled with all of the tools someone would need to build a house.

The conversation could go like this:

Teacher: If we needed to put two pieces of wood together, which tool or tools would we use?

Student: Hammer and nails.

Teacher: Great. What if we needed to cut a piece of wood in half?

Student: Saw.

Teacher: Super. And what if I were going to put a hole in the wood?

Student: A drill.

Teacher: Excellent!

Reinforce students for knowing what tool to use in each of the situations when it was needed. Explain that social and emotional situations are the same. You need to know what the situation is and then which tool to use.

5. Distribute copies of the "Tools for the SDM/SPS Toolbox" worksheets.

Explain that today students are going to create their own Social Decision Making/Social Problem Solving toolboxes.

Tell them that their first job is to color the tools and cut them out. Then ask them to label their envelopes with their name, teacher's name, and "SDM/SPS Toolbox." They can also color or decorate their toolbox any way they like. Let them know that they will be keeping the boxes in or on their desks for future use. (If no drawing is provided for a skill or concept students choose to include in their toolbox, they may draw and color their own.)

6. Conduct a practice activity.

After students are done, explain that you are going to give them a chance to see if they are as good at choosing the right tool for social decision making as for building a house. Let them know that you will be reading descriptions of something that might happen to them, and they should hold up the tool that they would use in that situation.

What tool would you use if . . . ?

The principal is standing in front of the school in the auditorium waiting to start an assembly. (Speaker Power and Listening Position.)

Reinforce the idea that sometimes it's important to use more than one skill.

The fire alarm goes off. (Listening Power and Following Directions.)

Ask the class how they would put these tools to work.

You notice that a student who is new to our school is alone on the playground looking a little shy. (BEST, Giving Help.)

Ask the class how they would use these tools.

You notice that someone did a great job coloring their SDM/SPS Toolbox. (Giving Praise, BEST.)

Ask the class how they would use these tools. Partner students to show their toolboxes to each other. Ask them to look for something they like about how their partner colored or decorated their toolbox. Remind them to give and receive praise, using their BEST. Be sure to allow time for both participants to give and receive praise.

7. Distribute copies of the "How Am I Doing?" self-report worksheet.

Let the students know that you are interested in hearing from them what tools they are using and what tools they have a difficult time remembering to use.

Tell the class that you are going to be asking them to show you what tool they could use when situations come up throughout the week. Tell them to have their toolboxes ready!

8. Introduce a Reflective Summary.

As outlined in the Introduction, ask students to reflect on the question "What did you learn from today's lesson?" Reinforce key themes, then go over any follow-up work.

9. Follow up.

The following steps will help make sure that the students have a chance to continue working with the new concepts.

Assignment

Ask students to keep their toolboxes where they can see them as a reminder to use their skills. Tell them that you would be happy if they notice a time when a SDM/SPS skill tool could help in a situation and made that suggestion on the spot. Tell students that you will be asking them about the tools they have used at the next session.

Take-Home

Students can bring home copies of the SDM/SPS tools so that they can create a toolbox for use at home. Suggest that parents and guardians review the tools and remind their children to use their tools as situations arise.

Plans to Promote Transfer and Generalization of Skill

1. Before activities that involve group work, movement to a new area, or attending an event, ask students to think about their toolboxes and which tools they will use. Having the children take the tool out of their box (the envelope) to identify and explain why the tool would be helpful is a concrete way to prepare them for expected behaviors. Ask the children to bring their toolboxes with them. If people are forgetting to use their skills, a member of the group can volunteer to put their tool symbol in a place where it can remind people to use it.

2. Some students benefit from a visual reminder of a skill that they are having trouble remembering to use. If you notice someone forgetting a tool, have them put the tool symbol on their desk where they can see it.

3. Scan ahead for situations characters face in language arts, social studies, health lessons, or movies or videos when the use of social decision making skills would be beneficial. Encourage students to identify these as they come up.

4. Students can be asked to:

   ■ Think ahead about what tools a character might want to take out of their toolbox before heading into a situation.

   ■ Think about what tools a character used or could have used. What happened as a result of using or not using the tools?

TIPS FOR TEACHERS

1. This lesson is a great review and allows teachers to assess the skill gain of their students.

2. Skill gain requires time and practice. If teachers feel that their students need more practice and are not ready to proceed, then earlier activities or whole Topics can be reviewed or repeated to enable students to further practice these skills.

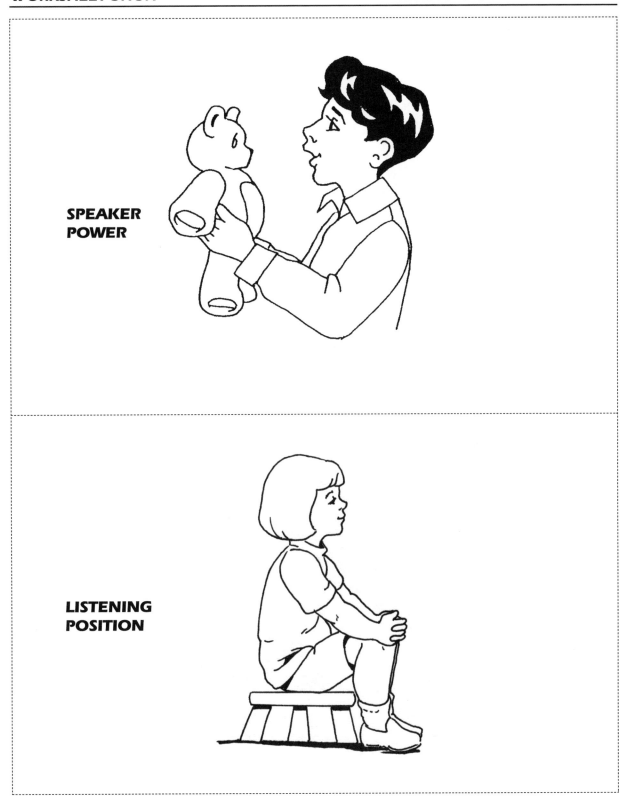

SPEAKER POWER

LISTENING POSITION

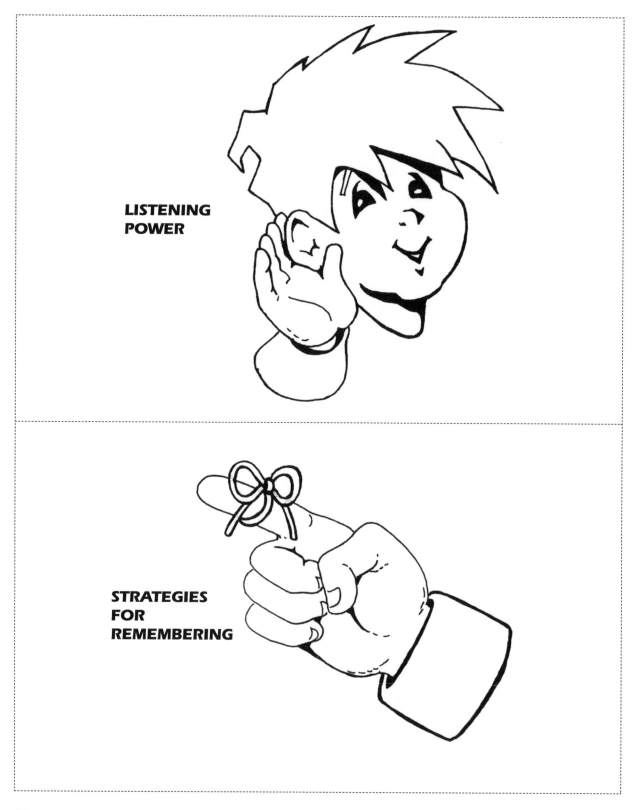

**LISTENING
POWER**

**STRATEGIES
FOR
REMEMBERING**

FOLLOW DIRECTIONS

BE YOUR BEST

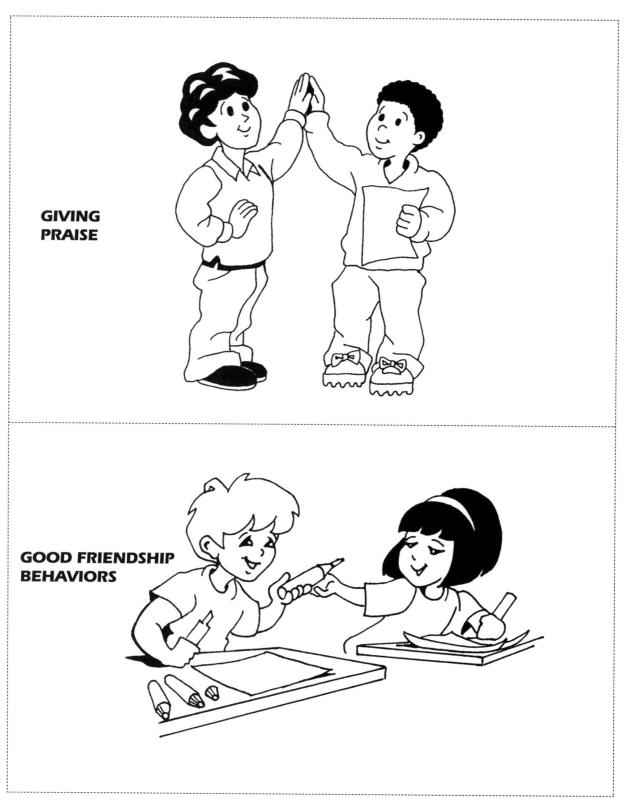

GIVING PRAISE

GOOD FRIENDSHIP BEHAVIORS

KEEP CALM

HELP

Student _____ Date _____

1. I used Speaker Power.

2. I used Listening Position.

3. I used Listening Power.

4. I Followed Directions.

5. I Praised Others.

6. I was Helpful.

7. I used Calm, Nice Words.

Topics 14–21

14 Identifying Feelings

OBJECTIVES
- To identify personal feelings and share feelings with others
- To attend to signs of feelings in others by "mirroring" them
- To build class cohesion

MATERIALS

Index cards

Copies of "Feelings Faces" Numbers 1–6 (Worksheets 3.14.1–3.14.6)

PREPARATION

Before beginning, prepare a set of "Feelings Flashcards" by writing a number of feelings words on small index cards. Some suggested words: *happy, lazy, terrific, satisfied, surprised, pleased, joyful, bored, important, proud, curious, excited,* and *carefree.*

INSTRUCTIONAL ACTIVITIES

1. Review Topic 13.

Begin by commenting about some positive ways that students have been remembering to use their SDM/SPS Toolbox. Have students give examples of times when they used their SDM/SPS tools.

2. Introduce the new skill by conducting a Sharing Circle.

Let children know that during this lesson the class will be playing some games that will help them learn about feelings. Ask them to take a minute and think of one word for a feeling that they felt already today, and share it with the class as Speaker Power is passed around the circle. Let them know that it is OK if their feelings word is the same as someone else's or different from what anyone else has used.

3. Talk about feelings as an experience.

Comment that feelings are something that everyone has every day, and people can have many different feelings during each day, depending on what is going on. Share an example of your own—something along these lines:

I felt sad this morning when I first woke up, and then I felt delighted when one of my favorite songs was on the radio on my way to school.

Or:

I felt excited about finishing a book I was reading, but later that day I felt worried when I lost my wallet. I was elated when I found it.

The example should be something you really felt; the class will be able to tell if you're just reading these words.

4. Conduct the Feelings Flashback activity.

Let students know that the first activity is a game called "Feelings Flashbacks." This game will help the students learn about feelings by remembering some feelings they have had.

Prepare the class for the activity by discussing and modeling each feelings card. Possibly this can be taught a day ahead of time. Tell the students they will each be responsible for selecting at least one feelings card and then sharing a time when they felt this way with the class. They will be asked to share a specific time or situation when they felt that way.

Complete the Feelings Flashbacks activity by having students take turns picking a feelings card and asking, "Can you tell about a time when you felt _____?" Have students volunteer their contributions. Continue with each feeling. Make sure that each student contributes at least one feeling flashback.

If you have more student participants than cards, place the cards in a container and have students pick a card out of the container in turn. Keep the stack of cards that have been used outside the container, and shuffle and replace them until everyone has had a chance to share a feelings flashback. An alternative is to keep the unused cards in one pile and used cards in another. Once all of the cards are in the used stack, reshuffle and start again.

5. Conduct the Mirroring activity.

Tell the children that the next game they are going to play is called "Mirroring." Divide the group into pairs, then say:

Here's how it works. I'll read a story, and you listen for feelings words. One of you in each pair will be called the Communicator, and whenever I say a feelings word, your job will be to act out or pantomime the feeling as if you were in the situation. The other will be the Mirror. What does a mirror do?

Let the class come up with some suggestions, then continue:

A mirror can only reflect what comes to it. So if you're playing the part of the Mirror, you must watch the Communicator carefully and portray accurately any changes in expression, movement, or position that you see the Communicator make.

Model "mirroring" before you start the class exercise: Have two students practice with you before the lesson, or ask for a volunteer to try it with you. Explain that the goal is to show the feelings, not to do a full role-play. People can stand up and move a little bit if they need to do so, but the focus is on showing the feeling when it is read.

Here's a sample situation:

*A girl was starting to feel **bored** because she was sitting on the bench for a long time waiting for a turn to play basketball. She was **happy** when the coach called her name to come and play. Someone passed her the ball, and her feelings went from **happy** to **excited**. She dribbled the ball up to the basket, threw the ball, and to her **surprise** it went in. Then she jumped for **joy**!*

When you read this example, the Communicator should slump as if sitting on a bench and looking bored—perhaps moving from looking down and glum to looking around distractedly, keeping a *bored* expression. Check to see that the Mirror is copying the Communicator's expression and movements before reading the next sentence. If the Mirror is having trouble, explain and model both parts until an example of communication and mirroring happens.

At the word *happy,* the Communicator's job is to look up alertly, stand, and pretend to be walking onto the basketball court without actually leaving the spot in front of the chair. When *"happy to excited"* is read, the Communicator should pretend to be catching a ball and look and act *excited* while moving slowly, again as if pretending to walk while dribbling the ball and then holding the ball and looking up as if under the basket. The next thing is to shoot the pretend ball in the basket and look *surprised.* Then jump for *joy.*

It is important when first modeling to keep movements slow and limited to help avoid silliness when students have a chance to try it.

Ask if anyone has any questions about how to be a Communicator or a Mirror.

Depending on the maturity of the class, have students split up into groups of two or three. In groups of three, one member would be the Mirror, one the Communicator, and one an Observer whose job is to notice how closely the expressions are matched. Roles can be switched every few minutes as time allows. Here are some practice situations:

- A student is *confidently* working on a math assignment, but comes across a problem he or she does not know how to do. The student feels *curious* and *wonders* how to go about it. After trying several solutions, the student solves the problem and feels *proud* and *satisfied.*

- A child has worked very hard in school and comes home feeling *lazy*. The child is *happy* and *relieved* when the adult in charge there suggests that he or she go outside before doing homework because it is such a beautiful day. The child feels *carefree* while walking to the park.

- A student is disappointed after swinging and missing on the first two balls during a baseball game, so it is a surprise when, on the third pitch, the student hits a home run. The student j*oyfully* runs around the bases.

- A student is asked to read out loud in class, but is *embarrassed* because he or she doesn't feel like a good reader. The student tries to read but stumbles over some words and becomes *angry*. The teacher praises the student for a good effort and he or she feels much more *self-confident*.

6. Introduce a Reflective Summary.

As outlined in the Introduction, ask students to reflect on the question "What did you learn from today's lesson?" Reinforce key themes, then go over any follow-up work.

7. Follow up.

The following steps will help make sure that the students have a chance to continue working with the new concepts.

Assignment

Feelings Find

Ask students to find (or draw) pictures of feelings to bring to the next lesson. Supply old magazines and handouts of blank Feelings Faces and help children distribute and choose materials they might want to work with. Let them know that they can look for pictures in things that they have at home, too, but to be sure and ask a parent or guardian before they cut anything out of books, magazines, or photographs at home.

Take-Home

It is a good idea to send a short note home explaining that students are learning to identify feelings in themselves and in others. Let parents or guardians know that the homework involves finding pictures of feelings to bring to the next lesson. Ask them to help their child decide what materials to bring. If there are old magazines or other pictures at home that they could use, it would be helpful—but it is not necessary. The children can use some materials distributed at school, and they can draw their own feelings faces, too.

Suggest helping the child with this activity by asking questions such as "Why did you choose (or draw) that picture?" "What feeling does it show?" "Could you use more than one feelings word to describe it?"

Plans to Promote Transfer and Generalization of Skill

Language Arts Applications

Teachers can scan ahead for feelings words in stories students will be reading and play Feelings Flashbacks as a way to introduce new vocabulary. It will also help students relate personally to the character who experiences the emotion in the story.

It's also useful to scan ahead for sections of a story where characters experience a variety of emotions and use "Mirroring" while reading that section aloud. It helps bring the story to life and is especially useful to students with auditory learning styles.

Other Applications

Students can be asked to describe how a character would be feeling during a critical event being studied in history, current events in the news, a discussion about a real-life "current event" that happened in the classroom or on the playground, or when considering choices in health-related situations. Additionally, students can be asked to share a feelings flashback for the feelings words generated. Again, this helps them to better understand another's experience.

TIPS FOR TEACHERS

1. It is recommended that teachers use positive or mildly negative feelings words when first introducing the "Feelings Flashbacks" and "Mirroring" activities. These activities can be used on an ongoing basis for developing a vocabulary for feelings. The rationale for starting with feelings on the more positive end is to help students who are not comfortable or familiar with sharing their feelings begin with things that may be more fun to share. We have also found that when offered a mixture of emotions, one student will pick *embarrassed,* for example, while another will get to share something they are proud of, a situation that could be uncomfortable for some children.

2. Some students benefit from beginning with a poster activity. Instead of flashcards, the teacher can begin a collection of pictures or cutouts from magazines that students can add to (see "Feelings Find" assignment). Feelings illustrations can be numbered, and students can share on the basis of the feeling that corresponds with the number they draw.

3. One of the most important ways to build students' feelings skills and the generalized use of those skills is to verbally model your own feelings states and talk about them with students, as in Step 3

of the "Instructional Activities" section. Doing this briefly on a daily basis is a highly powerful skill-building activity.

4. When identifying feelings, it's best to begin with positive or mildly negative emotions; the class doesn't need to work with high intensity words like *angry* and *terrified*.

I am feeling _____

I am feeling _____

I am feeling _____

I am feeling _____

I am feeling _____

I am feeling _____

15 Looking for Signs of Different Feelings

OBJECTIVE
- To learn to recognize signs of feelings in others and demonstrate signs of different feelings in oneself
- To learn that feelings can vary in their degree of intensity

MATERIALS
Chalkboard or easel pad

Whole-group display of "Feelings Words" (Worksheet 3.15.1; *optional*)

Whole-class display or copies of "Feelings Can Be . . ." (Worksheet 3.15.2)

Copies of "Feelings Faces" from Topic 14

Copies of the "Feelings" Take-Home (Worksheet 3.15.3)

INSTRUCTIONAL ACTIVITIES

1. Begin with a Sharing Circle about feelings.

Use an On-Topic question such as the following:

What is something that you find scary? How do you show that you are feeling scared?

2. Introduce the skill of looking for signs of different feelings.

Explain that good social decision makers and problem solvers learn to pay attention to the messages that other people send through the way they look and act. People let you know how they are feeling in many more ways than just words.

Ask for examples, and write them down on the chalkboard or easel pad. Make sure the list includes things people say, gestures, facial expressions, tone of voice, body posture, eye contact, and so on—enough to make the point about the importance of nonverbal communication.

3. Conduct a practice activity.

Have students share their Feelings Find assignment from Topic 14—the one where they were asked to draw or find pictures of people showing feelings.

Invite them to show their pictures to the group and tell what feeling they think the person is having in the picture. Then ask them to tell what they see that makes them think the person is feeling that way. Refer students to the display of Feelings Words as needed.

Depending on the maturity of the group, bring up the idea that in some pictures there might be more than one feelings word to describe what that person appears to be feeling. Ask the student and the rest of the group for any other words that match what they see. Again, ask:

What do you see that makes you think that the person is feeling that way?

4. Conduct another practice activity.

Introduce the idea that sometimes feelings can be very strong and sometimes they are not as strong.

Show students a whole-class display of "Feelings Can Be . . ." or distribute a copy to each student. Let students know that the sheet is a meter that they can use to rate feelings from 1 (Mild) through 5 (Very Strong). Tell them that you are going to read some statements to them, and then you would like them to show if they think the feeling would be 1, 2, 3, 4, or 5 by the number of fingers they hold up.

Read the following situations to the class one at a time, pausing after each situation to ask the questions listed after the first one. Notice if children differ in how strongly they feel about something. Let them know that this is what usually happens—people often have different levels of feeling about the same events.

- Someone took Kim's new bike for a ride without asking permission.

  How strong do you think the feelings would be on our rating scale or meter? Hold up your fingers to show the number you would rate the feeling.

  What feelings would the person in the story be having? How would you feel if the situation happened to you?

Other sample situations:

- You just found out that you were not chosen for a part in your school play.
- Your best friend just told you about plans to move far away.
- You were playing a game with your friend, and you won.
- A coach just yelled at you for not following directions.

- You were not invited to your friend's birthday party.

It is often useful to go through the situations again and ask how the other people in each situation might be feeling.

5. Introduce a Reflective Summary.

As outlined in the Introduction, ask students to reflect on the question "What did you learn from today's lesson?" Reinforce key themes, then go over any follow-up work.

6. Follow up.

The following steps will help make sure that the students have a chance to continue working with the new concepts.

Assignment

Ask students to pay attention to feelings when they watch television or movies, read a story, or work and play with teammates and friends in school and at home. They should note what people do to show their feelings.

Pass out blank Feelings Faces and ask the students to fill in the name of a person they saw, a drawing of the expression they saw on the person's face, and the word for the feeling it showed.

Tell students to bring at least one Feelings Face for the next meeting.

Take-Home

Send the "Feelings" Take-Home (Worksheet 3.15.3) to parents and guardians and follow up as desired.

Plans to Promote Transfer and Generalization of Skill

1. Keep an ongoing collection of feelings words and pictures and "Feelings Can Be . . ." ratings on display and use them to help children express both what they feel and how strong the feeling is.

2. Language arts, social studies, and health texts and topics provide ongoing opportunities for infusing practice of the identification of personal feelings and the feelings of others. The same questions used in this topic area can also be used daily within academic subjects and real-life situations:

   - How are you feeling?

   - How do you think (fill in character or person) might be feeling?

   - What other feelings words might help us understand how else someone might be feeling in that situation?

- How strongly do you feel (or do you think they might feel) about this situation? Use our "Feelings Can Be . . ." meter.

When students are writing, challenge them to avoid the words *mad, sad, happy,* and *scared,* unless no other word will work as well or better.

TIPS FOR TEACHERS

1. Expect that you will have to prompt students in an ongoing way for any of the following to happen:

   - Using new words for feelings
   - Increasing the expression of feelings in daily communication or in writing
   - Recognizing and labeling the feelings of other people

   Some teachers find it helpful to keep a list of questions to prompt feelings identification in plain sight as a reminder to use them when first getting started with this program.

2. After students share their Feelings Find homework, the pictures or drawings can be used in a variety of ways:

   - Made into (or added to) a bulletin board or other display of feelings.
   - Arranged into groups that are the same or similar (for example, *happy, excited, joyful,* and *proud* might be in the same cluster).
   - Made into a notebook or dictionary of feelings for the class to use as a reference.
   - Saved in students' social decision making portfolios or notebooks.

3. Scan ahead for academic content areas addressed during the week that lend themselves to infusing practice identifying feelings. Writing this activity into lesson plans as one of the objectives is also a helpful reminder.

SCARED	MAD	SAD	GLAD
Alarmed	Angry	Worried	Happy
Anxious	Bothered	Unsure	Excited
Cautious	Annoyed	Disappointed	Cheerful
Concerned	Stressed	Hurt	Surprised
Fearful	Frustrated	Regretful	Joyful
Frightened	Outraged	Sympathetic	Ecstatic
Horrified	Enraged	Mixed Up	Lovestruck
Jittery	Disappointed	Depressed	Confident
Nervous	Disgusted	Lost	Hopeful
Panicky	Troubled	Confused	Encouraged
Shocked	Overwhelmed	Lonely	Enthusiastic
Shy	Upset	Helpless	Determined
Suspicious	Aggravated	Guilty	Proud
Terrified	Furious	Dismayed	Amazed
Threatened			Content
Timid			Delighted
Uneasy			
Weak			
Worried			

Feelings Can Be . . .

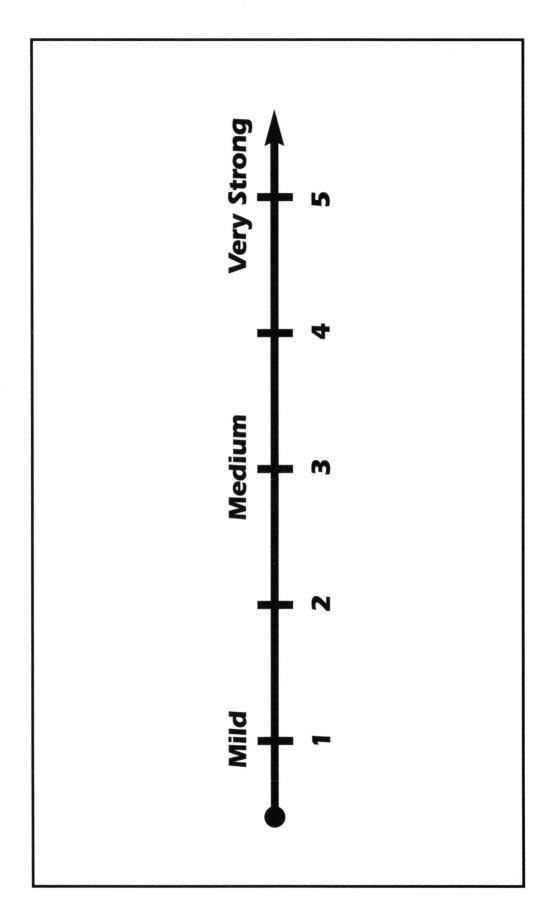

Mild   Medium   Very Strong

1   2   3   4   5

From *Social Decision Making/Social Problem Solving: A Curriculum for Academic, Social, and Emotional Learning* (*Grades 2–3*). Copyright © 2005 by Maurice J. Elias and Linda Bruene Butler. Research Press (800-519-2707; www.researchpress.com)

Feelings

Your child has been learning to pay attention to personal feelings and the feelings of others. At this age, children can learn how behaviors change the way people feel. They can also start to learn that people can feel more than one feeling at a time. For example, someone can be feeling excited and frightened about being on stage or angry and hurt if someone makes fun of them or teases them.

Children often use only a few words to describe how they feel. Having a broader vocabulary for feelings can help children understand themselves and others in a deeper way.

<u>Afraid</u>	<u>Mad</u>	<u>Sad</u>	<u>Happy</u>
Frightened	*Angry*	*Worried*	*Excited*
Nervous	*Annoyed*	*Unsure*	*Surprised*
Shocked	*Frustrated*	*Disappointed*	*Joyful*
Shy	*Outraged*	*Hurt*	*Confident*
Terrified	*Disappointed*	*Confused*	*Hopeful*
Uneasy	*Overwhelmed*	*Lonely*	*Enthusiastic*
Worried	*Upset*	*Helpless*	*Proud*
			Amazed

Feelings Flashback

For this family game, you will need a stack of index cards. On each card, write a feelings word. One person in the family picks a card and, for the feeling on it, shares a specific time or situation when he or she felt that way. One format is the question "Tell about a time when you felt _____." Everyone is permitted to ask a follow-up question. Be sure to ask your child, occasionally, how they knew they felt that way.

Your child may be asked in class to share what happened when you practiced this activity.

Thank you!

_____   _____

(Teacher signature)   *(Date)*

(Please sign and return this bottom section.)   **Feelings   3.15.3**

Student _____ **Date** _____

We tried Feelings Flashback.   ❒ Yes   ❒ No

If you did, how did it go?

_____

(Signature of parent or guardian)

TOPIC

16 Identifying Feelings in Stories

OBJECTIVES
- To practice identifying feelings of characters in the context of language arts
- To practice identifying internal feelings about stories that students read, hear, or observe in the media

MATERIALS
Copies of "Feelings Face 6" (Worksheet 3.14.6)

Crayons or markers

PREPARATION
This Topic provides a sample story, but you can also pull stories from common trade books, excerpts from language arts texts, short summaries of a movie or television show, or excerpts representing a common area of concern, such as teasing, bullying, or being left out of a group.

NOTE
You may use any of the Feelings Faces (Worksheets 3.14.1–3.14.6) in the "Assignment" portion of this Topic.

INSTRUCTIONAL ACTIVITIES

1. Begin with a Sharing Circle.

Have students show the Feelings Faces from the Topic 15 assignment and discuss the feelings represented.

2. Introduce the idea of using stories to build skills.

Ask for a show of hands if students like to read or listen to stories about other people. Then ask for a show of hands if they like to watch movies or television shows that tell a story about things that happen to other people.

Explain that students can use stories about other people as a great way to practice the skills they have been learning about feelings.

3. Conduct the Be a Storyteller activity.

Prepare students for the activity by telling them that during this meeting they will use a story to practice recognizing feelings and building their vocabulary for feelings. Tell them to pay attention and look for signs of different feelings.

Use a book as a story line that you can modify slightly to address current issues. For example, the *Berenstain Bears* series, by Stan and Jan Berenstain, has stories in which the bears encounter a wide variety of problems common in the lives of third graders (for example, teasing, fighting with siblings, bad dreams, not telling the truth, watching too much television, and many more).

Here is an example of a story constructed by looking at these books and attempting to turn some of the main story line into a story, using the teacher's own words. This example illustrates one way that practicing identifying feelings could be infused into this particular story:

> *There once was a little bear who lived in a wonderful big house in the country. The house was made by the little bear's father, who hollowed out a tree, so their house was inside a tree! It was a big, old tree filled with beautiful, cozy rooms. The kitchen had an old-fashioned stove where the Mama Bear made delicious meals. Upstairs, Mama and Papa Bear's room had a big, old comfy bed and a fireplace. Some nights when it was cold outside, Papa Bear and Little Bear would get under blankets and read stories in front of the fireplace to stay nice and toasty warm. Little Bear loved reading stories with Papa Bear in his room, but he also loved to be in his own room. It had a big window so he could look out and see the brook and the beautiful countryside. In his room he kept many of his favorite things, like his bat and ball (he loved to play baseball), all his favorite books, and a toy plane that he made all by himself. He also had a snug little bed that his father made for him when he was a little baby.*

Ask:

> *If you were to guess, how do you think Little Bear feels about his house in the country?*

> *What feelings words do you think of when you imagine what it would be like to live there? . . . What part of the story makes you imagine that feeling?*

After a brief discussion, continue the story:

> *One day, Little Bear woke up and had aches and pains in his knees and his legs. His father helped him figure out that he had gotten so big that he no longer fit in his bed. That very morning, Papa Bear told Little Bear that he could help make a new, bigger bed. They went outside right after breakfast to chop*

down some trees to make it. Little Bear could not help but wonder what would happen to his little bed. He asked his mother, and she said, "Don't you worry about that, Little Bear." Then he asked his father, but his father could not hear because he was sharpening his ax, and it made too much noise.

Ask students:

How do you think Little Bear is feeling? . . . How do you think you would feel if you were Little Bear and all of a sudden you were too big for your bed? . . . How do you think Little Bear felt when he asked his father a question and he did not answer?

End by asking the students to finish the story. Get a few ideas and then have a vote on an overall ending. Either work with the class to create one ending or have individuals or pairs of students write their own endings. Afterward, ask these questions:

- What are some possible feelings Little Bear could have had?
- How would you be feeling if you were Little Bear?
- How strong are Little Bear's feelings? What number on our "Feelings Can Be . . ." meter do you think his feelings might be?

Pass out copies of Feelings Face 6. Ask students to write their name at the top and "Little Bear" under the Feelings Face. Ask them to pick a feelings word that they think best describes the feeling Little Bear is having at this point in the story, write it at the top of the Feelings Face, and then draw what Little Bear's face might look like. (They can add Little Bear's ears if they wish.)

Have students share their pictures and describe their ideas.

4. Introduce a Reflective Summary.

As outlined in the Introduction, ask students to reflect on the question "What did you learn from today's lesson?" Reinforce key themes, then go over any follow-up work.

5. Follow up.

The following steps will help make sure that the students have a chance to continue working with the new concepts.

Assignment

Pass out blank Feelings Faces and ask students to watch for different feelings and do a Feelings Face, just as they did with Little Bear but for a person—someone they see on a television show or someone they know. Instruct them to write the person's name and a feelings word that seems to describe the feeling best, and then draw what the feeling looked like on the person's face. Have students bring their Feelings Face to share at the next session.

Take-Home

As part of how you typically encourage parents and guardians to read with their children, show them how they can help their children identify feelings by looking at pictures and reading the text together. Parents and guardians can ask children what feelings the characters are having and how they could tell. They could also ask children how they would feel if they were the character in the story.

Plans to Promote Transfer and Generalization of Skill

1. Find books that have particularly good illustrations of people's feelings. Read out loud, stopping to have children look at the pictures to tell you what feelings they see and what they see that makes them think the person feels that way.

2. Make up a story that works for you. Think of some ways that students are not as sensitive as you would like them to be about one another's feelings. Make up a story about other students as a way to help you teach them to think about how other people feel in situations that are relevant and familiar.

   For example:

   > *I heard a story the other day that made me wonder about how someone might be feeling. A third grader told his teacher that he was having fun on the tire swing on the playground, and another boy who is his friend jumped on the swing and knocked him off. He ended up scraping his elbow, and it really hurt. I was thinking that he might have some feelings about what happened to him.*

   You could ask students:

   - What are some feelings words that come to mind when you imagine what the student must have felt like when that happened?
   - What do you think his friend was feeling?
   - Can you imagine how you would feel if that happened to you?
   - How would you feel if you jumped onto the tire swing and knocked a friend off it?
   - Would feelings be different if the boys were not friends? How might feelings be different?

3. Have students share books from home or from the library that show characters with different feelings or emotions.

TIPS FOR TEACHERS

1. Another way to do the Feelings Face worksheets is to ask students to track the feelings of a character as they read (or you read) a story. After each paragraph, page, set of pages, or chapter, you can ask students to provide a label for the strongest (or most recent) feeling and then have them draw that feeling on the worksheet. You can also ask students to fold over the label and share their drawing with a partner to see if the other student can recognize the feeling. If not, perhaps students could work together on an improved version of either or both depictions.

2. Some school libraries have created sections for books that deal with feelings and other similar topics. Even if yours doesn't have a formal section, you can ask the school librarian to advise students on which books contain references to different feelings words to help increase the students' feelings vocabulary.

17 What Are Your Feelings Fingerprints?

OBJECTIVES
- To help students become aware of situations that trigger or elicit strong emotions *(Trigger Situations)*
- To increase awareness of the unique way strong feelings make their presence known internally *(Feelings Fingerprints)*
- To teach students how strong feelings affect the ability to think clearly
- To introduce the importance of taking responsibility by using Feelings Fingerprints as signs that students need to calm down before thinking and acting

MATERIALS
Whole-class display of "Feelings Words" (Worksheet 3.15.1)

Whole-class display of "Feelings Can Be . . ." (Worksheet 3.15.2)

Chalkboard or easel pad

Copies of "Feelings Fingerprints" (Worksheet 3.17.1)

INSTRUCTIONAL ACTIVITIES

1. Review the study of feelings.

Ask students to share their latest Feelings Faces.

2. Review vocabulary of feelings.

Introduce the lesson by directing students' attention to the list of feelings words. Ask students to find a word that they think would be rated 5 on the "Feelings Can Be . . ." meter. They are looking for an emotion or feelings word that would be very strong. Let them know that it is OK to pick the same word as someone else.

Explain that during this lesson they will start to learn about strong— or Number 5—feelings. Tell them that everyone at one time or another has a problem that needs to be solved. These can be problems with parents, teachers, brothers, sisters, or friends. Ask if any children who have brothers or sisters have ever had a time that one or both of them had Number 5 feelings because of a problem that they were having.

Tell students that sometimes people jump right in and try to solve the problem before they are ready. If this happens, nothing gets accomplished because they are too upset and their feelings get in the way of being able to think clearly. Add:

> To make the "BEST" decision, we need to calm our feelings so we can use our brains to think about what we can or want to do.

3. Introduce Trigger Situations.

Define *Trigger Situations* as events or situations that cause a Number 5—very strong—feeling.

Have the class share examples of some things that could happen that cause very strong feelings for them. Provide some examples, such as giving a speech, getting into an argument, and so on—and brainstorm a variety of common Trigger Situations with the group. Prompt children if needed to include emotions in categories other than anger, such as fear, nervousness, sadness, or being so excited or upset that they think they will jump out of their skin.

Record the situations on the chalkboard or easel pad.

4. Introduce physical signs of stress.

Ask if any of the students who received instruction in second grade remember what a Feelings Fingerprint is. If so, use their explanations as you make the following points:

> Our bodies send us signals when we are very stressed or upset. The name for this kind of signal is "Feelings Fingerprint." Everyone has their own set of Feelings Fingerprints.

> The first step toward being your BEST is to know what your Trigger Situations are so that you can try to think about ways to handle them before they happen.

> The next step is also very important. You need to know your own Feelings Fingerprints.

Explain that everyone has their own special way that feelings show up. When people run into a Number 5–feeling Trigger Situation, they all experience physical reactions, but the place each one feels the reaction can be different from the place someone else feels it.

5. Identify personal Feelings Fingerprints.

It will help students to brainstorm their Feelings Fingerprints, their personal physical signs of stress, if you share your own experiences when faced with Trigger Situations.

This kind of openness may be difficult, but students often respond well when teachers self-disclose an example (real or close to real) of their own Feelings Fingerprints. For example:

> *Once I was on my way to school and I got a flat tire. When I thought that I was going to be late and of you worrying about me, I got a tight feeling in my chest. That is my Feelings Fingerprint. When I get upset and worried, my chest gets tight, and it's hard to breathe.*

After they get the idea, have the students brainstorm their own Feelings Fingerprints, or physical signs of stress, by sharing what they experience when faced with Trigger Situations. The list may include headache, increased heart rate, upset stomach, sweaty palms, tense shoulders, rapid breathing, shaky knees, and so on.

6. Talk about the general experience of Feelings Fingerprints.

Mention people with different jobs and ask why, when, and how they might feel Feelings Fingerprints: athletes, musicians, police officers, firefighters, librarians, cashiers, and any others who fit the background and experience of your students.

Have each student choose one of the Trigger Situations listed in Step 3 and identify their own Feelings Fingerprint for that trigger. You may suggest that children close their eyes and try to remember being in that situation. Ask them to try to visualize the experience and feel how their bodies felt at the time.

Pass out the "Feelings Fingerprints" worksheets and ask the children to draw where Feelings Fingerprints show up in their body. After they finish, ask them to share their picture with a partner. Then ask for volunteers to show and describe their personal Feelings Fingerprints.

7. Introduce a Reflective Summary.

As outlined in the Introduction, ask students to reflect on the question "What did you learn from today's lesson?" Reinforce key themes, then go over any follow-up work.

8. Follow up.

The following steps will help make sure that the students have a chance to continue working with the new concepts.

Assignment

Ask students to be on the lookout for Feelings Fingerprints and let them know that the next topic in the series involves learning skills that help them calm down strong feelings so that they can use their brains and respond to the "Be Your BEST" prompt. Tell students to be prepared to share a Trigger Situation and Feelings Fingerprint that happened to them recently.

Take-Home

Parents and guardians can review the "Feelings Fingerprints" worksheet and have a family discussion in which every family member identifies one of their Feelings Fingerprints and the emotion that causes it. You can introduce this idea during a face-to-face meeting at school or send home the "Feelings Fingerprints" worksheet with a brief note.

Plans to Promote Transfer and Generalization of Skill

Help students to recognize any Trigger Situations and Feelings Fingerprints throughout the week. Ask them to draw or write about it.

TIPS FOR TEACHERS

1. This is a very important lesson for children, especially for those with issues of anger management and self-control. When generating a list of Trigger Situations, a Sharing Circle is a good way to ensure that every child understands the concept of a Trigger Situation and can identify at least one of their own Trigger Situations. Sometimes it is the children with the most problems who have the most difficulty identifying or realizing what triggers them. If this occurs, you can gently suggest a situation that you have seen trigger the child in the past.

2. It can be helpful to explain to students that human bodies are equipped to respond to upsetting situations with a "fight or flight" reaction. What happens in a Trigger Situation is that the body makes a chemical called adrenaline that causes physical reactions and provides a lot of energy. When strong feelings happen, it is a lot easier for someone to use fight or flight behavior than to think because another thing adrenaline does is make it hard to use the strongest part of our brain. It is important to be able to recognize times when it is difficult to "Be Your BEST" because of strong feelings—and know what to do about it.

3. If you make a list of Feelings Fingerprints, there is no need to include names of the people who contribute each item; the list will still be useful because students may have several in common. The list can be posted for future use.

4. Some teachers have students work in small groups to outline one team member's body on a large sheet of paper and work together to put their initials where a Feelings Fingerprint for each student in the group is located.

Student _____ Date _____

T O P I C

18   A Strategy for Keeping Calm

OBJECTIVES
- To point out problematic situations in which students can use self-control to calm down before reacting
- To teach students how to get calm and keep their self-control in a problematic situation
- To practice a deep-breathing exercise called *Keep Calm.*

MATERIALS
Copies or whole-class display of "Stages of Anger" (Worksheet 3.18.1)

Whole-class display of the steps in "Keep Calm" (Worksheet 3.18.2)

Copies of the "Keep Calm" Take-Home (Worksheet 3.18.3)

INSTRUCTIONAL ACTIVITIES

1. Begin with a Sharing Circle.

Review Topic 17 by having students share a Trigger Situation and that situation's Feelings Fingerprint.

2. Introduce the Keep Calm exercise.

Explain:

> *Today we are going to learn about the importance of keeping calm. It is possible to handle almost every type of problem or difficulty better if you are able to keep calm. To help us learn to keep calm, we are also going to learn a specific strategy called "Keep Calm." This strategy can help you through a problem situation without saying or doing something you later wish you hadn't.*

3. Discuss the progression of anger.

Distribute the Stages of Anger worksheet or direct students' attention to a whole-class display. Discuss how anger can progress from *irritated* to *upset,* then *angry,* then *furious,* and finally *enraged.* Describe Keep Calm as a skill people can use to stop and calm down before their feelings get all the way to Number 5. They can also use it if they find them-

322

selves with a Number 5 feeling already and want to bring down the strong feeling so as to better figure out how to handle the situation. But this takes a lot of practice.

4. Talk about consequences.

Ask:

What happens when we lose our temper and yell or hit people or things?

After some discussion, repeat the promise:

Today we are going to learn what you can do before you do something that could get you into trouble.

5. Present the Keep Calm steps.

Ask if anyone already knows Keep Calm. If so, let them help you explain what it is.

Direct students' attention to the whole-class display of the steps in Keep Calm:

1. Tell yourself to STOP.

2. Tell yourself to KEEP CALM.

3. Slow down your breathing with two long, deep breaths.

4. Praise yourself for a job well done.

6. Model behavioral and cognitive components of the skill.

It's useful to provide examples of people your students will relate to—sports figures or heroes in stories you know they're following. Continue:

Athletes, performers, and people who do martial arts have used methods like Keep Calm to help them achieve their best.

Model the skill by describing and demonstrating the steps to the class by following this procedure: Present a situation in which you could be irritated or nervous. Describe the situation, then say:

First, I would tell myself, "STOP."

Then I would tell myself, "Use Keep Calm to calm down."

Then, I would take two long, deep breaths. First, I would let out all the air in my lungs through my mouth. Then I would take a slow and smooth breath of air in through my nose to the count of five. I would hold that breath for the count of two and then slowly let the air out through my mouth to the count

*of five, while still saying to myself on the inside, "Keep Calm."
Then I would do the breathing again.*

When I felt better I would say to myself, "Good job." Using self-control can be hard work, and you need to praise yourself.

Ask students to watch carefully while you model how to breathe before they try. Demonstrate the procedure, counting with your fingers to five while taking a breath in. Count to two again while holding your breath and again to five while breathing out. Then repeat the breathing. Bring your hands down to your sides while you are releasing the breath through your mouth—indicating that you are saying, "Keep Calm." Smile after completing the breathing to indicate you are telling yourself "good job" on the inside.

Also, show students how Keep Calm should *not* look (puffed out cheeks, breath holding, silliness).

7. Conduct a practice activity.

Have everyone try the procedure. Look for students who are doing the procedure correctly. Be specific in praising—"Nice, smooth breathing." If children need correction, state it positively, with information about what to do. For example, say, "Slow down your breathing" rather than "Don't go so fast."

Tell students that using Keep Calm does not need to be loud or obvious to others. Ask them for examples of times they could use Keep Calm. After every example, have the whole group pretend that they are in the situation and again practice doing the Keep Calm steps.

Generate situations when Keep Calm may be used. Most situations fall into three main categories.

- When you are nervous. (Before a test, up at bat, giving a speech, or during other types of performance.)

- When you really need to concentrate. (Working on a test, working after recess, when you are distracted by noise in the room.)

- When you are angry or frustrated and about to lose your cool. (Beginning to yell during an argument or when you feel like you will do something that will get you into trouble.)

8. Conduct additional practice activities.

If time and interest permit (and it may be useful to apply this topic across two sessions), some additional practice activities often prove useful:

- Have students write situations where Keep Calm could be used. Keep their examples on hand for future practice.

- Present students with situations through staging role-plays, acting out a situation yourself, or showing a video or pictures and then having students add examples of their own to those presented. The following situations may be used:

Feeling fidgety and talking in class

Feeling nervous about a test or a report

Being lost in a shopping center

Going to a new school

Competing in a sports event

- Introduce an object (a stuffed animal, a pen, a swatch of soft cloth like velvet or velour) called "Keeping Calm." Make sure it is something quite different from the Speaker Power object. When an incident occurs in class and a student is upset, you can give them the object to hold to remind them to keep calm.

- Have the students draw a picture of someone before and after using the Keep Calm exercise.

9. Introduce a Reflective Summary.

As outlined in the Introduction, ask students to reflect on the question "What did you learn from today's lesson?" Reinforce key themes, then go over any follow-up work.

10. Follow up.

The following steps will help make sure that the students have a chance to continue working with the new concepts.

Assignment

Encourage students to find a time when they can use Keep Calm and try it. Let them know that you will expect an example of how they used Keep Calm at the next session.

Take-Home

Students can create posters with the Keep Calm steps as well as bring the Keep Calm worksheet to their parents or guardians. Parents and guardians should be encouraged to review the steps and hang the poster and handout in a place where their child needs to remember to use Keep Calm, such as by the TV, in their room, or on the refrigerator. Parents and guardians should also be encouraged to remind their child to use the Keep Calm technique, as well as to be alert to Trigger Situations and Feelings Fingerprints.

Plans to Promote Transfer and Generalization of Skill

1. Make several posters of the steps of Keep Calm and have students decorate them. Place them in areas of the room where they can best be used by students to guide them through the steps while the skill is still new to them.

2. Use Keep Calm skill prompts when a child is upset or is beginning to lose control. Say:

   Use your Keep Calm steps.

   Stop and think about what's happening.

   Let's Keep Calm and get focused.

   Let's take a look at what's going on—describe what is happening and how you are feeling.

   Take a deep breath and Keep Calm—then we can talk about it.

3. In language arts, find characters who are experiencing strong emotions and could use the Keep Calm exercise. Ask students how the story could have changed if the character had used Keep Calm.

4. Remind children about Keep Calm before potentially stressful situations and changes in class, such as transitions to art, music, physical education, lunch, and playground period.

TIPS FOR TEACHERS

1. Some students may need a real-life example of what it is like to be nervous, antsy, or lose their temper. This can be illustrated in several ways: Use a mirror to show differences in physical appearance before and after using Keep Calm. Jogging in place to increase breathing can also help show the contrast before and after Keep Calm.

2. Some students may have difficulty conceptualizing the breathing component of this strategy. Using "Smell the Pizza" cards (see Worksheet 2.21.3) is helpful for these children. They can pretend that they are holding a slice of pizza. They can breathe in to smell how good the fresh pizza smells, pause to enjoy it, and then they can blow on the hot, fresh pizza to cool it down. (This approach can be helpful either with or without the reminder cards.)

3. Some students will learn to use their Feelings Fingerprints as a signal to use Keep Calm. Others will be prompted by Trigger Situations or other sets of cues. Regardless, the lesson is designed to introduce the concept. The skill will be learned to the extent that students are prompted and reminded to use the skill in salient everyday situations.

4. The goal of Keep Calm is to have students use the skill before they lose their self-control and not wait until after they are already very upset.

5. Regularly discuss and reinforce the use of Keep Calm and find occasions to talk about the use of the skill. These discussions will promote future use of self-control.

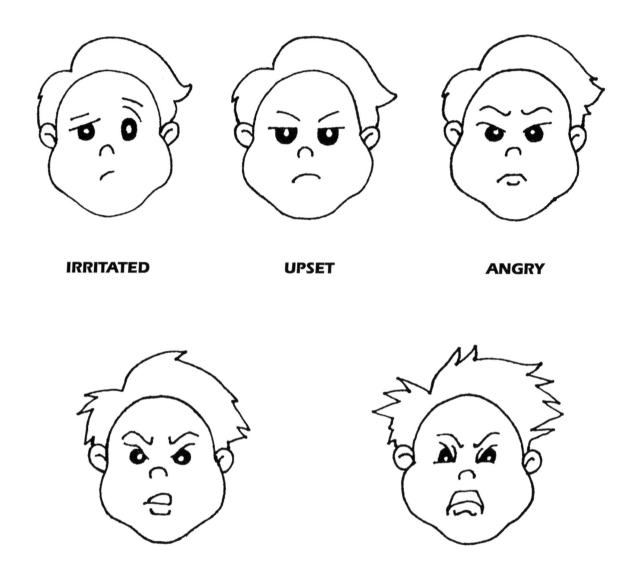

IRRITATED   **UPSET**   **ANGRY**

FURIOUS   **ENRAGED**

Keep Calm

1. Tell yourself to STOP.

2. Tell yourself to KEEP CALM.

3. Slow down your breathing with two long, deep breaths.

4. Praise yourself for a job well done.

From *Social Decision Making/Social Problem Solving: A Curriculum for Academic, Social, and Emotional Learning* (Grades 2–3).
Copyright © 2005 by Maurice J. Elias and Linda Bruene Butler. Research Press (800-519-2707; www.researchpress.com)

Keep Calm

Your child has been learning a valuable skill called Keep Calm, along with some other terms.

- **Trigger Situation:** A trigger is a situation in which a person has a strong feeling, such as nervousness, anger, fear, or excitement.

- **Feelings Fingerprints** are physical signs of stress, such as headache, feeling hot or flushed, clenching fists, or rapid heartbeat. Everyone feels stress in a different way, just as we each have different fingerprints.

- **Keep Calm** is a stress management technique that helps a person calm down to think clearly and problem solve.

   The steps in Keep Calm are as follows:

   1. Tell yourself to STOP.

   2. Tell yourself to KEEP CALM.

   3. Slow down your breathing with two long, deep breaths.

   4. Praise yourself for a job well done.

Keep Calm at Home

Hold a family meeting and make a list of Trigger Situations, having everyone add one or more of their triggers to the list. Also, make a list of the Feelings Fingerprints that accompany these situations. Discuss ways that family members can help remind each other to use Keep Calm. Also, discuss any ideas for solving some of these problems, so that some of the triggers can be avoided in the future.

Your child may be asked in class to share what happened when you practiced this activity.

Thank you!

_____   _____

(Teacher signature)   *(Date)*

- -

(Please sign and return this bottom section.)   **Keep Calm   3.18.3**

Student _____ **Date** _____

We tried Keep Calm.   ❒ Yes   ❒ No

If you did, how did it go?

_____

(Signature of parent or guardian)

19 Introduction to Problem Diaries

OBJECTIVES
- To provide students with practice in dealing with conflicts and criticism by keeping calm and using BEST
- To introduce and practice using a Problem Diary to self-monitor
- To practice Keep Calm and "Be Your BEST" skills

MATERIALS
Copies of the "Problem Diary" (Worksheet 3.19.1)

Copies of the "Problem Diary (Alternate 1)" (Worksheet 3.19.2) and "Problem Diary (Alternate 2)" (Worksheet 3.19.3) *(optional)*

INSTRUCTIONAL ACTIVITIES

1. Review Topic 18 in a Sharing Circle.

Ask the students to share situations when they used Keep Calm. Allow students time to share their efforts and recognize any successes. Remind them that remembering to use Keep Calm when emotions are strong is hard for everyone. As needed, review the components of Keep Calm and BEST (body posture, eye contact, speech, and tone of voice) and practice the behavioral components of these skills.

2. Demonstrate the practice activity.

Choose two children to role-play one of the next two situations, demonstrating both Keep Calm and Be Your BEST.

- You are riding your bike with your friends. You slip on a wet spot in the road and your front tire hits another bike, causing one of your friends to fall and get hurt. Your other friends think you caused the crash on purpose and are angry at you.

- You are on the playground and two children start making fun of your shirt.

Give the chosen pair of students time to practice. While they are practicing, divide the rest of the class into four groups. Assign each a different task. One group is to concentrate on the body posture, one on eye contact, one on speech, and one on tone of voice.

After the role-play, review it by discussing each component of BEST. Here are some useful discussion questions:

- Were the students calm?
- Did they have an even tone of voice?
- Did they look at each other or away?
- Did they use nice speech?
- Did they stand tall, or were they slumped over or hunched?

3. Introduce the Problem Diary.

Distribute copies of the "Problem Diary" (Worksheet 3.19.1) to each student. Explain that the Problem Diary is something to use when there's no one around to help manage a Trigger Situation.

4. Apply the Problem Diary.

Have students fill out a Problem Diary, using the most recent role-play situation. Let children know that they are all going to pretend that they are the student who role-played the part of the person being faced with a Trigger Situation. Say:

> Let's imagine that we are [name of student] and are going to use a Problem Diary to review how well we think we remembered and used Keep Calm and BEST.

Together, read each question and discuss possible answers. After each question, give students a chance to write their answers. Repeat with another role-play as time allows.

5. Conduct additional practice activities.

Continue to role-play situations as time allows. Here are some role-play situations that you can use in this lesson or at other times:

- You spent a lot of time working on a math paper. Instead of subtracting, you added all the numbers. The teacher tells you to do it over again. You are very frustrated.
- Two kids want you to take something out of someone's desk. You know it is wrong and say no. They make fun of you for being a chicken. You are very upset.
- Today you need to bring a signed note to school so you can go ice skating with your class. You love to go ice skating. You remember to check for the note five minutes before the morning school bus will arrive. You know that you had a signed note, but now you can't find it. If you don't have the note you cannot go skating. The bus will be here in four minutes now!
- Your class has to stay inside during lunch hour because it is rain-

ing, and several classmates start to play a game together. You ask to join them, but they say you can't because they have enough people to play already.

6. Introduce a Reflective Summary.

As outlined in the Introduction, ask students to reflect on the question "What did you learn from today's lesson?" Reinforce key themes, then go over any follow-up work.

7. Follow up.

The following steps will help make sure that the students have a chance to continue working with the new concepts.

Assignment

Distribute clean copies of the Problem Diary. Have students complete them for homework, using a Trigger Situation that arises during the upcoming week. Tell students that they will be sharing their Problem Diary with the class.

Take-Home

Send home a copy of the Problem Diary. Include with it a note saying something like:

This is a Problem Diary. I use it in class when students are upset or having a problem they need to solve. Feel free to make copies of this worksheet and ask your child to fill it out when he or she is having a problem around the house (for example, with homework, chores, siblings, or friends).

In addition to the general suggestions listed, add some personal recommendations for individual students you feel would be helpful for their parents or guardians. Many parents and guardians have used Problem Diaries as a tool to help their children deal with Trigger Situations at home.

Plans to Promote Transfer and Generalization of Skill

1. Continue to provide opportunities for students to practice using their skills through short role-plays, using situations listed in Step 5 or short hypothetical situations that represent a common problem for students in your class. You can use these activities as a transition to or from playground and recess or as time allows through the course of the school day.

2. Problem Diaries are also useful tools for guidance counselors, child study team members, principals, and vice principals to help students in dealing with difficult situations. Some schools have had success providing lunch and playground aides with a Keep Calm area and a stack of Problem Diaries. Children benefit most from interventions that help them link reflection about their behavior to the immediate situation.

3. Have students with conflicts fill out Problem Diaries before entering into peer mediation or conflict resolution. Doing so helps them think rather than simply react, and having the brain activated in a task brings them out of that high emotional state. Have students read each other's Problem Diaries prior to mediation, or have them complete one from the point of view of the other person as well as their own.

TIPS FOR TEACHERS

1. Have a stack of blank Problem Diaries available for use when Trigger Situations arise. Some teachers set up a Keep Calm corner where skill step posters are displayed so students can reflect on their behavior, practice Keep Calm, and complete a Problem Diary.

2. When students encounter a problem or Trigger Situation, they can complete the worksheet. Students can keep the completed worksheets for themselves in a social decision making portfolio or notebook to assess skill gains, or they can use them to confer with the teacher to help solve their problem and avoid future difficulties.

3. Some teachers leave a box for completed Problem Diaries to be turned in and used as future hypothetical situations for social problem solving and social decision making lessons.

4. Problem Diaries have been given different names by different schools (for example, Trouble Tracker, Hassle Log, Trigger Journals, In Retrospect). As long as all the teachers in your school agree, at least at a given grade level, feel free to rename the form.

5. If students seem to be having difficulty with the Problem Diary and role-play practice, try using one of the alternate forms (Worksheets 3.19.2 or 3.19.3), which are less complex.

Student _____ **Date** _____

Time: ❏ Morning   ❏ Afternoon   ❏ Evening

Where were you?

SCHOOL   HOME

❏ Classroom   ❏ House
❏ Hallway   ❏ Street
❏ Lunchroom   ❏ Playground
❏ School bus   ❏ Other (specify) _____

What happened?

❏ Somebody teased me   ❏ Somebody started fighting with me
❏ Somebody took something of mine   ❏ Somebody did something wrong
❏ Somebody told me to do something   ❏ Other _____
❏ Somebody was doing something I didn't like

Who was that somebody?

❏ Another student   ❏ Teacher   ❏ Parent   ❏ Another adult   ❏ Sibling

What did you do?

❏ Hit back   ❏ Told adult
❏ Ran away   ❏ Walked away calmly
❏ Yelled   ❏ Talked it out
❏ Cried   ❏ Told peer
❏ Broke something   ❏ Ignored
❏ Was restrained   ❏ Other _____

How did you handle yourself? *(Circle one.)*

1	2	3	4	5
poorly	not so well	OK	well	great

How upset were you? *(Circle one.)*

1	2	3	4	5
mad	really upset	pretty upset	a little upset but still OK	not upset at all

What could you do that would help you stay calm and in control?

_____

_____

Student _____ Date _____

What happened?

How did you feel?

**What did you want
to have happen?**

**What is something you
could have done to
make that happen?**

Student _____ Date _____

Trigger Situation _____

_____

KEEP CALM   😊 😐 ☹️

Body Posture   😊 😐 ☹️

Eye Contact   😊 😐 ☹️

Speech (Say something nice.) 😊 😐 ☹️

Tone of Voice   😊 😐 ☹️

What did you like about how you handled the situation? _____

_____

_____

What would you do differently? _____

_____

_____

TOPIC

20   Using Problem Diaries in Our
      Lives: Part 1

OBJECTIVES
- To continue to practice using the Problem Diary, applying it to real-life Trigger Situations
- To establish ways that the Problem Diary will be used as a tool to keep track of Keep Calm and BEST skills in daily life and team-work situations

MATERIALS   Copies of the "Problem Diary" (Worksheet 3.19.1)

NOTE   If students have not come with Problem Diaries, give them time to complete one, using a recent situation in which they faced a Trigger Situation.

INSTRUCTIONAL ACTIVITIES

1. Conduct a Sharing Circle.

Ask students to share a Problem Diary situation or recent Trigger Situation. Review listening skills and components of Keep Calm and Be Your BEST, as needed. Tell students that during this lesson they will continue to practice ways to use Problem Diaries, Keep Calm, and Be Your BEST in real-life situations.

2. Practice using the Problem Diaries.

Divide the class into pairs and instruct each pair to share their Problem Diaries. Students should give feedback on their partner's situation and then switch roles. After they have done so, invite volunteers to share their situations with the whole class.

3. Select a situation and conduct a role-play.

Choose a situation from those volunteered and help the student who volunteered it choose coactors from the class to perform a role-play. Ask the students to role-play either what they did to use Keep Calm and BEST or—if they did not remember to use these skills—how they could have used them in the situation. Guide the role-play according to the suggestions in Topic 7. Assign the audience the task of watching for specific components of BEST.

4. Discuss alternative solutions and conduct additional role-plays.

Have the class analyze the role-play and talk about whether the solution role-played worked to solve the problem. Have students create alternative solutions that might resolve the situation and role-play those as well. Perform additional role-plays as time permits.

5. Introduce a Reflective Summary.

As outlined in the Introduction, ask students to reflect on the question "What did you learn from today's lesson?" Reinforce key themes, then go over any follow-up work.

6. Follow up.

The following steps will help make sure that the students have a chance to continue working with the new concepts.

Assignment

Distribute a new copy of the Problem Diary and have students complete it for homework, using a situation that arises during the upcoming week. Tell students that during the next session you will be role-playing some of these situations.

Plans to Promote Transfer and Generalization of Skill

Have students complete Problem Diaries from the point of view of characters in literature and social studies. Assess how well the characters managed their emotions and communicated effectively.

TIPS FOR TEACHERS

1. Use the version of the Problem Diary you feel is most appropriate for your students (Worksheet 3.19.1, 3.19.2, or 3.19.3).

2. Problem Diaries can be shared with parents during conferences or disciplinary meetings.

3. Role-play situations that you feel are most relevant to your students. Emphasize that there is always more than one way to handle a difficult situation. This activity is getting the students ready for more advanced problem solving and decision making.

21 Using Problem Diaries in Our Lives: Part 2

OBJECTIVES
- To continue to practice using the Problem Diary in real-life Trigger Situations
- To develop an understanding of respect, fairness, and good citizenship
- To create a list of specific behaviors related to good citizenship

MATERIALS
Copies of "Problem Diary (Alternate 1)" (Worksheet 3.19.2)
"Good Friendship Behaviors" list (generated in Topic 12)
Poster board and markers

NOTE
When the group has determined their final list of "Good Citizenship Behaviors," write or have students write them on a sheet of poster board and display them in the classroom. Students can also help by illustrating the poster.

INSTRUCTIONAL ACTIVITIES

1. Conduct a Sharing Circle.

Ask students to talk about what these words and phrases mean to them: *respect, being fair,* and *good citizenship.* Make and post a chart of students' ideas. As time allows, compare and contrast with the "Good Friendship Behaviors" list made earlier.

2. Discuss Trigger Situations.

In groups of four, have students share Trigger Situations they have experienced recently. Ask each group to pick one and complete a Problem Diary with these extra instructions:

When you think of what you want to have happen and what you might do, be sure your answers are respectful, fair, and show good citizenship.

Walk around and help the groups and listen to how they try to incorporate ideas about good character into problem solving.

Conclude by sharing the best examples you hear and encouraging the students to be respectful and fair and to show good citizenship when they solve problems.

3. Introduce a Reflective Summary.

As outlined in the Introduction, ask students to reflect on the question "What did you learn from today's lesson?" Reinforce key themes, then go over any follow-up work.

4. Follow up.

The following step will help make sure that the students have a chance to continue working with the new concepts.

Assignment

Distribute new copies of the "Problem Diary" worksheet and have students complete them for homework, using a situation that arises during the upcoming week or something that happens to a character in a book, movie, or other media performance. Ask them to check to see that their answers are respectful and fair and show good citizenship. Emphasize that there is always more than one way to handle a difficult situation. Remind students that this activity is getting them ready for more advanced problem solving and decision making.

TIPS FOR TEACHERS

1. Problem Diaries can be shared with parents and guardians during conferences or disciplinary meetings. Provide them with blank copies they can use at home, if needed.

2. Support staff such as cafeteria aides, classroom aides, and after-school care workers can be taught to use the Problem Diary so that they can prompt students to use this tool when problems arise.

3. When conflicts arise in the classroom and solutions are suggested, ask students to reflect on whether their ideas show respect, fairness, and good citizenship.

SOCIAL DECISION MAKING
AND SOCIAL PROBLEM SOLVING

Topics 22–26

22   Introduction to FIG TESPN

OBJECTIVES
- To introduce students to step-by-step problem solving (FIG TESPN)
- To learn and practice the first three steps (FIG)

MATERIALS
Whole-class display of the "FIG TESPN Ladder" (Worksheet 3.22.1)
Copies of the "FIG Worksheet" (3.22.2)
Chalkboard or easel pad

INSTRUCTIONAL ACTIVITIES

1. Begin with a Sharing Circle.

Briefly review past lessons by having students share recent Problem Diaries.

2. Introduce the new topic.

Tell students that they have learned many important skills that will help them to solve problems and work together as a team. Today's new skill will let them use a step-by-step process to think about what they can do to solve a problem.

3. Ask the students to tell you what the word problem means.

After a few answers, take out a dictionary and use it and what the students said to provide a definition. As part of the definition, indicate that a problem is something that happens to someone or between people that usually makes them feel unhappy or uncomfortable.

4. Lead in to the new skill components.

Start by asking students:

What skills have you learned that may help you solve a problem?

Say that those skills are even better if they're used in an organized way. Display the FIG TESPN Ladder and introduce FIG TESPN as a step-by-step way to get out of a problem situation and get back on top with success:

FIG TESPN stands for each one of the rungs on this ladder. If we use it step by step, we can solve a problem and feel like the frog in the picture. How does the frog look? . . . We can feel that way, too.

Ask students to read each of the steps of the ladder along with you, starting at the bottom.

F —Find the Feelings

I —Identify the Problem

G—Guide Yourself with a Goal

T —Think of Many Possible Solutions

E —Envision Consequences

S —Select the Best Solution

P —Plan and Be Prepared for Pitfalls

N—Notice What Happened (Now What?)

Explain that as you go down the list (and up the ladder), each skill builds on the one before it.

For example, the step from F to I works like this: Rather than stopping when we identify the feelings word, the next step teaches us to describe the problem in a specific way. In this way, "I feel silly" becomes "I feel silly because I did my math homework but forgot to bring it in."

5. Work with F and I.

Ask students for possible problems for the following feelings:

■ I feel sad because . . .

■ I feel annoyed because . . .

■ I feel nervous because . . .

Ask the class to recall what they learned about how strong feelings affect a person's ability to think clearly. Summarize by saying:

Strong feelings influence how we might think about a problem. If feelings are strong, Keep Calm is the first step to clear thinking. Keep Calm, however, does not solve the problem. Keep Calm helps a person become ready to think and go up the ladder and problem solve. FIG TESPN is a strategy that can help people learn to think clearly about a problem and come up with a plan for how to make things better.

6. Introduce the first three FIG steps.

Tell the class that these first steps help to set up a problem in a clear and constructive way. If students have been learning to set up word problems in math, ask them what would happen if you set up the problem incorrectly. As in math, if the problem is not set up right, it would be very difficult to come up with the right solution. Explain that the first three steps can also help them become better communicators.

Take the students up the FIG (Feelings, Identify the problem, Goal) part of the ladder by using the sample problem given in this step.

List F, I, and G on the chalkboard or easel pad, as displayed on the FIG Worksheet. Record responses generated by the group.

Sample problem:

> Judy has a lot of trouble reading and goes to a special teacher. The other students in the class are pages or even books ahead of her. One day as she is returning to class, she overhears some other students say, "Judy is really dumb. She can't read at all."

Feelings

First, start at the bottom skill (F) and turn it into a question. Ask first what feelings Judy would have. Generate several feelings words. Refer children to a list of feelings words, if needed. (You may want to ask the children what the other students might be feeling, but only record feelings for Judy on the worksheet because the goal is to use FIG to set up the problem from Judy's point of view.)

Identify the Problem

Then move on to the next skill (I). Have students tell what they think the problem is. Be careful not to confuse the problem with the goal or a possible solution. The problem is a clear, objective description of what is making Judy unhappy. For example, the problem is not "Judy needs to ignore them" (a possible solution) or "Judy wants them to stop gossiping and treat her with respect" (a possible goal). Instead, state the problem in terms like these: "The children are making fun of Judy" or "Judy is a poor reader." Both of these are clear and objective, factual statements that describe the problems that Judy has.

Goal

Once the problem is established, it's much easier to deal with the third skill (G). Ask students:

> What does Judy want to have happen? . . . What would it be like if the problem were solved? . . . You have to know what you want to have happen before you can think about what to do. There are many ways to solve problems, and you have to really think to be sure you have the right answer for you.

Review the responses generated by the group for Judy. Ask them if they think Judy's problem is now clear.

*Once a problem is clear and we understand the goal, we can
start to think about what can be done to reach the goal. Using
social problem solving skill steps can help Judy and all of us
to be clearer thinkers and more successful problem solvers.*

7. Conduct a practice activity.

As time allows, use the sample problems below to have students
practice going up the first three steps of the FIG TESPN Ladder.
Distribute the FIG Worksheet and have students complete responses
to describe the feelings, identify the problem, and generate a goal from
the point of view of the lead character (Paulo in the first problem and
Keisha in the second). Students can work individually, in pairs, or in
small groups.

- Paulo has been looking forward to the regional playoff game all
  week. He is the third baseman. The day before the big game he
  trips and sprains his ankle. He cannot play baseball for three
  weeks.

- Keisha has been best friends with Sandy since first grade. They
  spend most of their free time together. Now a new kid has come
  into Sandy's class, and Sandy is spending a lot of time with the
  newcomer, excluding Keisha.

8. Introduce a Reflective Summary.

As outlined in the Introduction, ask students to reflect on the question "What did you learn from today's lesson?" Reinforce key themes,
then go over any follow-up work.

9. Follow up.

The following steps will help make sure that the students have a
chance to continue working with the new concepts.

Assignment

Distribute more copies of the FIG Worksheet and have students make
a list of all the problems and decisions that they encounter in a day
or in a week. Have them be prepared to share one or more of these
problems or decisions using FIG during the next session.

Take-Home

Send home a copy of the FIG TESPN Ladder. In a cover letter, ask parents and guardians to review it with their children. Parents and
guardians can help children practice by guiding them up the first three

steps of the ladder (FIG) before they come up with ideas about how to resolve a problem that the child has encountered.

Plans to Promote Transfer and Generalization of Skill

Social Application

Over the next week, when a visible situation occurs that involves an embarrassing or teasing remark, take time with the whole class to generate a FIG to better understand what people feel and want in these situations.

Language Arts Application

1. In creative writing, ask the class to use their imaginations to complete the following statements. Any one of these could be the opening sentence of a paragraph or short story.

   - Tran felt disappointed because . . .
   - The policeman felt confused because . . .
   - Robert was overjoyed because . . .
   - The baseball player felt thrilled because . . .
   - The Johnson family felt very pleased when . . .

2. During reading, ask students what a character's feelings and problem and goal might be by stopping at critical points as stories are read. This can also be done during reading in social studies.

TIPS FOR TEACHERS

1. In the third grade, most children reach a stage of cognitive development when they can begin to "think about the way they think." Developmentally, it becomes possible for them to begin to learn cognitive strategies that can guide their problem-solving thought process. This topic area provides students with an introduction to an eight-step problem-solving strategy called FIG TESPN. In the beginning, teachers should expect that students will need a lot of prompting and coaching from adults to use their thinking skills. It is only through extensive practice that children will begin to internalize and independently self-monitor their thinking.

2. The primary objective for skill building in the third grade is to provide extensive practice in the first three steps of problem solving (FIG). The FIG steps provide a solid base to beginning problem solving that is also realistic, given students' emerging cognitive abilities.

3. The use of the concept of a *problem* has special value. First, it encourages children to describe social matters with the same familiar language that they use in math or science. Second, placing a social difficulty into a problem context suggests optimistically

that it may be solvable. By generating a goal, a problem is turned into a statement of something that can be achieved instead of something that is wrong or unclear.

4. Another important aspect of this skill is that if students can put what is bothering them into words, a seemingly overwhelming situation becomes manageable. "I feel sad" becomes "I feel sad because I forgot to feed the dog."

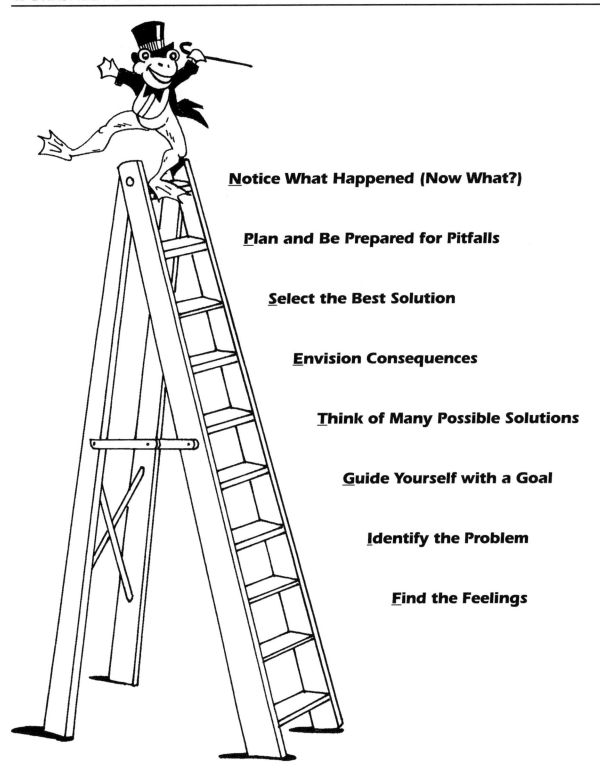

Notice What Happened (Now What?)

Plan and Be Prepared for Pitfalls

Select the Best Solution

Envision Consequences

Think of Many Possible Solutions

Guide Yourself with a Goal

Identify the Problem

Find the Feelings

Student _____ Date _____

F eelings

(List as many as you can.)

_____

_____

_____

_____

I dentify the problem

(Use clear and descriptive statements.)

_____

_____

_____

_____

G oal

(What would you like to have happen?)

_____

_____

_____

_____

23 Using FIG to Give Constructive Criticism

OBJECTIVES
- To identify the difference between positive (that is, constructive) and negative criticism
- To link constructive criticism with the first three steps of problem solving and with "I-messages"
- To practice giving criticism in a constructive manner, using FIG, Keep Calm, and BEST

MATERIALS
Whole-class display of the "FIG TESPN Ladder" (Worksheet 3.22.1)

Copies of "Using FIG to Give Constructive Criticism" (Worksheet 3.23.1) and the "Using FIG" Take-Home (Worksheet 3.23.2)

INSTRUCTIONAL ACTIVITIES

1. Conduct a Sharing Circle.

Review the FIG TESPN Ladder and ask students for examples of how they used the first three steps (FIG).

2. Introduce the idea of kinds of criticism.

Obtain students' interest by telling them that you would like to share a couple of stories with them. Then present these contrasting stories:

- Students are playing kick ball during recess. Marco is playing first base. He is not paying attention when the ball is thrown to him to make the third out. The winning run scores! Sheila, Marco's team captain, runs toward him, yelling, "You idiot! You don't know how to play kick ball! You'll never be on my team again!"

- Students are playing kick ball during recess. Marco is playing first base. He is not paying attention when the ball is thrown to him to make the third out. The winning run scores! Sheila, Marco's team captain, runs toward him and says, "I'm mad because you were not paying attention when the ball was thrown to you, and now we lost the game. If you want to play first base, please remember to keep your eye on the ball."

Ask the class what Sheila was doing to Marco in these stories. (You'll get answers like "giving him put-downs" and "criticizing him.") Once the word comes up (and you should introduce it if the first three or four tries don't include it), ask the class what *criticism* is. (You're looking for answers like telling someone when you disagree with what they are doing or when they are doing something wrong, asking them to change or stop the behavior you do not like.) Then ask:

> *How did Marco feel in the first story when Shelia criticized him? . . . How do you think he reacted? . . . How did Marco feel in the second story when he was criticized? . . . How do you think he reacted this time?*

3. Talk about constructive criticism.

Continue by saying:

> *Sometimes it is important to ask someone to change what they are doing. Letting someone know that you have a problem with their behavior and asking them to change or stop is called criticism. It is important to criticize in the correct way so that the person will listen to what you have to say. In which story was it easier for Marco to listen to the criticism? Why?*

4. Review the first three steps of problem solving.

Refer students to the FIG TESPN Ladder and review the first three steps of problem solving:

Find the feelings (F).

Identify the problem (I).

Guide yourself with a *goal* (G).

Explain that to criticize in a positive manner, it's necessary to use all three steps, in that order:

F: Say what you see and feel.

I: Give a reason why you do not like it (that is, identify the problem).

G: Tell what you want instead (your goal).

5. Conduct a practice activity.

Read the second story again and review the procedure in Step 4. Ask:

> *What words did Sheila use to say what she saw? (You were not paying attention when the ball was thrown.)*

> *What words did Sheila use to show why she did not like Marco's behavior? (I'm mad. . . . We lost the game.)*

What words did Sheila use to show what she wanted instead?
(Keep your eye on the ball.)

6. Practice with the worksheet.

Distribute the "Using FIG to Give Constructive Criticism" worksheet and have students practice developing FIG statements to deliver constructive criticism in the situations provided. First, explain and model that sometimes you may not like something about a person:

If someone comes in with a new haircut and it does not look very nice, what could you do?

You could say nothing about it and talk about something else. Or you could say, "Boy, your hair looks funny," or "Hey, I see you got a haircut." Which would be the better thing to say? Why?

In this case, it is better to say what you see rather than saying how you feel. Why do you think it might be better to say what you see rather than what you feel? (Insults may hurt the other person's feelings and provoke them not to listen to what you have to say.)

Then have the students complete the worksheet. Review and share as time allows.

7. Introduce a Reflective Summary.

As outlined in the Introduction, ask students to reflect on the question "What did you learn from today's lesson?" Reinforce key themes, then go over any follow-up work.

8. Follow up.

The following steps will help make sure that the students have a chance to continue working with the new concepts.

Assignment

Have students practice giving constructive criticism during sharing of academic assignments, classwork, or projects by asking them to use the first three steps of FIG TESPN when they need to give feedback to others.

Take-Home

Distribute the "Using FIG" Take-Home. The worksheet describes FIG and suggests that parents and guardians try using FIG when they would like their children to change their behavior.

Plans to Promote Transfer and Generalization of Skill

Behavior Management

Model using FIG statements to engage students in problem solving a situation you have identified regarding the performance or behavior of a student or the class. Present children with a FIG statement that describes *your* feelings, identified problem, and goals or objectives linked with classroom or school rules or academic achievement.

If using a FIG in a problem situation, it is often good to begin by telling the class or student that you have a problem. You may also want to ask the class or child to use their Listening Power while you have Speaker Power. It is also often a good idea to begin the discussion by all using Keep Calm together, depending on the situation. Use FIG to frame the discussion. For example:

> *I have a problem and I am going to share it with you, using FIG.*
>
> *F—Feelings: I am feeling very frustrated right now.*
>
> *I—Identify the problem: We have a lot of work to finish, and many people are spending time off-task.*
>
> *G—Goal: We need to finish this work before lunch and recess time. I do not want to have you miss recess time to finish.*
>
> *How many of you want to finish so that we do not have to stay in from recess?*
>
> *What ideas do you have so that we can solve this problem?*

Engage the students in coming up with some ideas and as soon as several good ideas are generated, suggest that they try them.

Social Applications

Have students use FIG when they encounter problems or are giving feedback during cooperative learning activities, during physical education, and during recess.

TIPS FOR TEACHERS

1. Two of the skills covered in this curriculum (this Topic, "Using FIG to Give Constructive Criticism," and Topic 29, "Joining a New Group") base their skill components on behaviors that differentiate students who are effective in their peer relationships from

those who experience peer rejection. Giving criticism or negative feedback to someone and entering a new group are both difficult social situations, and sometimes even the most socially skilled students may experience an unsuccessful interaction or rejection.

Just as with the skill of BEST, it is important to stress that using BEST and constructive criticism gives students their best shot at being successful but does not guarantee success. After students have had an opportunity to role-play the skill of giving constructive criticism in scenarios where the recipient accepts it, it can be helpful to then have them anticipate potential obstacles or ways that someone might respond negatively to their constructive criticism. Planning ways to respond to those obstacles will help them be prepared for both positive and negative reactions. Stress the importance of knowing that they are being their BEST and that these skills give them their best chance of success.

2. We have found that focusing on a motivation goal enhances the success of an adult-delivered FIG designed to address behavior management issues. Note, for example, in the situation illustrated under "Behavior Management" in the "Follow up" activity, the teacher is stating a personal goal for what should and should not happen. The goal is to appeal to the motivation of the students. Even if the behavior is currently a problem, a FIG can create a positive vision for what can be achieved. Often avoiding a negative consequence helps, too, but focusing on what you would like the children to do in a positive way with confidence that they can do it helps the students join in the goal you are setting as the authority figure. For example, a goal statement might be "What I would like us to do is work together to come up with a plan to help you remember to bring in your homework. You are in third grade now, and I know you are smart enough to solve this problem if we keep working at it." Depending on the class, you can describe a negative consequence you want to avoid: "I think we can do this together so I do not have to call a meeting with your parents." You could also refer to not wanting to take away privileges or points or other consequences—whatever the students are likely to find less attractive than fulfilling your goal.

3. The first three steps of FIG TESPN also overlap with skills labeled "I-messages" in a wide variety of cooperative learning and conflict resolution skills curricula. These materials (adapted when needed) can provide valuable supplemental and extension activities for skill practice.

4. Especially because students are learning to give constructive criticism, they may be more "critical" than "constructive." Sometimes it is a good idea to use a Sharing Circle or naturally occurring opportunities to talk about receiving criticism. The basic steps are to listen carefully, use Keep Calm, ask yourself if the criticism is true, and use your BEST skills to answer the person who gave you

the feedback. Role-playing practice can take place during academic feedback activities to add this aspect of SDM/SPS skills.

Student _____ **Date** _____

1. **You and a friend play soccer on different teams. Today your team lost the game. When the game is over, your friends make fun of you for losing.**

<u>F</u>eelings: I feel _____

_____

_____

<u>I</u>dentify the Problem: (that is, because . . . or when . . .) _____

_____

_____

<u>G</u>oal: I want _____

_____

_____

2. **You're standing in line ready to go out for recess. All of a sudden, a student pushes right in front of you.**

<u>F</u>eelings: I feel _____

_____

_____

<u>I</u>dentify the Problem: (that is, because . . . or when . . .) _____

_____

_____

<u>G</u>oal: I want _____

_____

_____

Using FIG

Your child is learning to use the first three steps of our problem-solving ladder (which we call FIG TESPN) as a guide for putting problems into words in a clear, objective, and constructive way. These are the first three steps:

F: Find the Feelings (Say how you feel.)

I: Identify the Problem (Describe what is happening.)

G: Guide Yourself with a Goal (What is it that you would like to see happen?)

Try the following activities at home.

Coaching and Modeling

When your child is feeling upset, use the FIG steps to help your child express how it feels, clearly describe what it is that is causing the feeling, and then state what he or she wants to have happen. This helps frame the problem in a way that can guide problem-solving action.

Use the FIG steps when you have a problem with your child's behavior:

F (Find the Feelings): Tell your child how the problem behavior makes you feel.

I (Identify the Problem): Say what it is about the behavior that makes you feel that way. What are the consequences of the behavior for the situation?

G (Guide Yourself with a Goal): What is it that you need or want to have happen instead?

Then ask if your child will work on this with you. If your child agrees, ask for ideas that could you help reach your goal.

Your child may be asked in class to share what happened when you practiced this activity.

Thank you!

_____   _____

(Teacher signature)   *(Date)*

- -

(Please sign and return this bottom section.)   **Using FIG   3.23.2**

Student _____ **Date** _____

We practiced using FIG.   ❐ Yes   ❐ No

If you did, how did it go?

_____

(Signature of parent or guardian)

24 Using FIG to Understand Different Points of View

OBJECTIVES
- To introduce the concept of different points of view
- To introduce active listening skills
- To practice active listening skills and FIG
- To practice the "Footsteps" activity to resolve conflicts

MATERIALS
Chalkboard or easel pad

Colored construction paper and scissors

A bell or whistle to signal a change of place in the Footsteps activity *(optional)*

INSTRUCTIONAL ACTIVITIES

1. Introduce the idea of points of view.

Organize students in a Sharing Circle. Begin by saying:

Do we all see the same thing in the same way?

Pick an object in the room and ask students how it would look from where someone else is sitting if that person didn't turn to look at it. For example:

How does the easel look to Katie? What about Jamal? How about Yoni?

Pick students from different parts of the room to convey the idea that what they see depends on their "point of view."

Explain that everyone has a different point of view:

The way we see things can make a difference when we are trying to work out a problem. For example, when I look out at our classroom, I see a group of students. When you look out at our classroom, what do you see? . . . Exactly. Because I am the teacher, I have a different point of view. You see friends and classmates and a teacher, and I see students.

2. Explore the concept of different points of view, using a relevant situation.

Ask:

> *How many of you have a little brother or sister or cousin who sometimes likes to play with things that are yours? . . . What is your point of view? . . . How do you feel? . . . How would you describe this situation from your point of view? . . . What about your brother or sister or cousin? How do you think it feels from their point of view?*

List two columns on the board—one column for "Older Brother/Sister/Cousin" and one for "Younger Brother/Sister/Cousin" and write down the thoughts and feelings of several students who respond.

Some examples for older children:

> *Feelings:* I feel frustrated and worried.
>
> *Point of view:* I do not like my little brother messing with my things because he might break them.

Or:

> *Feelings:* I feel angry.
>
> *Point of view:* My mom wants me to share, but I want special things to be only mine.

Some examples for younger children:

> *Feelings:* I'm excited and happy.
>
> *Point of view:* I want to play with this stuff because it belongs to someone who is older and it's cool.

Or:

> *Feelings:* I feel angry.
>
> *Point of view:* I just want to see it. I like it, too, and I hate being told I am too little.

3. Extend the discussion.

Ask students if they can think of any other examples of times when people had different points of view. Prompt for both academics (history, language arts, social studies) and real-life situations. Be especially alert to current events examples.

Examples may include things like these:

a. The settlers wanted to move West, and the Native Americans did not want people taking over their territory.

b. Two characters in a piece of literature that the class is reading have different points of view about what's happening in the story.

c. My brother and I wanted to watch different TV shows.

d. Someone gets blamed for something they did not do.

4. Introduce the Footsteps activity

Tell students that they will learn more about different points of view when they play a game called "Footsteps." Have each child make a pair of paper feet to stand on in the game.

Display the following three steps on the chalkboard or easel pad, explaining that the idea is to finish each statement that ends in three dots:

Step 1: Use Speaker Power

I feel . . .

I think . . .

I want . . .

Step 2: Use Listening Power

I think I understand what you said.

You feel . . .

You think . . .

You want . . .

"Is that right?"

Step 3: Think of Solutions

"How about if . . .?" or "How can we . . . ?"

Point to the three steps and explain that these steps will be used in an activity to practice taking different points of view by standing in a different place. That is, the idea is to literally move across the floor so each person stands right where the other one started out for the second set of statements, then goes back to the original place for the third. Use your example to demonstrate the process.

Select two students to demonstrate the steps, using the following scenario while you read the viewpoints and step prompts. They should use the sample dialogue as a guide but come up with their own things to say.

Kevin wants the class to put on a show for the school and thinks that his class should be the only performers.

Donna is in Kevin's class and wants to put on a show, too, but she thinks they should invite other classrooms to be a part of the show.

Stage directions:

Step 1: Use Speaker Power

Each actor stands on a pair of paper footprints and explains one of the two points of view, using "I" sentences such as "I think," "I want," or "I feel."

After both have spoken, the students switch places so each stands in the other's footsteps. You should tell them to wait for your signal to switch places, so the one who spoke first isn't tempted to move too soon.

Step 2: Use Listening Power

The actors switch places (to help them get a different sense of perspective). Each person explains the other person's point of view as well as possible, using statements like these: "I think I understand what you said. You feel . . . " "You think . . . " or "You want. . . ." Follow up each sentence with the question "Is that right?" or "Is that how you think or feel?" or "Is that what you want?"

After both have spoken, the students switch places so each stands in their original footsteps. You should tell them to wait for your signal to switch places so the one who spoke first isn't tempted to move too soon.

Step 3: Think of Solutions

Pairs think of ways to work out the problem, taking both points of view into account and using sentences that start with "How about if . . ." or " How can we. . . ." For example:

Kevin: How about if we let our class figure out what kind of show we want to do?

Donna: We could try that, but how about if we come up with the kinds of acts, too, and see if there is any extra time for other classes.

Kevin: That's a good idea.

Donna: All right, I'll ask the teacher for a class meeting about the show.

The actors should then ask the class:

What "I" sentences did you hear us use? How about "you" sentences? What were our "How about if . . ." suggestions? Did we agree on a solution? What was it?

5. Conduct a practice activity.

Explain that students will use the same three steps to act out a problem you will give them.

Divide your group into pairs. Assign parts—one is Child A and one is Child B—in each pair.

Have pairs take their places on facing footsteps around the room.

Read this "Footsteps" problem out loud:

A and B both want the last two pieces of blue construction paper for their book report covers. The students playing A want the blue paper because blue is their favorite color, and the ones playing B want the blue paper because their book report is on oceans of the world.

Give students about one minute for each step, with all pairs acting out the situation at the same time. Remind them to take turns talking.

Walk around the room and listen to what students are doing. If necessary, help with suggestions.

6. Call the large group back together.

Choose one pair to act out the situation for the group.

Ask everyone the following questions:

What else could A or B have said to explain their point of view?

Did they seem to understand each other's point of view? What misunderstandings did you see?

What was the solution they came up with? Would both people reach their goal? What are some other solutions they could try?

7. Use additional practice situations, as time allows.

Have pairs act out one or more of the following situations and talk about each situation, using some of the same questions from Step 6:

- Ashley and Alex are having a misunderstanding. Ashley feels hurt because Alex said Ashley's new shoes were "different." Ashley likes the shoes and wants to wear them all the time. Alex didn't mean to hurt Ashley's feelings. He just thinks the shoes might be too fancy for their camping trip.
- Pick a situation involving two characters under current study in history, social studies, or language arts.
- Pick an example of a current problem from the classroom or playground.
- Use one of the additional scenarios listed under "Tips for Teachers."

8. Introduce a Reflective Summary.

As outlined in the Introduction, ask students to reflect on the question "What did you learn from today's lesson?" Reinforce key themes, then go over any follow-up work.

9. Follow up.

The following steps will help make sure that the students have a chance to continue working with the new concepts.

Plans to Promote Transfer and Generalization of Skill

1. Stop at critical points of a story in language arts, social studies, or other lessons and ask students to role-play—using Footsteps—the different points of view.

2. When conflicts occur on the playground, prompt students to use Keep Calm, and then try using Footsteps to help them think of a way that they could solve their problem.

TIPS FOR TEACHERS

1. Footsteps can also be combined with FIG, especially if students have a hard time taking one another's point of view.

2. Additional conflict situations:

   - One student calls another a name in a humorous way, but the other sees nothing funny about it.

   - Two students want to read the same book. One student says he needs it for a report. The other says it is his favorite book and he wants to read it again.

   - Two students are arguing over a very fancy pen. One says that it looks like the one she bought with her allowance. The other says that it looks like the one given to her by her favorite aunt.

3. Keep two sets of laminated footsteps available to use whenever students are involved in a conflict. That will let you establish "Drop the Feet" as a prompt, directing the students to literally drop the feet and stand on them to carry out the Footsteps procedure. This can also be done at a critical point in a story by asking two students to play the role of two characters who encounter a conflict.

25 Practice Using FIG to Tackle School and Life Problems

OBJECTIVE
- To introduce and practice using FIG TESPN problem-solving steps in a way that can be used on an ongoing basis as a group to help solve real-life problems or make a decision

MATERIALS
Chalkboard or easel pad

Whole-class display of the "FIG TESPN Ladder" (Worksheet 3.22.1)

PREPARATION
Before conducting a lesson on this topic, first choose or prepare a situation that you feel would be appropriate and helpful for the group. This can be done by having students submit situations for the group to solve or by taking a situation that recurs in your class or school. Change the names, make it into a hypothetical story, and have the students solve it. Playground, bus, and gym class are possible trouble spots around which a story can be formulated.

INSTRUCTIONAL ACTIVITIES

1. Start with a Sharing Circle.

Ask if any of the students had an opportunity to use any of the skills they learned in class recently. Reinforce any examples shared. As time permits, ask if anyone had a time during the last week when they wished they had remembered to use their problem-solving skills. Ask what skill or skills they could have used and how they think the situation would have been different if the skills were used.

2. Introduce the Topic.

Remind the students how important it is to remember to use the skills being taught during the social problem solving lessons when they are faced with a problem to solve or a decision to make in their own lives. Listening Power, BEST, FIG, Problem Diaries, and the Keep Calm and Footsteps exercises will all help them to be successful.

3. Display the FIG TESPN Ladder.

Tell the students that today's activity will use the FIG TESPN Ladder to solve everyday problems that children their age might have. Let them know that they will start at the bottom of the ladder and then use the skill steps together to see if they can reach the top with a good solution to the problem.

4. Present a problem.

Choose a problem from suggestions from the class or use a hypothetical situation that describes a common problem situation for children in third grade.

Sample hypothetical situation:

> *Aldo drew a picture in art class that he felt very proud of. He worked hard on it, and when the art teacher passed by his desk, she complimented him on it and asked him to hold it up for the class to see.*

Ask students how they think Aldo might be feeling at this point, then continue:

> *Aldo asked for a pass to get a drink of water, and when he returned to his desk the picture was gone.*

5. Use facilitative questioning to take students up the FIG TESPN Ladder.

Point to the first FIG TESPN step—F, at the bottom of the ladder—and then write "Feelings" on the chalkboard or easel pad. Write the key words of FIG TESPN, in turn, before recording student responses. Turn the problem-solving steps into questions that you ask the group.

Find the feelings:

> *What are all the different feelings Aldo might be having when he returned to his desk?*

Expect answers such as mad, upset, puzzled, betrayed, sad, furious.

Identify the problem:

> *What is Aldo's problem? What is a clear and descriptive problem statement?*

Aldo's picture is missing.

Guide yourself with goals:

> *What do you think Aldo wants to have happen? What is his goal?*

Aldo wants his picture back. Do not accept possible solutions (find out who took it, ask the teacher, and similar statements) as the goal. If students propose that sort of thing—and they probably will—ask:

> *Is that a goal or a solution? A goal is what we want to have happen, not the ways to make it happen. We have to stand on the goal rung to get to the next step on the ladder, thinking of solutions. Let's set up a good goal statement for Aldo so we know what it is he wants to have happen.*

Think of many possible solutions:

> *What can Aldo do to reach his goal? What can he do to solve his problem? What ideas do you have?*

Accept and record all responses without judging. The brainstorming momentum is important. Shorten and paraphrase as you record. Ask for clarification if needed. Try to avoid giving your opinions or ideas. If you must contribute your own ideas, let the children know that it is a break in the activity. For example, you might say:

> *I would like to stop for a minute and take a look at this list. Our brainstorm is getting full of lots of ideas about how to hurt the other person. Can anyone think of another idea?*

Generate a list of possible solutions from the students. Compliment them for having many ideas.

Envision outcomes:

> *Now let's take a look at solutions and think about what might happen if Aldo does each one. We want to think of all the good things that could happen and all the bad things that might happen.*

If the list is not exceptionally long, review each of the possible solutions and consider possible positive and negative consequences. This can be valuable practice in the skill of consequential thinking.

Here's a shortcut that can be used when you face time constraints (as so often happens in real life):

> *Now let's take a look at solutions and think about what might happen if Aldo does this. We want to think of all the good things that could happen and all the bad things that might happen. Let's go back to our goal. Keeping Aldo's goal of getting his picture back in mind, review the solutions on our list. Can we nominate and agree on three ideas that you think might have the best chance of solving the problem?"*

Rather than three ideas, you can call for whatever number you have time for. You can also include nominations for solutions to eliminate when considering Aldo's goal. In the process of answering this question students generally use consequential thinking, but in a more streamlined way.

Select the best solution:

Which solution do you think has the best chance of getting to Aldo's goal?

Plan and be prepared for pitfalls:

Once a solution is agreed upon, point out that it has to be carried out well for it to work. Ask,

What are some things to think about before trying to make this solution work? What might make it not work? How can BEST skills help?

Notice what happened (Now what?):

After you try to carry out a solution, it is important to think about what you have learned that you want to remember for next time.

Have students role-play how they could use their BEST when they tell the teacher something important. Have observers give praise and suggestions for making BEST even better. Then apply it to Aldo's situation. Make the point that the observers' feedback is like the last step of the FIG TESPN ladder.

6. Conduct additional practice activities, as time allows.

Continue to help students climb up the FIG TESPN problem-solving steps by using facilitative questions linked to the eight skill steps to guide and coach their thinking.

Additional situations:

- Every day, when Maria gets on the bus, Janine gets on at the next stop, sits near Maria, and pesters her. Janine whispers put-downs, raps Maria on the head, and pulls on her clothing, much to the amusement of the other kids. How do you think Maria is feeling?
- Tamara and Jake have been best friends since kindergarten, and now they are in the third grade. They live in the same apartment building and always play together after school. A new girl, Sudha, has moved into the neighborhood, and Tamara begins to spend all her free time with this girl. How do you think Jake is feeling?
- Rondall and three of his friends are playing in Rondall's garage. It is filled with neat stuff—an old motorcycle, newspapers, paint cans, a barbecue, bikes, and more. One of Rondall's friends, Frankie, pulls out matches and suggests lighting them. How do you think Rondall is feeling?

7. Introduce a Reflective Summary.

As outlined in the Introduction, ask students to reflect on the question "What did you learn from today's lesson?" Reinforce key themes, then go over any follow-up work.

8. Follow up.

The following steps will help make sure that the students have a chance to continue working with the new concepts.

Plans to Promote Transfer and Generalization of Skill

1. Continue to use the FIG TESPN Ladder to address real-life situations that occur in the classroom or on the playground.

2. Provide students with opportunities to submit school-related problems for teacher review that can then be used for group input and support in solving a problem or making a decision.

TIPS FOR TEACHERS

1. This topic and its practice activities are intended to help illustrate a strategy that can be used in an ongoing way. Begin with problem situations that are not too complex to serve as an initial illustration.

2. It is important not to use problems recognizable as belonging to particular students in a group problem-solving situation unless the student with the problem has either asked for or agreed to identification ahead of time. The maxim "Criticize in private and praise in public" is true about problem solving in a group as well.

3. Exposure and structured practice applying social problem solving skills to hypothetical situations can help children participate more fully in adult-led problem facilitation or peer-led mediation of a real-life conflict. Use facilitative questions to go up the FIG TESPN ladder at various times during the week. Start off with hypothetical situations and gradually extend to actual situations. What you are doing is beginning to extend the FIG process to FIG TESPN.

4. Expect that students will need your support and coaching in using cognitive strategies in early stages of practice. You will probably see a gradual increase in their ability to access these skills independently.

TOPIC

26

Review SDM/SPS Tools and Celebrate Success

OBJECTIVES

- To provide students with an opportunity to review their social decision making and social problem solving skills

- To provide teachers and students with an opportunity to assess skill gains

- To anticipate and plan ways that to use social decision making and social problem solving skills in the next grade

MATERIALS

Whole-class display of "Our SDM/SPS Tools: Grade 3" (Worksheet 3.26.1)

Copies of the following worksheets:

"More Tools for the SDM/SPS Toolbox" (3.26.2)

"SDM/SPS Certificate of Achievement" (3.26.3)

"Student Progress Report" Take-Home (3.26.4)

"SDM/SPS Summary and Recommendations" (3.26.5)

Students' SDM/SPS Toolboxes (from Topic 13)

Crayons or markers, drawing paper, scissors *(optional)*

NOTE

This lesson may be divided over several sessions, but all components should eventually be completed.

INSTRUCTIONAL ACTIVITIES

1. Conduct a Sharing Circle.

Direct students' attention to the whole-class display of the updated SDM/SPS tools list. Explain that this lesson will give students a chance to think about all of the skills and concepts they have learned so far as a part of social decision making and social problem solving.

The skills and concepts learned during Grade 3, and the Topics in which they were introduced, are as follows:

- Sharing Circle; Speaker Power (Topic 1)

- Listening Position (Topic 2)

- Listening Power (Topic 4)
- Strategies for Remembering (Topic 5)
- Following Directions (Topic 6)
- Learning to Role-Play (Topic 7)
- Be Your BEST (Topic 8)
- Giving and Receiving Praise (Topic 10)
- Giving and Receiving Help (Topic 11)
- Good Friendship/Not-Good Friendship Behaviors (Topic 12)
- Trigger Situations; Feelings Fingerprints (Topic 17)
- Keep Calm (Topic 18)
- Problem Diaries (Topics 19–21)
- FIG; FIG TESPN (Topics 22–24)

2. Distribute the "More SDM/SPS Tools" worksheet.

Explain that the worksheet provides more tools students can put in their toolboxes. Instruct students to color and cut out their new tools. (If there is a skill or concept not pictured, students may create their own drawing of it.)

3. Conduct a practice activity.

In small groups, have students take turns picking a new skill symbol that everyone else will also hold up. When they pick up the skill symbol, their job will be to describe the skill components and share a time when they used the skill or a time when they are going to use the skill. Then everyone can pack that skill symbol into their toolbox. Go around the group repeating the process until all the new skill symbols are packed away.

4. Review progress and look ahead.

Let the students know that you are interested in hearing what tools they are using and what tools they have a difficult time remembering to use. Ask students how they feel about going into the fourth grade. Then brainstorm some possible problems they might have.

In small groups, have students use FIG TESPN to create goals and plans for coping with problems that they are concerned about regarding their transition to the next grade. (If possible, spend several sessions on this subject.)

5. Wrap up and celebrate the unit.

Praise students for their accomplishments. Ask students if they have any praise for the accomplishments of the team.

Conduct a final Sharing Circle, asking everyone to praise the person that they pass the Speaker Power object to about some way that person was a good teammate. Be sure that all students are able to give and receive a compliment.

As time permits, the group can pass Speaker Power to whoever raises their hand to offer more praise to a team member or to the group.

End with a ceremony in which every member of the team is presented with a Certificate of Achievement. Wrap up with a round of applause for the great teamwork they have shown all year.

6. Introduce a Reflective Summary.

As outlined in the Introduction, ask students to reflect on the question "What did you learn from today's lesson?" Reinforce key themes, then go over any follow-up work.

7. Follow up.

The following steps will help make sure that the students have a chance to continue working with the new concepts.

Assignment

Have students take their toolboxes with them as a reminder to use their skills during the summer and in the next grade. Remind students to help one another use and practice their skills.

Take-Home

1. Send the Student Progress Report home to give parents and guardians a summary of student skill gains and recommendations for helping their children celebrate their achievements and continue building skills.

2. Student portfolios or notebooks can be sent home as a reminder of skills and record of all that was learned and achieved throughout the year.

Plans to Promote Transfer and Generalization of Skill

Students should practice using their skills in various academic and social settings for the remainder of the school year. It is recommended that teachers continue to adapt lessons accordingly.

TIPS FOR TEACHERS

1. Students can continue practicing their FIG TESPN steps, using problems regarding the transition to a new grade for the remainder of the school year.

2. Teachers may also want to spend more time on transition problem solving if students will be moving to another school in the district—for example, from an elementary to a middle school setting.

3. Complete and distribute the "SDM/SPS Summary and Recommendations." This form is designed for you, as the sending teacher, to let receiving teachers know what their students have covered, and provides recommendations for maintaining and building on skill levels attained, as shown in an end-of-year assessment.

Our SDM/SPS Tools: Grade 3

1. Sharing Circle
2. Speaker Power
3. Listening Position
4. Listening Power
5. Strategies for Remembering
6. Following Directions
7. Role-Playing
8. Be Your BEST
9. Giving and Receiving Praise
10. Giving and Receiving Help
11. Good Friendship/Not-Good Friendship Behaviors
12. Trigger Situations
13. Feelings Fingerprints
14. Keep Calm
15. Problem Diaries
16. FIG
17. FIG TESPN

Worksheet 3.26.1

FEELINGS FINGERPRINTS

KEEP CALM

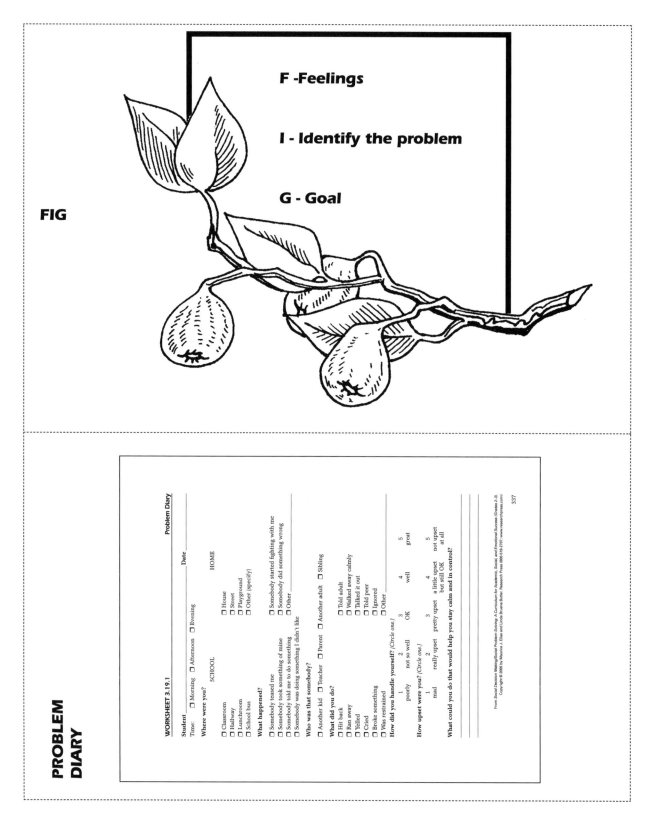

FIG

F -Feelings

I - Identify the problem

G - Goal

PROBLEM DIARY

FIG TESPN

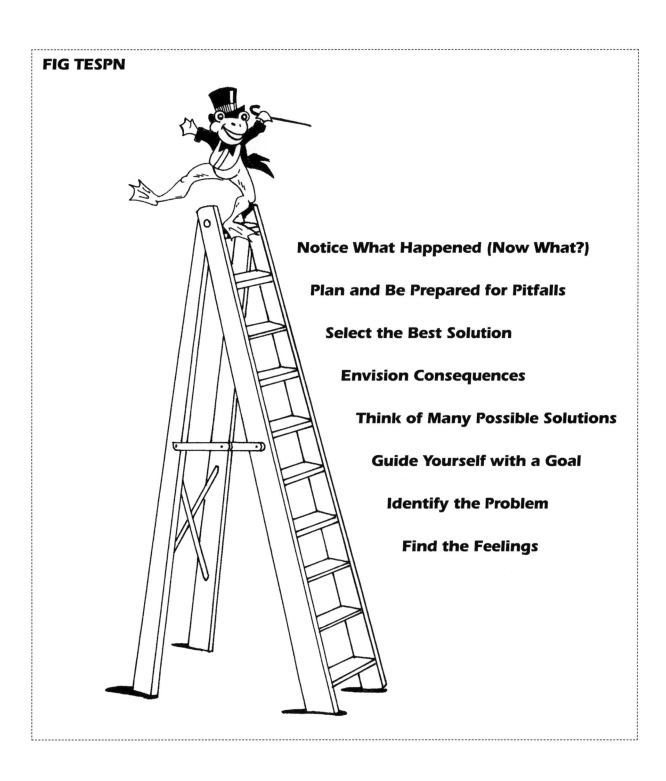

Notice What Happened (Now What?)

Plan and Be Prepared for Pitfalls

Select the Best Solution

Envision Consequences

Think of Many Possible Solutions

Guide Yourself with a Goal

Identify the Problem

Find the Feelings

SDM/SPS
Certificate of Achievement

_____

(Student)

Has successfully developed many Social Decision Making and Social Problem Solving skills

Sincerely,

_____   _____

(Teacher)   (Date)

Student Progress Report

 I appreciate your support and partnership as we have worked this year to help your child develop social decision making and social problem solving abilities. As the school year comes to a close, I would like to share my assessment of your child's progress and make some recommendations to you about ways that you can help to continue the development of these skills through the summer months.

Skill improvement

_____

_____

_____

Suggestions to help you reinforce and continue skill development

_____

_____

_____

Additional comments

_____

_____

_____

_____

Thank you!

_____

(Teacher signature)

(Please sign and return this bottom section.)   **Progress Report   3.26.4**

Student _____ **Date** _____

We received the report.   ❒ Yes   ❒ No

Comments:

_____

(Signature of parent or guardian)

Teacher _____ **Date** _____

Students in my class worked on a Social Decision Making and Social Problem Solving (SDM/SPS) team this past year to develop a variety of skills. I have attached a copy of all of last year's SDM/SPS Topics we covered. The numbers of those we covered fully are checked; an *X* appears beside Topics we touched upon but that might need some review. In addition, I have noted below accomplishments and areas of focus for particular students:

1. **Students with general strengths in SDM/SPS:**

    _____   _____

    _____   _____

    _____   _____

2. **Students needing overall growth in SDM/SPS:**

    _____   _____

    _____   _____

    _____   _____

3. **Students with strengths in particular SDM/SPS areas:**

    Student   *Area*

    _____   _____

    _____   _____

    _____   _____

4. **Students needing skill development in particular SDM/SPS areas:**

    Student   *Area*

    _____   _____

    _____   _____

    _____   _____

SDM/SPS Topics Covered

Becoming a Problem-Solving Team

- ☐ 1. Introduction to Social Decision Making/Social Problem Solving (SDM/SPS) Lessons
- ☐ 2. Learning to Listen Carefully and Accurately
- ☐ 3. Exercises to Pull Your Team Together
- ☐ 4. Listening Power
- ☐ 5. Strategies for Remembering
- ☐ 6. Following Directions
- ☐ 7. Learning to Role-Play
- ☐ 8. Be Your BEST
- ☐ 9. Using Your BEST to Stop Bullying and Teasing
- ☐ 10. Using Your BEST to Give and Receive Praise
- ☐ 11. Using Your Best to Give and Receive Help
- ☐ 12. What Makes a Friend a Friend?
- ☐ 13. Packing Your SDM/SPS Toolbox

Feelings

- ☐ 14. Identifying Feelings
- ☐ 15. Looking for Signs of Different Feelings
- ☐ 16. Identifying Feelings in Stories
- ☐ 17. What Are Your Feelings Fingerprints?
- ☐ 18. A Strategy for Keeping Calm
- ☐ 19. Introduction to Problem Diaries
- ☐ 20. Using Problem Diaries in Our Lives: Part 1
- ☐ 21. Using Problem Diaries in Our Lives: Part 2

Social Decision Making and Social Problem Solving

- ☐ 22. Introduction to FIG TESPN
- ☐ 23. Using FIG to Give Constructive Criticism
- ☐ 24. Using FIG to Understand Different Points of View
- ☐ 25. Practice Using FIG to Tackle School and Life Problems
- ☐ 26. Review SDM/SPS Tools and Celebrate Success

Supplemental

- ☐ 27. Using FIG in Language Arts
- ☐ 28. Using FIG in Social Studies
- ☐ 29. Joining a New Group

Topics 27–29

27 Using FIG in Language Arts

OBJECTIVES
- To provide students with an opportunity to practice FIG problem-solving steps on decisions facing characters in literary works
- To provide students with an opportunity to empathize with characters who have experiences and points of view different from their own
- To begin to help students identify "critical points in a story" when characters face a decision to make or a problem to solve
- To introduce and practice FIG methods that can be used in language arts in an ongoing way

MATERIALS
Copies of the following worksheets:
"FIG TESPN Literature Discussion Guide" (3.27.1)
"Using FIG to Plan Your Story" (3.27.2)
"Respond and Revise" (3.27.3)
"Problem Journal" (3.27.4)
"Character Choices" (3.27.5)
"Reading for Problem-Solving" Take-Home (3.27.6)

PREPARATION
Select a short story or a story from the language arts text or a trade book and mark it at a critical point in the story. Identify a "critical point in the story" when the reader has enough information to identify the problem but before the character makes a decision about how to solve it. Plan either to stop at this point if reading aloud or to instruct students to stop reading at this specific point.

A list of stories that have successfully been used in third-grade classrooms. An example of a critical point in the story can be found in the "Tips for Teachers" section of this topic.

INSTRUCTIONAL ACTIVITIES

1. Conduct a Sharing Circle as part of a language arts lesson.

Ask a question related to the book you are or will be reading. For example, if you are beginning a story, you could briefly introduce the main character and what the story is about, and then ask the children to share one thing they would like to learn more about or what kind of feelings they think the character might have in this situation.

If you are reading a book aloud in sections, tell children to imagine they could meet one of the characters in the story. Ask:

Who would you most like to meet?

If you could ask or say something to one of the characters in our story, who would you choose and what would you say?

Let the class know that you are going to read the story until characters face a critical point where they have to make a decision or solve a problem. Ask the students to keep the following questions in mind as they hear the story:

How is the character feeling?

What is the problem the character is facing?

2. Go through the story to the identified critical point.

Either read aloud or give students specific instructions regarding where to stop reading. Students can read aloud, read in small groups, or read individually.

3. Lead the class in a discussion.

Use the "FIG TESPN Literature Discussion Guide" (Worksheet 3.27.1) to help the class consider the problem faced by the character. Depending on the maturity of the group, you can distribute copies of the worksheet to familiarize them with the process, which can be used repeatedly in various subject areas.

Use the FIG steps as follows, naming the character where appropriate.

F: Feelings

How is the character feeling? Think of as many feeling words as you can.

I: Identify the problem

What is the problem that the character faces? Describe what is happening as clearly as you can.

G: Goal

What is the character's goal? What does that character want to have happen?

What are some things the character might do to solve this problem?

Return to the story. Compare and contrast students' ideas with what the character chooses to do.

4. Conduct additional practice activities for creative writing and careful reading in everyday lessons.

    a. Incorporate "Using FIG to Plan Your Story" (Worksheet 3.27.2) within creative writing assignments. The worksheet helps students use FIG to storyboard the feelings and identify a problem and a goal for a character they plan to write about.

    b. After students write a story, distribute "Respond and Revise" (Worksheet 3.27.3) and have the students work in pairs or small groups to read and provide feedback to the author. Again, FIG provides a framework for problem solving and constructive criticism as a guide for providing feedback on the author's work.

    c. To vary the way students practice applying FIG steps to think about the point of view of a character in a story, use the "Problem Journal" handout (Worksheet 3.27.4). This handout is designed to be folded into a four-sided booklet. Students are asked to pretend that they are the character in the story and to write what they think the character would write if this was the character's own journal or home diary. The Problem Journal has a cover page, a page with a blank feeling face for students to draw the character's feelings, a page to write the problem or what happened, and then a page to write about what the character wants.

    d. Distribute a copy of "Character Choices" (Worksheet 3.27.5). Assign the reading of another section of the story or a new story and have students complete the worksheet for a new character, specifying the point in the story where they should end their reading. An alternative assignment is to assign a new reading and ask students to identify a critical point in the story when the character is faced with a problem to solve or a decision to make. Ask students to complete the journal as if they were in the shoes of the focal character.

5. Introduce a Reflective Summary.

As outlined in the Introduction, ask students to reflect on the question "What did you learn from today's lesson?" Reinforce key themes, then go over any follow-up work.

6. Follow up.

The following steps will help make sure that the students have a chance to continue working with the new concepts.

Take-Home

Distribute the "Reading for Problem Solving" Take-Home (Worksheet 3.27.6). Let the children know that you are sharing the same questions used during this topic with their parents and guardians to use when they read at home. Parents and guardians are encouraged to read with their children and use the same problem-solving discussion questions when a character in the story is faced with a problem to solve or decision to make.

An alternative assignment is to send home a cover letter to parents or guardians with a copy of the FIG TESPN Literature Discussion Guide or Character Choices worksheet and ask them to fill the worksheet out with their child as they read a story together. They can also model the problem-solving steps by sharing with their child a story that they are reading that may be of interest to and appropriate for their child.

Plans to Promote Transfer and Generalization of Skill

Continue using the worksheets from this lesson and from the additional practice activities as an ongoing part of language arts lessons and assignments. Multiple and varied opportunities to practice using problem-solving steps will help your students internalize these skills.

Academic Activities

Continue to look for critical points in situations when a decision needs to be made or a problem solved in other academic topics such as math, health, or science. Take time to identify this point and ask, "How is the person feeling?" (Or, "How are you feeling?") "What is the problem? What is the goal?" Brainstorm different ideas about how the problem will be solved, as time allows, before moving on to find out how another person decides to solve a problem or how the children engage in solving the problem themselves.

Real-Life Activities

1. Look for opportunities to point out to children times when they or the class are facing a critical point. Stopping to point out that a problem or decision-making situation is occurring is the most powerful way to illustrate that the critical thinking and problem-solving skills they are learning in the classroom and practicing in academic subject areas can also be applied in daily life.

2. The Problem Journal can be used in real-life situations as a way to share a point of view with another person or as a personal journal to help children clarify their thinking about a problem. Teachers can use the Problem Journal to provide students with constructive criticism in an unobtrusive way. This also provides adult modeling of the use of FIG to help solve a problem or make things better.

TIPS FOR TEACHERS

1. The FIG steps can also be used to promote literacy and critical thinking about characters in other media, such as television shows, videos, and movies.

2. In some stories, there may be more than one character with a significant point of view at the place you choose to stop reading. In this case, you can assign different members of the class different characters to focus on in developing a FIG. Discuss the similarities and differences in how each character perceives the same situation.

   If the situation chosen involves a problem of bullying, assign students to develop a FIG for the victim, the bully, and any bystanders who may be present.

3. Examples of "critical points" in stories used in third grade are as follows.

Bullying

The Recess Queen, by Alexis O'Neill and Laura Huliska-Beith

A critical point in the story takes place when Queen Jean catches up with Katie Sue after charging after her on the playground and lets her know that no one swings or kicks or bounces until after she (Queen Jean) does. Stop after "and she figured that would set the record straight." Develop a FIG from the point of view of Katie Sue, Queen Jean, and the other children who were bystanders.

Internal Conflict and Survival

The Sign of the Beaver, by Elizabeth George Speare

A critical point in this story comes when a thirteen-year-old boy named Matt talks with some American Indians (a friend named Attean, in particular), who ask him to join their clan rather than stay to guard his family's cabin in the wilderness. Matt has been left by his father to guard their newly built cabin while he goes to get the family. Dad is gone longer then expected, and Matt meets Attean, who teaches him to survive in the woods and talks about his way of life and problems facing his Beaver Clan. At this critical moment, many points of view can be assigned for developing FIG. The concept of an internal conflict can be introduced by having students do a FIG for the side of Matt that would like to go away with the Indians and the side of Matt that would like to stay and guard his family's cabin. FIG statements can also be generated from the points of view of Attean and of the father if he learns that Matt chooses to leave.

Hatchet, by Gary Paulsen

A critical point in this story occurs when Brian, who is troubled by his parents' divorce, is in a plane crash while on the way to visit his father. Stop at the point when he is trying to decide if he should or should not dive to the bottom of the lake where the crashed plane and dead pilot are. Again, students can develop a FIG for two points of view, using the voice of Brian. What are the feelings, problem, and goal he might have, considering both options?

Friend Trouble

Ruby the Copycat, by Peggy Rathmann

A critical point to stop in this book is when Ruby stands behind her new friend, Angela, and recites a poem that is very similar to one that Angela wrote and just read to the class. The teacher, Miss Hart, says about Ruby's poem, "What a coincidence." At this point in the story, Ruby has copied what Angela does many times. Students can develop a FIG that considers the points of view of Angela, Ruby, and the teacher.

Prejudice and Stereotyping

Felita, by Nicholas Mohr

Felita is a girl from a biracial family that has moved to a new neighborhood because the parents value a good education for their children. One critical point in the story occurs when Felita has been the victim of discrimination and racial slurs and tells her mother that she wants to return to their old neighborhood. Develop a FIG from the point of view of the mother, Felita, and the other children.

Molly's Pilgrim, by Barbara Cohen

A critical point in this story is when Molly tells her mother that other children are making fun of her because she is different. Develop a FIG from the point of view of the mother, Molly, and the other children.

Problem Solving

Holes, by Louis Sachar

Stanley is an unlucky boy from a family with a history of bad luck who ends up at a juvenile detention center for an unlikely crime. A critical point in the story is when Stanley finds a gold tube while working on the 5' × 5' hole that each boy at the camp must dig each day. When he arrived at the camp he was told that they were digging holes all day to build character. They were also told that if they ever found anything interesting and gave it to the warden, they would be given a day off. To maintain his social status in the group of boys, Stanley allowed another boy (called X-Ray) to claim the find and get the day off. In addition, the warden appeared for the first time and treated the boys better than on any other day but had them change their routine to work together in the area where she thought X-Ray had found the gold tube. Stop right before you get to the end of chapter 15, where the warden calls a halt for the day and says that since it has taken this long to find the tube, she can wait another day. Do a FIG for Stanley. It is possible at this point to do one for the immediate situation and for the general situation he finds himself in.

Be a Perfect Person in Just Three Days! by Stephen Manes

Milo finds a book called *Be a Perfect Person in Just Three Days!* when it falls off the top shelf in the library. He decides that it is worth a try, but what the book tells him to do on the first day is to wear a stalk of broccoli around his neck for the first twenty-four hours. Do a FIG from Milo's point of view when he reads about his first assignment.

Student _____ **Date** _____

The character I am thinking about is named _____.

F: Find the FEELINGS

How is _____ feeling? Think of as many feelings words as you can.

_____

_____

I: IDENTIFY the problem

What is the problem that _____ faces? Describe what is happening as clearly as you can.

_____

_____

G: Guide yourself with a GOAL

What is _____ 's GOAL? What does _____ want to have happen?

_____

_____

What are some things that you might do to solve this problem?

_____

_____

_____

Now go back to this problem and continue reading to find out what happens.

Using FIG to Plan Your Story

Student _____ Date _____

Main character in my story _____

FEELINGS

IDENTIFY THE PROBLEM

GOAL

How is the character feeling?

What is the problem?

What does the character want to have happen?

_____

_____

_____

Author's name _____ Reviewer's name _____

Reviewer

1. How did you feel about what you read?

   _____

   _____

2. In one or two sentences, tell what the writing is about.

   _____

   _____

3. What was the author's goal for this piece of writing?

   _____

4. What could be added to help you understand the writing better? Think about what was expected for this assignment.

   _____

   _____

5. Plan some changes that you might make in this writing and write them down.

   _____

   _____

   _____

6. Now hand this work back to its author.

Author

After your writing has been reviewed, think about how you could make it even better. Write down improvements you will make. Now rewrite your paragraph on the back of this page, including these new ideas.

_____

_____

_____

From *Social Decision Making/Social Problem Solving: A Curriculum for Academic, Social, and Emotional Learning (Grades 2–3)*.
Copyright © 2005 by Maurice J. Elias and Linda Bruene Butler. Research Press (800-519-2707; www.researchpress.com)

Problem   **Feeling**

I want . . .

PROBLEM JOURNAL

Name _____

Student _____ **Date** _____

My character _____

1. How was the character feeling?

   _____

   _____

   _____

2. What was the problem?

   _____

   _____

   _____

3. What did the character want?

   _____

   _____

   _____

4. How was the problem solved?

   _____

   _____

   _____

5. How else could the problem have been solved?

   _____

   _____

   _____

Reading for Problem Solving

Our class is learning about how to solve problems and make decisions. You can help your child practice these important skills at home while reading stories.

Before starting a story, ask your child to keep the following question in mind:

How do the people in the story feel, and what makes them feel that way?

As you read, stop at times to ask:

What do you think _____ is feeling?

What is the problem or decision _____ is facing?

What is _____'s goal? What does _____ want to have happen?

What ideas do you have about how _____ might solve this problem?

Say: Now let's go back to the story and see what _____ decides to do.

After finishing the story, ask:

What was the solution that _____ chose to solve the problem? How well did it work?

Now that you've learned what happened, would you have handled this situation any differently? If so, what would you have done?

Your child may be asked in class to share what happened when you practiced this activity.

Thank you!

_____

(Teacher signature)

- -

(Please sign and return this bottom section.)   **Reading   3.27.6**

Student _____ **Date** _____

We used these questions.   ❐ Yes   ❐ No

Comments:

_____

(Signature of parent or guardian)

From *Social Decision Making/Social Problem Solving: A Curriculum for Academic, Social, and Emotional Learning (Grades 2–3)*.
Copyright © 2005 by Maurice J. Elias and Linda Bruene Butler. Research Press (800-519-2707; www.researchpress.com)

28 Using FIG in Social Studies

OBJECTIVES
- To apply FIG and a decision-making approach to a current issue or historical event
- To identify critical points of decision making and problem solving in current events

MATERIALS
Copies of "FIG TESPN: Thinking About Important Events" (Worksheet 3.28.1)

Copies of "Problem Solving in the News" Take-Home (Worksheet 3.28.2)

INSTRUCTIONAL ACTIVITIES

1. Conduct a Sharing Circle during a social studies lesson.

Ask:

Who has heard an interesting story in the news this week? Just describe in one sentence what the story is about.

Explain to the students that today they will be using their social problem solving skills to think about important events in the news. Explain that some events that were once current news have such an impact that people study them far into the future. Ask for a show of hands on whether the story just shared might go down in history.

2. Introduce the exercise.

Distribute the "FIG TESPN: Thinking About Important Events" worksheet.

Take up an existing reading in history or current events and proceed until you reach a critical point in a situation that the class is currently studying. Using the worksheet, help the children put the event into words. Help the students develop objective and clear problem statements for the individuals or groups that they are studying. Help them to take the perspective of these individuals or groups and then to identify the feelings and goal of each.

For example, if you are studying Martin Luther King Jr., introduce the issues that you will be discussing about Dr. King. For each issue, stop to consider the problem he was trying to solve, the feelings he might have had, and what his goal was. Identify other individuals or groups involved to examine their perspective or point of view as well.

3. Conduct a practice activity.

Have student groups share their answers on the worksheet and help them be clear about what they have read and how it relates to what they said.

Continue by brainstorming all of the different ways that the characters or groups could solve the problem.

Then proceed, stopping (or not) as desired at other critical points to engage students in problem solving.

4. Introduce a Reflective Summary.

As outlined in the Introduction, ask students to reflect on the question "What did you learn from today's lesson?" Reinforce key themes, then go over any follow-up work.

5. Follow up.

The following steps will help make sure that the students have a chance to continue working with the new concepts.

Take-Home

Distribute the "Problem Solving in the News" Take-Home, which provides parents and guardians with a series of questions that they can use to help children think critically about situations they see and hear in the news.

Plans to Promote Transfer and Generalization of Skill

Use FIG TESPN discussion questions or the "Thinking About Important Events" worksheet when talking to students about discoveries in science or other subjects.

What is the event that we are thinking about? When and where did it happen?

F: Feelings

Ask students, "How do you think this person was FEELING? Think of as many feelings words as you can."

I: Identify the problem

Ask students, "What is the PROBLEM that _____ was trying to solve? We need to describe what was happening as clearly as we can."

G: Goals

Ask students, "What was _____'s goal? What did they want to have happen? What were they trying to achieve?"

Ask students, "What are some ways that _____ might have tried to solve this problem?"

Reinforce students for thinking about possible solutions before returning to the event of study to learn about what happened (or current status, if it is a part of something that is still in progress). Conclude by pointing out how discoveries in science or other fields often emerge from using FIG TESPN to solve important problems.

TIPS FOR TEACHERS

1. These activities are designed to be used throughout the year, integrated within academic subject areas repeatedly, with changing content.

2. Try to provide multiple opportunities for students to practice the FIG steps in both academic and social settings.

Student _____ **Date** _____

The person or group I am thinking about is _____.

F: Feelings

How is the person or group FEELING? Think of as many feelings words as you can.

_____   _____

_____   _____

_____   _____

_____   _____

I: IDENTIFY the PROBLEM

What is the PROBLEM that _____ faces? Describe what is happening as clearly as you can.

_____

_____

_____

_____

G: GOALS

What is _____ 's GOAL? What does _____ want to have happen?

_____

_____

_____

_____

Problem Solving in the News

In class, your child is learning to practice problem-solving skills while thinking about characters we are studying in history or current events. One way that you can help your child practice problem solving is to discuss situations in the news.

After watching a segment on the news on television, listening to a news story on the radio, or reading an article in the newspaper, ask your child the following questions.

Problem-Solving Questions

1. How do the people in the story feel, and what makes them feel that way?

2. What do you think _____ is feeling?

3. What is the problem or decision _____ is facing? How would you put this problem into your own words?

4. What do you think _____'s goal is (or was)?

5. What ideas do you have about how _____ might solve (or have solved) this problem?

6. If you could say something to _____ or ask a question, what would you say or ask?

Your child may be asked in class to share what happened when you practiced this activity.

Thank you!

_____

(Teacher signature)

(Please sign and return this bottom section.) **News 3.28.2**

Student _____ **Date** _____

We had a problem-solving discussion about something in the news. ❏ Yes ❏ No

Comments:

_____

(Signature of parent or guardian)

From *Social Decision Making/Social Problem Solving: A Curriculum for Academic, Social, and Emotional Learning (Grades 2–3)*.
Copyright © 2005 by Maurice J. Elias and Linda Bruene Butler. Research Press (800-519-2707; www.researchpress.com)

29 Joining a New Group

OBJECTIVES
- To teach students guidelines for joining a group
- To increase awareness of the problems that may be encountered when joining a group
- To discuss responsibilities of group members when accepting new members

MATERIALS AND Whole-class display of "Joining a New Group" (Worksheet 3.29.1)

INSTRUCTIONAL ACTIVITIES

1. Introduce the issue.

Begin by telling students that you are going to tell them a story about a student who is just about their age and in the third grade. Say something along these lines:

Jim has just moved to a new town, so he has to go to a new school. He does not know anyone. During recess, everyone went out to play kickball. Jim wants to play but does not know how to join the group. Let's help him learn to join the group.

Ask if anyone has ever had to join a group of people that they have never met before. How did it feel?

2. Develop the idea of using a planned set of steps to get into a new group.

Explain:

Jim can learn some steps to help him join the group. The first thing Jim should do is observe the feelings and actions of the children. Why should he do that? (Some reasons may be to learn the interests of the children, understand the rules of the game, to get to know the children, and so on.)

Where would be the best place for Jim to watch from? (Close by—so the children in the group can see his interest.) *Now he should find a way to join in. How could he join in?* (Start a conversation by commenting on what is going on, introduce himself, ask to join, or look for a way to help or contribute.)

Have children role-play each of the ways Jim could join. Refer to Keep Calm and BEST elements to provide feedback when students are conducting a role-play to model what they would do to enter a group.

3. Discuss possible problems.

Say:

> *Sometimes children want to join a group so badly that they may do the wrong things. Sometimes a child may want to observe a group with intentions to join, but may be too shy and stand and stare too long.*

Model a timid body posture and hovering stance, and ask:

> *Why isn't this a good idea?* (It makes the others uncomfortable.) *This is an example of passive behavior.*

Brainstorm other ways that would be wrong when joining a group. Some examples: calling attention to oneself in a disruptive way, interrupting at the wrong time, and disagreeing with or negatively criticizing the children.

> *These would be examples of aggressive behavior.*

4. Point out that nothing is guaranteed to work at once or all the time.

Continue the discussion by explaining:

> *Sometimes even when you do the right things, the children may ignore you at first. Why may they do that?* (They may be involved in what they are doing. They may feel shy about newcomers, too.) *What should you do?* (Don't take it personally and try again.)

5. Summarize the steps.

Say:

> *Now let's look at Jim's situation again. If you were part of the group, what could you do to make it easier for Jim?* (Introduce yourself, start a conversation, introduce him to others, ask him to join.)

Make connections between the behaviors that help someone enter a new group successfully and BEST.

Show the "Joining a New Group" display and review the steps:

- Focus on the ongoing activity.
- Keep Calm and observe.
- Look for a way to help or contribute.
- Be your BEST and introduce yourself.
- Ask if you can join.

6. Role-play some situations where children are asking to join a group.

Here are some possibilities:

- Cindy and Brian are playing a game. Alex wants to join. How could Alex ask? What could Cindy and Brian do?
- Terrell is entering middle school. Walking up to the school on the first day he sees only students that he does not know. What can Terrell do while waiting outside for the doors to open?
- Lisette invites Amy to a birthday party. Lisette is the only person Amy knows. How could Amy meet more people? What could Lisette do?
- Willie is new at school. The teacher asks him to find a place to sit at lunchtime. How should Willie join a lunch table? What should children at the table do?
- Jackie was in a special classroom and is being mainstreamed to a regular science class. The day she begins the class they are working on a project in groups of four. How can Jackie join the three other students in the group?

7. Introduce a Reflective Summary.

As outlined in the Introduction, ask students to reflect on the question "What did you learn from today's lesson?" Reinforce key themes, then go over any follow-up work.

8. Follow up.

The following step will help make sure that the students have a chance to continue working with the new concepts.

Plans to Promote Transfer and Generalization of Skill

A review of this activity is useful as part of preparation for transition to a new grade or school, but it can also be used at any time—especially if there are cliques in your class or new students entering.

TIPS FOR TEACHERS

1. As with Topic 23 ("Using FIG to give Constructive Criticism"), "Joining a New Group" discusses a difficult skill. Sometimes even the most socially skilled child may experience difficulty or rejection when attempting the techniques it recommends. Research on children's successful entry behavior has consistently found that when children take time to observe a new group before making any bids to enter, they are most likely to be successful. This observation allows the new child an opportunity to learn about the group and develop a frame of reference for doing what the group is doing. In contrast, prematurely trying to redirect the group is a high-risk strategy.

   Persistence is also important, as entry is a difficult task for all children, but group acceptance is more likely over time. The skill components targeted in this topic are based on social skills that will help increase children's success, but it is also important to prepare them for the fact that success may take time. Because of this, it can be helpful to have children anticipate obstacles or ways that their attempts to enter a group might not be successful. Brainstorming and role-playing ways to handle those situations as well will help them to cope with a range of possible outcomes.

2. For further reinforcement, have students write a short story about or discuss situations concerning joining a group that they have experienced (for example, new neighborhoods, classes, sports teams, scouting, and after-school activities). Ask how they felt, if they experienced any problems, and what their goals were. Ask them to remember what they did and what the outcome was. What was successful and what did not work? What would they do differently the next time?

Joining a New Group

1. Focus on the ongoing activity.

2. Keep Calm and observe.

3. Look for a way to help or contribute.

4. Be your BEST and introduce yourself.

5. Ask if you can join.

From *Social Decision Making/Social Problem Solving: A Curriculum for Academic, Social, and Emotional Learning* (Grades 2–3).
Copyright © 2005 by Maurice J. Elias and Linda Bruene Butler. Research Press (800-519-2707; www.researchpress.com)

Appendix A

The SDM/SPS Curriculum Approach: Evidence of Effectiveness

OUTCOME EVALUATIONS

The following is a summary of our evaluation data, which we have gathered over three decades. The data are organized around four claims of effectiveness. It is the research that produced this data that forms the basis for our program's being one of the few character education and social-emotional learning programs to have been validated as an Exemplary Program by the U.S. Department of Education's Program Effectiveness Panel. More recently, it has been granted Promising Program status by the Department of Education's Expert Panel on Safe and Drug Free Schools and the Character Education Partnership, and has also been designated as a Select SEL (empirically validated social-emotional learning) program by the Collaborative for Academic, Social, and Emotional Learning and as a Model Program by the New Jersey Center for Character Education (see Bruene Butler et al., 1997). (Note that these data are not exhaustive. For example, Thurston [1998] has studied the impact of SDM/SPS on special education populations, and Norris [1998] has evaluated the impact of SDM/SPS in a multicultural setting. Additional data are still being collected in urban implementation sites.)

Claim 1: Following training, teachers improve in their ability to facilitate children's social decision making and problem solving.

Fourth- and fifth-grade teachers from Middlesex, New Jersey, were given the Assessment of Responses of Teachers to Hypothetical Classroom Situations, a series of hypothetical school-based problem situations derived from the work of Irving Sigel and of George Spivack and Myrna Shure. Responses were classified according to a hierarchy ranging from *inhibitory* of children's representational competence (authoritarian responses) through *moderately facilitative* (providing consequences or alternatives to choose from) to *highly facilitative* of children's cognitive abilities (open-ended questions that encourage reflection on the possibilities and options). The results showed that, after training, teachers significantly increased their use of questioning strategies found to be highly facilitative of problem-solving thinking, with a significant difference ($p < .001$) between the experimental and untrained control groups. (The control group was later trained in the techniques as well.) Completing the instructional phase was associated with a significant reduction in the use of inhibitory responses (57 percent reduction by the experimental group; 61 percent by the control group after training) and a corresponding increase in the use of moderately to highly facilitative responses. Table 4 represents data from several further districts indicating gains in facilitative questioning by teachers. Teachers' inhibitory responses in these sites were reduced by a mean of 52 percent, while facilitative responses showed a mean increase of 58 percent.

Claim 2: Children receiving the program improve their social decision making and social problem solving skills relative to controls.

Self-Control and Social Awareness Phase

We have assessed the Readiness Phase of the curriculum by applying the measure "Getting Along With Others," using an expert rating scale we have developed and a scoring system that permits

Table 4   Summary of Change in Teachers' Inhibitory and Highly Facilitative Responses Following SDM/SPS Training

	N	Site*	Inhibitory			Facilitative		
			Pre	Post	-%	Pre	Post	+%
Center School	9	U U/S	17%	6%	-65%	46%	81%	+76%
Bartle School	7	U U/S	22%	9%	-59%	32%	52%	+63%
Clifton School	13	U/S	29%	14%	-52%	33%	46%	+39%
AK	16	R	20%	11%	-45%	52%	60%	+15%
OR	4	S	17%	8%	-53%	29%	63%	+117%
Mean			21%	10%	-52%	38%	60%	+58%

* Site: S = suburban; U/S = urban/suburban; U = urban; R = rural.

computerized statistical analysis. The measure yields scores for each of the eight questions that have been judged to reflect *average, competent,* or *at-risk* responses by a panel of experts in the field. For example, to be judged competent in response to the question "Name three things you do when someone is bugging you or bothering you," a child has to give at least two responses indicating either polite assertiveness (for example, "ask them to please stop") or a means of finding a solution by talking it out. However, if any one of the child's responses refers to aggression (for example, "punch them") or a display of anger or revenge, the child is coded as at-risk for this question. Other behaviors, such as telling someone rather than asking them to stop, physically leaving, or ignoring the person would be rated as average responses. These scores are then combined to provide a risk, average, and competence score for each child. We present three pretest/posttest, control group–design studies documenting the effectiveness of the Readiness Phase. In each case, there were no differences between the experimental and control groups at pretest. All data were analyzed using the nonparametric Wilcoxon rank-sum test for an approximate t-test result, using two-tailed tests. Interrater reliability exceeded 90 percent.

Study 1

Fourth-grade teachers at the Watsessing School in Bloomfield, New Jersey, were trained in February 1993. Bloomfield is an urban/suburban site, with a 41 percent minority student population at the Watsessing School. Thirty-two percent of the students qualify for free or reduced-price lunches. A control group (n = 22) was obtained from the Berkeley School in Bloomfield, which has comparable demographics.

From Table 5, it can be seen that the experimental group (n = 46) made a significant gain in competence by posttest in June 1994 (p < .0001), while the control group's competence score did not improve. By posttest, 54 percent of the experimental group were rated as low in risk and high in competence, based on their combined responses, while only 14 percent of the controls received that rating and 46 percent were in fact rated as high in risk and low in competence. For example, 74 percent of the experimental group could provide four characteristics that they look for in a friend, with over 60 percent providing qualities that result in reciprocal friendship or citing compatibility as an important characteristic, while 50 percent of the control group were unable to think of more than two qualities, with only 32 percent discussing reciprocity.

Study 2

In the Bartle School, Highland Park, New Jersey, the students of two trained third-grade teachers formed the experimental group (n = 32), with an in-school control of three classes of nontrained third-grade students (n = 59). Highland Park has the dual rating of urban and urban/suburban, with a 47 percent minority population, composed

Table 5   Summary of Mean Competence Scores and Statistics from the Three Studies of the Readiness Phase of the Curriculum

			PRE	POST			
STUDY	GROUP	N	MEAN (SD)	MEAN (SD)	Z	p <	Effect Size
Bloomfield, New Jersey	Experimental	46	1.64 (1.22)	3.17 (1.34)	5.08	.0001	1.25
	Control	22	1.85 (1.22)	1.68 (1.09)			
Highland Park, New Jersey	Experimental	32	1.95 (1.26)	3.50 (1.22)	4.56	.0001	1.23
	Control	59	1.77 (1.21)	2.20 (1.39)			
Litchfield, Arizona	Experimental	23	1.38 (1.17)	3.35 (1.15)	4.54	.0001	1.68
	Control	18	2.07 (1.21)	2.61 (1.46)			

ES = (Experimental posttest mean – Experimental pretest mean) / Experimental pretest SD. These effect sizes are considered to be significant in that for each study they exceeded one standard deviation.

primarily (28 percent) of African-American students. Fifteen percent of the third graders were eligible for free or reduced-price lunches.

Again, Table 5 shows that the experimental group's competence score improved significantly ($p < .0001$) by posttest in May 1994. By posttest, 78 percent were rated as low in risk and high in competence, compared with only 23 percent at pretest. At that time over 46 percent were actually rated high in risk and low in competence. This score was retained by only two experimental children (6 percent) at posttest. For example, at pretest, sixteen children from the experimental group are unable to identify a way of knowing when they are upset, and ten children had no strategy for talking to another person who was upset. By posttest, only three children were unable to provide ways of knowing when they are upset and only one child had no strategy for approaching an upset person. Within the experimental group, at pretest, 20 percent were unable to name even one characteristic that they look for in a friend, and 46 percent could think of only two. By posttest only one child (3 percent) was unable to list anything and twenty-eight children (87.5 percent) could name, as requested, four characteristics that they look for in a friend. In contrast, at posttest, only 37 percent of the control group was rated as low in risk and high in competence, with twenty-one children (36 percent) scoring high in risk and low in competence.

Study 3

The fifth-grade teacher at Litchfield School, Arizona, became a certified trainer in June 1993, and agreed to conduct a Readiness Phase study with her students ($n = 23$) during the 1993–1994 academic year. The experimental site is rural, with a 39 percent minority population, composed mainly of Hispanic students (30 percent). The students are predominantly the children of enlisted personnel from a nearby air force base, and 40 percent qualify for reduced-price or free lunches. In this study, the control group ($n = 18$) represents a higher socioeconomic group, with fifth graders from a more affluent school that serves officers' children in a suburban district. Students' pretest scores were not statistically significantly different, although the controls' scores were higher. By posttest, in May, the experimental group outperformed the controls in terms of competence, despite the pre-existing inequalities. At posttest, 74 percent of the experimental group scored low in risk and high in competence, compared with 28 percent of the control group.

For all three studies, at posttest, the experimental group differed significantly in competence from the control group ($p < .0001$, $.0001$, and $.05$, respectively). Table 5 also includes the effect size for each study, which was calculated using the formula ES = (experimental posttest mean – experimental pretest mean)/ experimental pretest SD. These effect sizes are considered to be significant in that for each study they exceeded one standard deviation.

Instructional and Application Phases

The Group Social Problem Solving Assessment (GSPSA) was used to assess the Instructional and Application Phases of the curriculum. Summary data from the fourth grades of two districts (Clifton and Berkeley Heights, New Jersey) are included, and results by grade are available from an additional district (Bloomfield, New Jersey). Clifton is an urban/suburban district that introduced the program with the training of fourteen teachers and phased the program into all first- through fifth-grade classrooms, serving approximately three thousand children. The fourth grade has a 29 percent minority population, with 27 percent of the students qualifying for free or reduced-price meals. Berkeley Heights is a suburban district with a 15 percent minority population; it serves students from the upper middle class, with complete implementation of the program in the district for Grades 3 through 6. In Study 4, we present data from these two sites, using data from a control district (Middlesex, New Jersey) for comparison purposes because SDM is taught districtwide and within-district controls could therefore not be obtained. (Middlesex is a blue-collar, multiethnic, but predominantly white town of about fifteen thousand in central New Jersey.) Scoring of this measure has not changed, and it is therefore a valid comparison. One hundred and forty-seven Clifton fourth graders and seventy-seven Berkeley Heights fourth graders completed the GSPSA pretest in September, prior to training in the Instructional Phase, and the posttest in May. The non-parametric Wilcoxon rank-sum test was again used to obtain approximate t-test results, with two-tailed tests, and interrater reliability exceeded 90 percent. The results presented in Table 6 indicate that children trained in SDM/SPS continue to make substantial gains in Interpersonal Sensitivity, Problem Analysis (which reflects a child's ability to examine a problem, define it, set goals, and consider alternative solutions), and Planning (which includes evaluating consequences and realistically assessing obstacles to problem resolution). In fact, the magnitude of effects for the current data exceeds that found in our original study.

A further study was conducted with fourth, fifth, and sixth graders in Bloomfield, New Jersey. Demographics for Bloomfield are presented under Study 1 in the Readiness section of this claim. As Table 7 shows, fourth graders again made significant gains in all three areas of social problem solving concepts, outperforming the original validation group (also shown in Table 7, for comparison). Following training, the fifth graders demonstrated significantly better knowledge of problem analysis and specificity of planning, while sixth graders demonstrated significant improvements in sensitivity to others' feelings and planning. Sixth graders' mean pretest score on problem analysis exceeded 14 points, which is the criterion for being rated highly skilled in this domain. While these students made gains in this skill by posttest, the nonsignificance of their result can be attributed to ceiling effects.

Table 6   Change in Fourth Graders' Mean Interpersonal Sensitivity (I.S.), Problem Analysis (P.A.), and Planning (PLAN) Scores Following Training in the Instructional Phase of SDM/SPS

	Middlesex (n = 120)			Clifton (n = 147)				Berkeley Heights (n = 77)			
	PRE	POST	ES	PRE	POST	Z	ES	PRE	POST	Z	ES
I.S. (sd)	9.89 2.20	10.29 1.54	.18	9.95 2.19	10.70 1.88	3.31*	.34	10.99 1.62	11.96 1.09	4.03**	.60
P.A. (sd)	10.37 3.62	12.47 3.72	.58	9.86 3.95	12.16 3.56	4.95**	.58	10.42 4.13	15.81 2.82	7.68**	1.3
PLAN (sd)	4.83 1.63	5.51 1.27	.42	5.55 2.08	6.56 1.91	4.06**	.49	6.20 1.76	7.61 1.72	4.65**	.80

*$p < .001$, ** $p < .0001$; ES = Effect Size

Table 7   Change in Mean Scores for Interpersonal Sensitivity (I.S.), Problem Analysis (P.A.), and Planning (PLAN) by Grade: Bloomfield

	4th grade (n = 45)				5th grade (n = 25)				6th grade (n = 31)			
	PRE	POST	$Z\ p <$	ES	PRE	POST	$Z\ p <$	ES	PRE	POST	$Z\ p <$	ES
I.S. (sd)	10.10 (1.97)	11.22 (1.28)	3.00 .003	.57	10.55 (1.50)	10.96 (1.56)	n.s.		11.12 (1.51)	11.94 (1.00)	2.17 .033	.54
P.A. (sd)	8.31 (4.04)	12.84 (3.74)	4.80 .0001	1.12	11.35 (3.73)	13.84 (3.02)	2.75 .008	.67	14.47 (3.10)	15.55 (2.53)	n.s.	
PLAN (sd)	5.14 (2.33)	7.22 (1.88)	4.24 .0001	.89	6.68 (2.26)	7.88 (2.05)	2.02 .048	.53	7.15 (1.42)	8.06 (1.57)	2.19 .032	.64

ES = Effect Size

Claim 3: Students receiving the program in elementary school show more prosocial behavior in school and greater coping with stressors upon transition to middle school, when compared with controls.

Assessment of the generalizability of the program involved an examination of the impact of receiving full, partial (instructional only), or no exposure to the curriculum on reactions to stressors encountered upon transition to middle school. Elias et al. (1986) conducted a study involving 158 fifth-grade students (80 boys and 78 girls) in four elementary schools for whom parental permission was obtained (98 percent of the population). Academically, students averaged approximately one year above grade level on standardized academic tests. All fifth-grade teachers were involved in carrying out the program under a delayed control design. Within the larger project, it was agreed that sufficient quality control could not be maintained while beginning implementation in all fifth-grade classrooms simultaneously; it was decided to begin instruction in two schools and use the two other schools as a delayed comparison group, while simultaneously meeting the concerns of parents that their children receive a high-quality program before entering middle school. To examine the nature of adjustment among children who received no SDM training, a control group consisting of children entering middle school during the prior year was used. Thus there were three quasi-experimental conditions: (a) no training, (b) full training, and (c) partial training (Instructional Phase only).

For the purpose of this study, two primary assessments were made. The first involved assessment of children's transition to middle school. The instrument used, the Survey of Middle School Stressors, consists of twenty-eight commonly occurring situations in middle school identified through behavioral analytic procedures as leading to difficulty, distress, or upset feelings (Goldfried & D'Zurilla, 1969). Examples of these stressor situations range from logistical concerns such as forgetting a locker combination and learning the way around a larger new building to mastering new academic routines (having many different teachers, more homework, greater academic pressures) and new relationships with peers (being teased or asked to do things one does not want to do, being approached to smoke or drink, not being part of a desired group, undressing in a locker room). For each stressor, children were asked to rate either that it was not a problem, a small problem, a medium problem, or a large problem for them since coming to middle school. In addition to patterns of response on the twenty-eight stressors, summary indices included Problem Frequency (number of stressors rated as a small, medium, or large problem) and Problem Intensity (number of stressors rated as a large problem). The present measure has an internal consistency coefficient greater than .90 across different samples and has been predictive of Piers-Harris Self-Concept scores (Piers & Harris, 1984), school attendance, and teacher ratings of school adjustment using the AML (Elias, Gara, & Ubriaco, 1985). In October of their first year in the sixth grade, all children who received social problem solving instruction were administered the survey. The preceding year, a comparison cohort entering the same middle school received the survey. The second primary assessment involved children's social problem solving skills. The instrument used was the GSPSA.

For the three groups of children, it was found that those entering without training were differentiated from those receiving at least some training in both the extent and severity of situations they considered to be problematic, with regression analyses significant at $p < .05$. Stressors such as peer pressure, academic demands, coping with authority figures, and pressure to become involved in behaviors such as smoking and substance abuse were felt to be significantly more difficult by children in the untrained group. Further, a significant discrimination could also be made between children with different amounts of training, in the expected direction, multivariate $F(282\ 107) = 1.62, p < .04$. Perhaps most important, a canonical analysis of the relationship of all children's social problem solving abilities to their responses to stressors indicated a significant inverse relationship of Problem Analysis and Action and Specificity of Planning with severity of stressors, multivariate $F(9, 326) = 2.00, p < .04$.

Overall, the results indicate a positive association between level of training and children's reports of coping with stressors and adjusting to middle school, and suggest that training in social decision making and social problem solving is an important aspect of this shared variance. These results cannot be accounted for by preexisting differences related to the children's elementary schools nor to marked differences in the degree of stressors encountered by students from one year to the next. Empirical support was found to suggest that a consistent mediating factor in children's responding to stressors was their social problem solving skills—most specifically, Problem Analysis and Action. These findings were obtained approximately four months after the conclusion of any formal training, including an intervening summer. None of the cues traditionally associated with the maintenance of an intervention (physical environment, prompts by a trained teacher, continued contact with the group within which training occurred) were available to the children. Furthermore, they were subjected to a transitional life event—middle school entry—with well-documented destabilizing influences on a "normal" population (Elias et al., 1985; Lipsitz, 1977; Toepfer & Marani, 1980).

Further, we have examined the function of explicit practice in SDM skills on the reduction of stress in the same situation, the transition to middle school, with the goal of exploring the difference between mere exposure to the social problem solving language, skills, and concepts, and systematic training in the use of those skills. We feel that the practice provided in the Application Phase, which is not included in many other problem-solving programs, is important in developing reflection and self-regulation, which ensure that the skill will be accessible in novel, real-life situations.

For this study, we chose a site, Clifton, where SDM/SPS is taught throughout the district. Half the students studied had formed an original control group for pilot studies and had never been explicitly trained. However, in a district of approximately three thousand first to fifth graders, which is thoroughly permeated with the program and language (including classroom posters of the problem-solving steps), it was unlikely that the sixth-grade control group would be oblivious to program concepts. We therefore decided to undertake an analysis of the strength of relations between knowledge of SDM skills and real-life outcomes, comparing sixth graders with exposure to problem-solving concepts and language with those who had received explicit training and opportunities to practice their skills. The staff hypothesized that by sixth grade there might be few differences between the two groups on a paper-and-pencil measure like the Group Social Problem Solving Assessment, but that real differences would emerge in terms of how well that knowledge would mediate stress or predict self-esteem. The new analysis, therefore, is in more depth, focusing on mediating factors.

All 623 sixth graders entering the two middle schools in the Clifton district completed the Survey of Middle School Stressors (which was used in our original validation study), the Piers-Harris Self-Concept Scale, and the Group Social Problem Solving Assessment (also used in the original study). Since Clifton is a district with a highly mobile population, the staff screened out students who had transferred into the district after third grade. This resulted in an experimental group of 175 students with three or more years of SDM/SPS training and a control group of 159 students who had been exposed to program concepts but had never been explicitly trained to use them.

As anticipated, the GSPSA did not discriminate between the two groups. Nor did their scores differ for the Survey of Middle School Stressors or the Piers-Harris. However, real differences emerged when we examined the strength of relationships within each group. The Survey of Middle School Stressors (SMSS) provides reliable subscales for stress arising from four different sources: conflicts with authority and older students, peer relationships, academic pressure, and substance abuse (alphas = .61 to .93). For the control group, there were no relationships between scores on the three GSPSA subscales (Interpersonal Sensitivity, Problem Analysis, and Planning) and scores on the SMSS subscales, with the exception of a counterintuitive positive relationship between Problem Analysis and stress from peer relationships (r = .18, p < .03). In contrast, as Table 8 shows, those sixth graders who had received three or more years of explicit SDM training had significant negative relationships between scores on both Interpersonal Sensitivity and Problem Analysis with stress from conflicts with authority and from academic pressure. Planning was also significantly negatively related to experiencing stress from academic pressure.

Similarly, when we examined the relations between self-esteem and social problem solving skills, a sharp distinction emerged between the two groups. The Piers-Harris contains eighty true-false items covering areas such as intellectual and school status, positive behavior, popularity, low anxiety, happiness, and physical attractiveness. A modified forty-four–item scale was used, in which all cross-loading items had been eliminated. The modified scale has an internal consistency of .85 and a six-month test-retest reliability of r = .73, and it has been used by other researchers in previous studies. Again, there were no relationships between the GSPSA subscales and the Piers-Harris score for the control group. However, as Table 8 shows, performance on all three GSPSA subscales related to the Piers-Harris Self-Concept score for the experimental group. A further examination of the relationships indicates that when children are explicitly trained in social problem solving skills, a good command of problem analysis predicts their sense of their intellectual and school status (r = .30, p < .0001), while planning skill is associated with positive behavior (r = .21, p < .005), low anxiety (r = .16, p < .04), and intellectual and school status (r = .29, p < .0001). Highly developed skills in interpersonal sensitivity are related to happiness

Table 8   Correlations Between GSPSA Subscales and Survey of Middle School Stressors and Piers-Harris Scores for the Experimental Group

	Interpersonal Sensitivity	Problem Analysis	Planning
SMSS: Conflicts with Authority	−.22**	−.18*	−.14
SMSS: Academic Pressure	−.23**	−.22**	−.31***
Piers-Harris	.43***	.25**	.29***

* p < .05, ** p < .005, *** p < .0001

$(r = .29, p < .0002)$, low anxiety $(r = .17, p < .03)$, positive behavior $(r = .31, p < .0001)$, and intellectual and school status $(r = .42, p < .0001)$. Clearly, students who have highly developed interpersonal and problem-solving skills as a result of explicit training and practice are in a better position to cope with real-life stresses such as the transition to middle school, and they have improved self-esteem.

Claim 4: After receiving varying amounts of exposure to the program in elementary school, students followed up in high school showed high levels of positive, prosocial behavior and decreased antisocial, self-destructive, and socially disordered behavior, when compared with controls who did not receive instruction.

The design of the study (Elias et al., 1991) involved a comparison of three cohorts of students who received social decision making and social problem solving instruction in elementary school. Cohorts received different amounts or different levels of instructional fidelity to the program, according to the distribution shown in Table 9.

Children did not know the purpose of the study, and the participation rate exceeded 95 percent. The measures used were the National Youth Survey (NYS) of Antisocial and Delinquent Behaviors (Elliot et al., 1983) and the Youth Self-Report (YSR) Rating Scale (Achenbach & Edelbrock, 1987). Both are self-report, standardized, and have been validated against external behavioral indices. The NYS consists of forty-two items covering vandalism; theft; use of various illegal substances; aggressive behavior toward

Table 9   Experience of High School Follow-Up Group

Grade in High School at Time of Follow-Up[a]	Time Elapsed Since End of SDM Program (years)	Program Received[b] (years)	Components[c]
Grade 9	3	2 (H,P vs. C,W)	2R + 2I + A
Grade 10 (a)	4	2	R + 2I + A
Grade 10 (b)	4	1.5	2I + A
Grade 11 (a)	5	1	I + A
Grade 11 (b)	5	.5	I

[a] For grades 9–11, there was a no-treatment control.

[b] Of the four schools per grade (H, P, C, and W), implementation fidelity was consistently rated higher at two schools (H and P).

[c] R = Readiness, I = Instructional, A = Application; 2 = repeated in Grades 4 and 5.

parents, peers, and other adults; cheating at school; lying about one's age; facilitating others' lying about their age; and school-based discipline problems. The YSR taps six factors: depression, unpopularity, aggression, delinquency, somatic complaints, and thought disorders (an additional factor, self-destruction/identity problems, is scored for boys only). There is also a competence assessment, including overall social competence and positive social activity.

Results of analyses of variance indicated that, relative to ninth-grade controls, ninth-grade program students made significantly less use of alcoholic beverages; had fewer self-destructive/identity problems; had higher scores in overall social competence, membership, and participation in positive social organizations; a higher level of participation in nonsports activities; and a higher level of quality of on-the-job work. Tenth-grade control students were significantly higher than tenth-grade program students in vandalism against school property, attacking persons with intent to injure, hitting or threatening other students, self-destructive/identity problems, and unpopularity. They also showed lower scores in overall social competence. Eleventh-grade control students were significantly higher than eleventh-grade program students in vandalism against parental property, hitting or threatening parents, and use of chewing tobacco. Across grades, male controls significantly exceeded male program recipients in petty theft and in buying or providing alcohol for someone else. The overall pattern of findings also indicated that students receiving the higher-fidelity program implementation generally showed better goal attainment than those receiving lower-fidelity implementation. It should be noted that these results reflect generally low base rates, as well as no correction for attenuation and no program of follow-up in the middle school.

PROGRAM SATISFACTION QUESTIONNAIRES

From the inception of the program of research, students, teachers, parents, and administrators have been given our Program Satisfaction measures to complete. The general format of these surveys involves asking how much the lessons were liked and how much they should be used in the future. In addition, specific components of the program are listed and respondents are asked to rate the extent to which components are liked or seen as effective. Also, open-ended questions elicit nominations of which children are more or less affected (and why), and respondents are asked for suggestions regarding how the program can be improved.

Program Satisfaction measures are recommended for all first-year implementation efforts, along with measures to monitoring implementation. We also recommend that student outcome measures ideally be added to the battery in the second year of implementation rather than the first year (unless funding or other reasons make this impossible) due to a contamination in the first year of student skill gains with teacher professional skill gains. Program Satisfaction results, however, are very valuable in every phase of implementation, as important input to assess program effectiveness and to target areas in need of modification.

All district-level evaluations ever done since the start of our work in 1979 would be impossible to collect for this report, as many of those we collected are now archived or have remained in in-house district documents. In general, districts report that student and teacher satisfaction normally ranges over 95 percent in areas of enjoyment and recommendations to continue. In addition, more than 90 percent of teachers and students report using the skills that they have been learning to solve everyday life problems. These responses have been extremely valuable as face-valid data in presentations to the school board, parent groups, and funders. Teacher reports most often describe the use of skills to solve peer relationship problems, while student reports in the first year focus on the use of self-calming to avoid the escalation of a conflict with a sibling or peer.

ANECDOTAL EVIDENCE

Perhaps the most satisfying aspect of our work comes from the large numbers of stories staff members hear from those implementing SDM/SPS. As mentioned, the consumer satisfaction surveys provide great examples, ranging from a class coming together to share feelings and help one another cope with the death of a family member, classmate, or even a pet, or with a national tragedy such as that occurring at Columbine High School. Student anecdotes are heartwarming and describe coping with a difficult person, a stressful situation, or their own feelings. A third grader once reported using "Keep Calm" to help him in a baseball game when up to bat with two strikes. Besides reporting that his use of self-calming had helped him to make a hit, he added, "And so, when I am an all star hitter for the Yankees, I will always think back to the third grade when I learned Keep Calm."

Anecdotes just as often speak to how the procedures and methods help group functioning and productivity. A first-grade teacher reported how a small group of boys came in from the playground and told her that they needed to have a Sharing Circle. On their own they formed a circle of chairs in the back of the room, chose a Speaker Power object and took turns giving their point of view about something that had happened on the playground. She said she watched in awe. After about ten minutes of serious exchange the group brought their chairs back to their desks and let her know that they were finished. Just a few days later, a group of girls requested some time to have a circle, too. The teacher reported that the students had exceeded her expectations for taking responsibility for their own feelings and relationships once she had established the procedures and introduced the class to some tools.

A principal of a northern New Jersey school reported a variety of anecdotal indicators that she uses to monitor the effectiveness of programming in her building. "I'm not spending all my time dealing with uncomfortable situations, but instead spend more time working on improving the school, improving communications with parents by explaining what the child is doing in the area of social-emotional learning, and teaching them the program's language. Detention used to contain twenty kids before the program; now there are about two. It used to take fifteen to twenty minutes to calm everyone down enough after lunch to start class. Now, any bickering stops once they walk in the door. My Peer Peacemakers tell me there are fewer physical fights, not as many arguments, and the students are calmer."

"I can also see a difference in self-esteem," the same principal added. "Children aren't easily able to fall into peer pressure. They aren't afraid to speak out. There is better behavior at home. Children understand the common language and the expectations. The students use it every day in situations not just at school but on the playground and at home with siblings. They try to live up to it, and though they may not always do it, you can tell that they are trying. They feel a sense of responsibility. They feel a sense of community and pride for the school, the teachers, and other students. They even use it to help out the teachers. A teacher reported to me, 'I was getting upset, and one of the kids told me to Keep Calm. It does come back to you!'"

An independent site visitor (Elias et al., 1997) obtained the following interview report, which quotes a central New Jersey community's recreation director, as cited in a local newspaper article, regarding his participation in a community sharing circle of city officials including the mayor's office and town counsel and sixth-grade students. "Our town, like so many other communities, had been experiencing an increase in incidents of vandalism. Most vandals are early to mid-teenagers. I felt that getting sixth graders involved in controlling vandalism could raise their level of awareness and, hopefully, prevent them from turning into future vandals themselves."

The response of the school district, according to this recreation leader "took his overture and turned it into a full-scale symphony." The sixth-grade students worked together over a course of the school year, using their social decision making skills to develop proposals to solve this problem, and their efforts culminated at the end of the year in a convocation where student representatives gave presentations of the proposals they had developed. After the presentations, the director said, "I was very impressed with the seriousness with which the students pursued this. I was overwhelmed with the response. I will provide a written report to the mayor and town council, and I believe they will approve these suggestions. I think that what the kids are learning through this process is far more significant than the proposals. I told them that what they are learning are life skills: Compromise, sharing, teamwork, seeking advice from peers" (Denker, 1999, p. 18).

Appendix B

Tools for Program-Level Assessment

SDM/SPS Curriculum Feedback

Teachers/leaders _____ **Date** _____

Class period and group worked with _____

1. General outline of lesson or class activities:

   _____

   _____

2. Student reactions to this session (for whom was it most or least effective):

   _____

   _____

3. Most effective or favorable aspects of this session:

   _____

   _____

4. Least effective or favorable aspects of this session:

   _____

   _____

5. Points to follow up in the next meeting:

   _____

   _____

6. Points to follow up in the following weeks outside group meetings (that is, in other class periods, other school settings, outside of school):

   _____

   _____

7. Suggested changes in this activity for the future:

   _____

   _____

From *Social Decision Making/Social Problem Solving: A Curriculum for Academic, Social, and Emotional Learning (Grades 2–3)*.
Copyright © 2005 by Maurice J. Elias and Linda Bruene Butler. Research Press (800-519-2707; www.researchpress.com)

Profile of Social Decision Making/Social Problem Solving Strengths

Student _____ Date _____

Observer _____ Title/position _____

Record your observation for each student by using this simple mastery rating, adjusted to appropriate age, grade, and ability expectations.

1 = Clearly does not demonstrate a satisfactory level

2 = Level in this area is uncertain

3 = Clearly demonstrates a satisfactory level

	To what extent can this child:		**Observation** *(circle one)*	
A. Readiness Area				
1. Self-control	1a. Listen carefully and accurately	1	2	3
	1b. Remember and follow directions	1	2	3
	1c. Concentrate and follow through on tasks	1	2	3
	1d. Calm himself or herself down	1	2	3
	1e. Carry on a conversation without upsetting or provoking others	1	2	3
2. Social Awareness	2a. Accept praise or approval	1	2	3
	2b. Choose praiseworthy and caring friends	1	2	3
	2c. Know when help is needed	1	2	3
	2d. Ask for help when needed	1	2	3
	2e. Work as part of a problem-solving team	1	2	3
B. Social Decision Making/Social Problem Solving Area				
1. Feelings	1a. Recognize signs of personal feelings	1	2	3
	1b. Recognize signs of feelings in others	1	2	3
	1c. Accurately describe a range of feelings	1	2	3
2. Problems	2a. Clearly put problems into words	1	2	3
3. Goals	3a. State realistic interpersonal goals	1	2	3
4. Alternatives	4a. Think of several ways to solve a problem or reach a goal	1	2	3
	4b. Think of different types of solutions	1	2	3
	4c. Do (a) and (b) for different types of problems	1	2	3

		To what extent can this child:	**Observation** *(circle one)*		
5. Consequences	5a.	Differentiate short- *and* long-term consequences	1	2	3
	5b.	Look at effects on self *and* others	1	2	3
	5c.	Keep positive *and* negative possibilities in mind	1	2	3
6. Choose	6a.	Select solutions that can reach goals	1	2	3
	6b.	Make choices that do not harm self or others	1	2	3
7. Plan and Check	7a.	Consider details before carrying out a solution (who, when, where, with whom, and so on)	1	2	3
	7b.	Anticipate obstacles	1	2	3
	7c.	Respond appropriately when plans are thwarted	1	2	3
8. Learn for Next Time	8a.	Try out ideas	1	2	3
	8b.	Learn from experience or from seeking input from adults and friends	1	2	3
	8c.	Use previous experience to help next time	1	2	3

References

Achenbach, T., & Edelbrock, C. (1987). *Manual for the Youth Self-Report and Profile*. Burlington: University of Vermont, Department of Psychiatry.

Bruene Butler, L., Hampson, J., Elias, M. J., Clabby, J. F., & Schuyler, T. (1997). The improving social awareness—social problem solving project. In G. Albee and T. Gullotta (Eds.), *Primary prevention works: Issues in children's and families' lives* (Vol. 6). Thousand Oaks, CA: Sage.

Denker, M. (1999, May 27). Vandalism as a learning tool. *Newark, New Jersey, Star Ledger*, p. 18.

Elias, M. J., Gara, M., Schuyler, T., Branden-Muller, L. R., & Sayette, M. A. (1991). The promotion of social competence: Longitudinal study of a preventive school-based program. *American Journal of Orthopsychiatry, 61*, 409–417.

Elias, M. J., Gara, M., & Ubriaco, M. (1985). Sources of stress and coping in children's transition to middle school: An empirical analysis. *Journal of Clinical Child Psychology, 14*, 112–118.

Elias, M. J., Gara, M., Ubriaco, M., Rothbaum, P. A., Clabby, J. F., & Schuyler, T. (1986). Impact of a preventive social problem solving intervention on children's coping with middle-school stressors. *American Journal of Community Psychology, 14*(3), 259–275.

Elias, M. J., Zins, J. E., Weissberg, R. P., Frey, K. S., Greenberg, M. T., Haynes, N. M., Kessler, R., Schwab-Stone, M. E., & Shriver, T. P. (1997). *Promoting social and emotional learning: Guidelines for educators*. Alexandria, VA: Association for Supervision and Curriculum Development.

Elliot, D. et al. (1983). *The prevalence and incidence of delinquent behavior: The National Youth Survey Report No. 26*. Boulder: Behavioral Research Institute.

Goldfried, M., & D'Zurilla, T. (1969). A behavioral-analytic model for assessing competence. In C. Spielberger (Ed.), *Current topics in clinical and community psychology*. New York: Academic Press.

Lipsitz, J. (1977). *Growing up forgotten: A review of research and programs concerning early adolescence*. Lexington, MA: Lexington Books.

Norris, J. A. (1998). *Promoting social competence and reducing violence and negative social interaction in a multicultural school setting*. Unpublished doctoral dissertation, Graduate School of Education, Rutgers University, New Brunswick, NJ.

Piers, E. V., & Harris, D. B. (1984). *Piers-Harris Children's Self-Concept Scale—Revised manual.* Los Angeles: Western Psychological Services.

Thurston, C. J. (1998). *A systems approach to the evaluation of a social and emotional development program for emotionally disturbed elementary school students in a private special education facility.* Unpublished doctoral dissertation, Graduate School of Applied and Professional Psychology, Rutgers University, New Brunswick, NJ.

Toepfer, C., & Marani, J. (1980). School-based research. In M. Johnson (Ed.), *Toward adolescence: The middle school years. Seventy-ninth yearbook of the National Society for the Study of Education.* University of Chicago Press.

About the Authors

MAURICE J. ELIAS, Ph.D., is professor, Department of Psychology, Rutgers University, and directs the Rutgers Social-Emotional Learning Lab. He is vice chair of the Leadership Team of the Collaborative for Academic, Social, and Emotional Learning (www.CASEL.org) and senior advisor for Research, Policy, and Practice to the New Jersey Center for Character Education. He devotes his research and writing to the area of emotional intelligence in children, schools, and families. His books for parents include *Emotionally Intelligent Parenting: How to Raise a Self-Disciplined, Responsible and Socially Skilled Child* (Three Rivers Press, 2000) and *Raising Emotionally Intelligent Teenagers: Guiding the Way for Compassionate, Committed, Courageous Adults* (Three Rivers Press, 2002), both published in several languages. His recent releases are *Engaging the Resistant Child Through Computers: A Manual for Social-Emotional Learning* (available through www.nprinc.com), *Building Learning Communities with Character: How to Integrate Academic, Social, and Emotional Learning* (Association for Supervision and Curriculum Development, 2003), and *EQ + IQ = Best Leadership Practices for Caring and Successful Schools* (Corwin Press, 2003), as well as *Bullying, Peer Harassment, and Victimization in the Schools: The Next Generation of Prevention* (Haworth, 2004). Dr. Elias is married and the father of two children.

LINDA BRUENE BUTLER, M.Ed., has worked on the development of school-based programs in social and emotional learning for over two decades. Currently, she is director of the Social Decision Making/Social Problem Solving (SDM/SPS) Program at the Behavioral Research and Training Institute of the University of Medicine and Dentistry of New Jersey, University Behavioral HealthCare's Behavioral Research and Training Institute. She has also served as adjunct faculty for courses in the area of social-emotional learning at the Department of Psychology, Rutgers University; Teachers College, Columbia University; and Department of Psychology, University of Illinois. Ms. Bruene Butler has published and lectured extensively in the area of social-emotional learning and has trained many others to become SDM/SPS consultants and trainers. Her current area of interest is exploring ways that distance learning methods can be used to share and evaluate innovative methods for promoting social-emotional learning.

ERIN M. BRUNO is clinician supervisor at the SDM/SPS Program at the Behavioral Research and Training Institute of the University of Medicine and Dentistry of New Jersey. After receiving her master's degree in drama therapy from New York University in 1997, Ms. Bruno worked as a therapist and school consultant in the area of social and emotional learning. She has extensive experience assisting schools in adopting the SDM/SPS curricula.

MAUREEN REILLY PAPKE is a program development specialist at the SDM/SPS Program at the Behavioral Research and Training Institute of the University of Medicine and Dentistry of New Jersey. In this role since 1989, Ms. Papke has provided training and consultation services to educators at all grade levels as they implement this social and emotional learning program.

TERESA FARLEY SHAPIRO, Ph.D., is a program development specialist and trainer for the SDM/SPS Program at the University of Medicine and Dentistry of New Jersey. Dr. Shapiro is a New Jersey–certified school psychologist. Within the school setting, she has provided a variety of counseling services utilizing SDM/SPS, with both regular and special education populations.